An Introduction to English Lexicology

Edinburgh Textbooks on the English Language

General Editor
Heinz Giegerich, Professor of English Linguistics, University of Edinburgh

Editorial Board
Laurie Bauer (University of Wellington)
Olga Fischer (University of Amsterdam)
Willem Hollmann (Lancaster University)
Marianne Hundt (University of Zurich)
Rochelle Lieber (University of New Hampshire)
Bettelou Los (University of Edinburgh)
Robert McColl Millar (University of Aberdeen)
Donka Minkova (UCLA)
Edgar Schneider (University of Regensburg)
Graeme Trousdale (University of Edinburgh)

TITLES IN THE SERIES INCLUDE

An Introduction to English Syntax, 2nd Edition
Jim Miller

An Introduction to English Morphology: Words and Their Structure
Andrew Carstairs-McCarthy

An Introduction to International Varieties of English
Laurie Bauer

An Introduction to Middle English
Jeremy Smith and Simon Horobin

An Introduction to Old English, Revised Edition
Richard Hogg, with Rhona Alcorn

An Introduction to Early Modern English
Terttu Nevalainen

An Introduction to English Semantics and Pragmatics
Patrick Griffiths

An Introduction to English Sociolinguistics
Graeme Trousdale

An Introduction to Late Modern English
Ingrid Tieken-Boon van Ostade

An Introduction to Regional Englishes: Dialect Variation in England
Joan Beal

An Introduction to English Semantics and Pragmatics, 2nd edition
Patrick Griffiths and Christopher Cummins

An Introduction to English Phonetics, 2nd edition
Richard Ogden

An Introduction to English Morphology, 2nd edition
Andrew Carstairs-McCarthy

An Introduction to English Phonology, 2nd edition
April McMahon

Visit the Edinburgh Textbooks on the English Language website at
www.edinburghuniversitypress.com/series/ETOTEL

An Introduction to English Lexicology

Laurie Bauer

EDINBURGH
University Press

Edinburgh University Press is one of the leading university presses in the UK. We publish academic books and journals in our selected subject areas across the humanities and social sciences, combining cutting-edge scholarship with high editorial and production values to produce academic works of lasting importance. For more information visit our website: edinburghuniversitypress.com

© Laurie Bauer, 2022
Edinburgh University Press Ltd
The Tun – Holyrood Road
12(2f) Jackson's Entry
Edinburgh EH8 8PJ

Typeset in Janson MT by
Servis Filmsetting Ltd, Stockport, Cheshire, and
printed and bound by CPI Group (UK) Ltd,
Croydon, CR0 4YY

A CIP record for this book is available from the British Library

ISBN 978 1 4744 7789 5 (hardback)
ISBN 978 1 4744 7791 8 (webready PDF)
ISBN 978 1 4744 7790 1 (paperback)
ISBN 978 1 4744 7792 5 (epub)

Contents

Figure and Tables

Preface

Lexicology is the study of words, in their many facets; English lexicology is the study of words in English. This book is thus a look at the fundamentals of words, and is envisaged as part of a course in English Language. As long as it is realised that the focus here is on English and that data from other languages is not presented in detail, the book can also be used for courses in Linguistics, Applied Linguistics and the training of English language teachers.

Words are a good place to start the study of a language. We all think we know what words are, though it soon becomes clear that the notion of word is not an easy one to deal with in a theoretical way. This is because there are enough difficulties with the notion to cast theoretical doubt on it as a notion, even while, in practice, we can function quite easily with it. More than that, words have different aspects. We can look at the very notion of word, and different types of word, we can look at the word as a meaning-carrying element, as a structured element (on several levels), as an element taking part in the evolution of language, and so on. The aim of an introductory book such as this one is not to cover all such aspects exhaustively so much as to give the student a glimpse of the breadth of the field and to give them an introductory vocabulary with which to tackle the field. In the exercises, I have tried to indicate ways in which the study might be taken further, in a fairly limited way, allowing students to start to understand the joys of making their own discoveries.

I should like to thank all those who have commented on earlier versions of the work, and the team at Edinburgh University Press for their support.

Transcription symbols

The symbols used in this book for the transcription of English vowels
are given in the table below.

FLEECE	iː		FACE	eɪ
KIT	ɪ		PRICE	aɪ
DRESS	e		CHOICE	ɔɪ
TRAP	æ		MOUTH	aʊ
STRUT	ʌ		GOAT	əʊ
PALM, START	ɑː		NEAR	ɪə
LOT	ɒ		SQUARE	eə
NURSE	ɜː		CURE	ʊə
THOUGHT, FORCE	ɔː		COMMA	ə
FOOT	ʊ		HAPPY	i
GOOSE	uː			

1 Words

1.1 What is a word?

Lexicology is the study of words as linguistic entities. Because we live in a literate society, and have a writing system which sets out words on the page, we generally feel that we know what a word is. This view, unfortunately, confuses cause and effect. In principle, we know how to write English because we know what the words are; we do not know what the words are because we can write English. If this latter view were true, the many languages which have no writing system would not have words, and neither would languages whose writing system does not put spaces between words. On the other hand, if we know where to put the spaces because we know what words are, we might expect that we would be able to reconstruct a way of arriving at that conclusion, but this does not appear to be the case – at least not where English is concerned.

We can certainly see some criteria that provide clues. The clues do not always agree, though. Let us consider a few.

A word is the smallest unit which can stand on its own as an utterance. This is not as simple as it looks. First, we have to distinguish between language **use** and language **mention**. In answer to a question like 'Is it inadvisable or unadvisable?', we might answer 'Un'. But we would not want to say that *un* is therefore a word; the objection would be that we are talking about *un*, not using it in its normal grammatical function. In this book, as in most linguistic texts, words that are mentioned will be put in italics. Even making that distinction, we have problems. In answer to a question such as *What do you hate most in the world?* We might give an answer *Cats*. So *cats* is a word. But it is hard to think of a place where we could have *cat* as an utterance by itself. **Grammatical words**, words which have a function in the grammar, like *of, and, if* or *the*, cannot be used as utterances by themselves unless they are mentioned. And if we think of something like *whiteboard*, which we write as one word, it is arguably made up of two units which could stand on their own as utterances.

A word is a unit which, when pronounced in isolation, has a single intonational focus point, or movement of pitch. That point in the word might be perceived as being louder, longer or more important than the surrounding material. In *isolation*, that point would include the sound corresponding to the letter *A*, in *movement* it would include the sound corresponding to the letter *O*. We can call this the **main stress** of the word, and we would probably say that the whole syllable, and not just the vowel, carries the main stress. In *whiteboard* there is just one such point, including the sound corresponding to the letter *I*. Again, there are problems with this criterion. A phrase like *in the beginning* has just one such point, but is not usually thought of as a word. For some speakers a very long word like *antidisestablishmentarianism* might be perceived to have more than one main stress, though this is controversial. And, perhaps most important of all, the position of the main stress seems to be something that fewer and fewer speakers are secure about.

The sound structure of a word is governed by fixed rules which do not apply beyond the word. For example, a word can begin or end with /st/ (as in *stir* and *mist*), but while a word can end /ft/ (as in *aft*), it cannot begin with /ft/. The sequence /sd/ cannot occur either at the beginning or at the end of a word, so if we meet that sequence, it must be over a word-boundary (as in *pats dogs*). This is known as phonotactic structure, or **phonotactics**. Note that on this criterion, *whiteboard* must be a sequence of two words, because /tb/ does not occur at the beginning or end of a word (and occurs in the middle only in just such instances).

A word has a single, unitary meaning. The trouble with this is that we have no definition of a single, unitary meaning. Is *put up* (a guest) a single word because *lodge*, which has the same meaning, is a word? Is *in the end* a single word because it has the same meaning as *finally*, which is a word?

A word is listed in the **dictionary**. Like the spelling convention, this is circular. Things are listed in the dictionary primarily because they are words. In any case, as we shall see below (Section 1.3), there are things that are longer than words which get listed in the dictionary, and some dictionaries also list things that are shorter than words, such as **prefixes** and **suffixes**.

The overall conclusion is that, although these criteria might provide insights into something about the nature of the word, they do not define it neatly. The result is that we are not entirely sure what a word is. For example, we might not know how to write /ɪnsəʊfɑːræz/. Is it one, two, three or four words? People disagree on how to write it. And there is a large set of words like *coffee-pot* or *rain-forest* that are sometimes written with a hyphen, sometimes as a single word and sometimes as two distinct words. The hyphen is also used where complex items occur in **attributive** position (that is, immediately before the noun it modifies). For example, *His position is well justified* corresponds to *His well-justified position.* This hyphen indicates syntactic constituency, but might also be taken to indicate wordhood.

Finally, we should note that what counts as a word is sometimes unstable, from a historical point of view. *Alright* has only relatively recently been accepted as a spelling of what was earlier *all right.* According to the *Oxford English Dictionary* (the *OED*), *after all* can be spelt *afterall* in the United States. In more recent times, we often see prefixes being written as separate words: things such as *mega deal.*

Despite all of this, there is a large amount of agreement among adult writers as to where words begin and end (children occasionally make what are, by adult standards, errors). There are a few places where there is variation, but people do not write *child ish*, even if they can use *ish* as a word in its own right: *Are you cold? Ish!* Even less do people write things like *diff icult, sim mer, ze bra*, where there is no prefix or suffix involved. Much of this is related to meaning: words are (usually) meaningful units, and things which are not meaningful are not treated as words. This means that even if we must acknowledge areas of insecurity, in most instances speakers seem to be fairly clear about where the words are, and can repeat a sentence one word at a time – for example, if it is required for dictation. At various points in this book, we will need to come back to whether things are or are not words, but in general we will accept the spelling conventions of English as defining words. This might not be terribly scientific, but it has the benefit of being practical.

1.2 Are names words?

A word is a linguistic item which helps us discuss the world around us. It is a unit which not only has **form** (a phonological structure or an orthographic one), but also meaning. In this sense, names are words. But names are different from other words in a number of ways.

They have unique reference. *Samantha* refers to one particular person in a given context. *Tree* refers to a set of items, one or more of which is relevant in the given context. *I saw Samantha at the opera* means that I saw a particular individual who we both/all know is called 'Samantha'; *I saw a tree with red flowers* means that I saw a particular tree, but all you know about it is that it is a member of the class of trees with flowers of a particular colour. You might imagine a rhododendron, when I actually saw a pohutukawa. We will agree that it was a member of the class of trees. One of the results of this is that *Samantha* is not easily made plural, while *tree* is easily pluralisable.

As a result of their unique reference, names are inherently definite. Sometimes names have a *the* in front of them (*The Hague, The Gambia, The Thames*) but there is rarely a contrast: we can have *Samantha* but not *The Samantha*, we can have *The Hague* but not *Hague*. Neither *Samantha* nor *The Hague* can mean 'any old Samantha/Hague'. Incidentally, this a fact about English: some languages do allow definite articles with names.

Both of those rules can be broken when a name is used as an ordinary word. This happens in sentences like those in (1). Precisely what happens in such cases is a matter of some dispute, but most authorities seem to agree that a proper noun (name) is treated as a common noun, and so takes on the grammar of a common noun.

(1)   This is not the Paris I used to know.
      I know the Manchester in New Hampshire, but not the one in England.
      We need another Einstein.
      Johnny is the new Patricia.
      There's a Mr Jones waiting to see you.

Matters are not this simple. There are plenty of unique descriptions which can be used as names: *The Netherlands, The Savoy, The Himalayas, The Duke of Wellington*. There are also unique entities which are named by ordinary nouns, which therefore become rather name-like: *the moon, fortune* (for example, in *Fortune favours the brave*), *hell* and so on. We should also note that while English spelling rules treat days of the week and months of the year as names, and use capital letters for them, other languages, such as French, do not.

Names, because of their meanings, also behave differently in regard to syntax from other words. Names, typically, act like a noun phrase rather than as a noun. *Kim*, in a sentence like *Kim read the entire book*, fills the whole subject function. We cannot add modifiers, defining relative clauses, quantifiers to it – or at least, if we do that, we end up with **constructions** like those in (1) where what was once a name has become a common noun. Even if we have a name that contains *the*, we cannot add adjectives or defining relatives without stopping it being a name: *The beautiful Hague, The former Argentine, The Gambia that I have come to love*. Most of our syntactic theories treat names as nouns, but we can argue that this is misleading.

All of this indicates that names are unusual words. But like normal words, they provide a phonetic (in sign language, a gestured) or written representation to a unit to which we assign a semantic interpretation. If that is true of things other than words, it is nevertheless at the heart of wordhood.

1.3 Multi-word expressions (MWEs)

So far, the words we have dealt with have mostly been independent of each other: *cat* and *dog*, *cat* and *sat*, *cat* and *independent* have their own meanings, their own usages, their own dictionary entries. But sometimes there are things listed in dictionaries that contain more than one orthographic word. These are called **multi-word expressions** (MWEs for short, although you may also come across the label *MWU* – short for *multi-word unit*).

As a simple example, consider *passion flower* (etymologically, *passion* here has to do with Easter, rather than with strong feelings). Unlike a *magnolia flower*, which could just as easily be a *magnolia blossom*, a *passion flower* is the name of the flower: it is a fixed expression. It happens to be written as two words, unlike *mayflower* and *sunflower* (and you may not even be sure how to write *cornflower*, *wall-flower* or *wild flower*), but the way it is written does not appear to be significant; if we wrote *passion-flower*, nothing else would change. While the spelling of such items is not entirely random in English, it is at least clear that for many such words the spelling is not fixed and does not indicate anything about the status of the construction. So let us say that *passion flower*, *sunflower* and *wall-flower* are items whose names behave just like *cat* and *dog*. But unlike *cat* and *dog*, these words have words as their elements, so they are word-like objects which are made up of (in the examples we have considered) two words. These, then, termed **compounds**, are the most straightforward of MWEs.

Having decided that there are MWEs which have a place in a dictionary, though, we find that there is a plethora of items which might (or might not) need to be treated in the same way.

Another type is provided by what are often called **phrasal verbs**. These are verbs that include a preposition, things like *do up*, *fall out*, *put up with*. Although these are written as two (or more) words in English, and can be divided by other words, as in *do your coat up*, which is a generally accepted sign of separateness for words, their meaning is not always predictable from the meanings of their individual elements. While *fall out* may have a predictable meaning in *My handbag fell out of the car*, it does not in *Kim and Lee fell out over which wine to serve*. Because these verbs have meanings which are often unrelated to the meanings of the verb and the preposition, and because they often have meanings which can be associated with single words (*He passed out* could be the same as *He fainted*), they seem to act as words, but they contain multiple words, and so are MWEs.

Lack of predictability of meaning is definitional of another class of MWEs, idioms. **Idioms** may be defined as constructions whose meaning is global (that is, the meaning attaches to the whole construction) rather than derived from the meanings of the elements of the construction. Consider the expression *piece of cake*. It does have a literal meaning, equivalent, perhaps, to *slice of gateau*, but in the sentence *The exam was a piece of cake*, the expression *piece of cake* can only be glossed globally as 'very easy'. It has nothing to do with pieces and nothing to do with cake. It is an idiom. As a second example, consider the Australian phrase *big bikkies*. This means 'a lot of money'. It has nothing to do with biscuits (*bikkies*). It can only be glossed globally. It is typical of idioms that they have a fixed form, and cannot be manipulated syntactically. *Kick the bucket* as an idiom means 'to die', but it would be very odd to say *The bucket was kicked by Kim* in this sense, or *What was kicked was the bucket*. *He jumped down my throat when I mentioned the loss* ('he got very angry with me') cannot be changed to *My throat was jumped down when I mentioned the loss*. Having said that, there are many examples which show that the lack of syntactic manipulation is not always absolute. Corresponding to *let the cat out of the bag* ('to divulge a secret unintentionally'), it might be possible to say *The cat has been let out of the bag*.

Some idioms are so obscure that, even if you can guess their meaning in context (such as *Here's mud in your eye* as a toast), you cannot explain how they came to mean what they mean. Others have meanings which can be worked out, with a bit of good will. *Talk the hind leg off a donkey* ('to talk excessively') is probably an expression whose meaning can be deduced, given that it is extremely unlikely to be literal. Equally, *When he saw he was caught, the spy came clean* ('told the truth') is probably a meaning that can be deduced. The term 'idiom' is used for the uninterpretable cases and for the cases which depend on some **figurative** use of language, but in terms of understanding, they are not equivalent.

Rhyming slang provides a different set of idioms. Rhyming slang is often attributed to Cockney English, but it is found in Glasgow and in Australia and New Zealand, as well as in London. And, as we shall see in a moment, some rhyming slang has become fairly general English. In rhyming slang, typically, a short phrase replaces the intended word. The last part of the phrase rhymes with the intended word. So, traditionally, instead of *kids* we find *dustbin lids* (occasionally, *teapot lids*) and more recently, instead of *throat*, we get *nanny goat*. Since the meaning of, say, *dustbin lids* is not semantically predictable from either *dustbin* or *lids*, we have to provide a global gloss, and that indicates an idiom. In a second level of rhyming slang, the rhyming word itself is omitted, so that *kids* are called *dustbins* and a *throat* is called a *nanny*. At this point, even the phonological motivation is removed, and a new **homonym** (a word which sounds the same as another word, but means something unrelated) is created. Because these homonyms cannot easily be reconstituted, it is often the case that we use rhyming slang without being aware of it. Some examples are provided in (2), all of them reasonably widespread.

(2)	*Usual expression*	*Full version*	*Meaning*
	a brass	a brass nail	'a piece of tail, a prostitute'
	blow a raspberry	blow a raspberry tart	'blow a fart'
	bread	bread and honey	'money'
	get down to brass tacks	get down to brass tacks	'get to the facts, get to the practicalities'
	have a butcher's	have a butcher's hook	'have a look'
	my old china	my old china plate	'my old mate'
	on your Tod	on your Tod Sloan	'on your own, alone'
	tell porkies	tell pork pies	'tell lies'
	use your loaf	use your loaf of bread	'use your head'

Note: Tod Sloan was a famous jockey at the turn of the twentieth century.

Once these have become established as new homonyms, they are no longer MWEs, but while they have the full version, they are MWEs.

Another place where we find relatively fixed, and not necessarily easily interpretable, usage is with proverbs. Proverbs often have to be interpreted figuratively, and are not always easily manipulable syntactically. *Too many cooks spoil the broth* may be abbreviated to just *too many cooks*, but it would be odd to make it passive (*The broth has been spoilt by too many cooks*) or to extract an element from the sentence (*The broth is what too many cooks have spoilt*). Other examples of proverbs are given in (3).

(3)   you can take a horse to water but you can't make it drink
      a bird in the hand is worth two in the bush
      make hay while the sun shines
      every cloud has a silver lining
      one man's meat is another man's poison
      you can't have your cake and eat it too

English has a large set of fixed similes, some of which we might expect (*white as snow*), others of which are unpredictable (*cool as a cucumber*, used only when *cool* means 'unflustered' rather than when it means 'slightly cold'). Some of these are less used today than they were a few decades ago, but many are familiar for at least some speakers. Some are given in (4). Note that other comparisons are possible, and are used; some are even well-established (*as busy as a one-armed paper-hanger*). These are just relatively fixed parts of the English language, and, to the extent that speakers know them, are MWEs.

(4)   as clean as a whistle
       as different as chalk and cheese
       as fit as a fiddle
       as flat as a pancake
       as honest as the day is long
       as long as your arm
       as quick as flash
       as snug as a bug in a rug
       as tough as old boots
       as warm as toast

Finally, we find a whole host of **collocations**, words which habitually occur together, some of which we probably want to classify as MWEs and some of which we probably do not wish to classify in this manner. We can begin with some extreme examples.

If you hear the word *kith*, you probably immediately think of *and kin*. *Kith* occurs, for all practical purposes, only in the phrase *kith and kin*. *Kith* is a **unique morph**, it occurs only in one place in the language. Except when the pattern is disturbed by the name of a cleaning powder, the same is true of *vim*. The phrase *vim and vigour* is the only place *vim* occurs. If *kith* or *vim* occurs without its supporting phrase, it is nearly always a joke. Here one word predicts another with almost 100 per cent accuracy, though the prediction goes only in one direction: *kin* does not predict the presence of *kith*.

At the other end of the scale, consider *in the*. *In the* occurs very frequently, largely because *in* is a preposition, prepositions nearly always occur in prepositional phrases, prepositional phrases are nearly always made up of a preposition and a noun phrase, and noun phrases often begin with *the*. *In* predicts (to some extent) the presence of *the*, but *the* does not predict the preceding *in*. This particular collocation is of value to someone who is programming a phone to support a user to write texts (SMS messages), but is not of great value in determining the meaning of a sentence. It is a collocation, but is probably not an MWE, because it is not lexical but determined by the grammatical system of the language.

In between these two extremes, there is a host of intermediate cases, sometimes with words that predict each other, sometimes where the prediction is in only one direction.

The class of proverbs, cited above, tails off into various classes of well-known expressions, some of which are quotations, some of which are fixed but not necessarily proverbial. Some examples are given in (5).

(5)   an eye for an eye
        curiouser and curiouser
        diamonds are a girl's best friend
        tomorrow is another day
        a little knowledge is a dangerous thing

There is also a set of binomials, two words linked by a coordinating conjunction (occasionally you find longer strings than this, but the most common are just two items long). Some of these have variable order, but mostly the order is fixed. Some examples are given in (6).

(6)   bed and breakfast
        black and blue
        born and bred
        cut and dried
        done and dusted
        down and out
        fruit and vegetables
        here and there
        life and limb
        loud and clear
        sink or swim

It is noticeable how many of the items in (6) either alliterate or rhyme, and this phonological aspect of the structure seems to be part of the appeal of these expressions. Note also that many **word-classes** are involved, and that the meaning of the whole is not necessarily predictable from the meanings of the parts.

And there are a whole set of different construction types which seem to be fixed expressions. Illustrated below are verbs with direct objects (7), prepositional phrases (8) and adjective–noun combinations (9), but virtually any syntactic structure can have fixed collocations within it.

(7)   bite the bullet
        change (one's) mind
        face the music
        pull (one's) leg
        shake a leg

smell a rat
upset the applecart

(8)   at home
        in cold blood
        in the open
        under the weather
        on the blink
        over the moon
        up the duff

(9)   black eye
        commanding officer
        fat cat
        fatty acids
        historical novel
        rhetorical question
        rich pickings

Another class, although one that potentially overlaps with others that have been discussed here, is the class of **formulae**, things which are just the way you say things. Some examples are given in (10).

(10)   all things considered
        as a matter of fact
        excuse me
        good afternoon
        I'm sorry to say
        in other words
        in the long run

A nice example is provided by the way in which we tell the time. To express the time 2:45, there are various possibilities, of which we probably use only one. Consider the versions in (11). Any of these is grammatical in English, but they are not what you say.

(11)   quarter to three (British English)
        quarter of three (American English)
        three o'clock less the quarter (French)
        quarter before three (German)
        three quarters three (German)
        three o'clock less fifteen (Japanese)

These are still fairly constrained, but the Danish for 3:20 translates as 'ten minutes in half four'.

All of this is important because of a general point it makes about linguistic theory. The approach to syntax advocated by Noam Chomsky and his followers assumes that each sentence is freely constructed from the elements that are available and the syntactic rules which allow those elements to be chained together. Examples like the ones that have been provided here suggest that our language is far more constrained than that: many things which appear to be options are not genuine options at all, but limited by the particular words involved.

1.4 Paradigms

In a sentence like *I like watching parrots* we can discern two sets of relationships. The first is the relationship between *I* and *like*, *like* and *watching*, *watching* and *parrots*. That is, there is a relationship between the elements that are strung together. Following Saussure ([1916] 1969), this is termed a **syntagmatic** (/sɪntægˈmætɪk/) relationship. In *I like watching parrots*, the syntagmatic relationship that has been drawn attention to is one between words, but syntagmatic relationships also exist between the elements /w/, /ɒ/ and /ʧ/ in *watch* and the *parrot* and *-s* elements in *parrots*. A syntagmatic relationship is one between elements which are all present in the stream of speech.

A different kind of relationship is one between elements of which only one is present in the stream of speech. Rather than *I like watching parrots*, we could have had *You like watching parrots*, *We like watching parrots* or *They like watching parrots*; equally we could have had *I hate watching parrots*, *I love watching parrots*, *I abhor watching parrots* and so on. In the first case we have a relationship between *I, we, you* and *they*, only one of which is present in the original sentence; in the latter case we have a relationship between *like, hate, love, abhor* (and any other words you can think of which would fit into the same slot). Following the Saussurean tradition, these are termed **paradigmatic** (/pærədɪgˈmætɪk/) relationships. Paradigmatic relationships are relationships of potential substitutability, and we can also call *I, you, we, they* a **substitution class**. As with the syntagmatic relationships mentioned above, paradigmatic relationships also hold between sounds, for example in the words *bat, cat, fat, hat, mat, gnat, sat, vat*, and with parts of words, for example in *employer, employee*.

Both syntagmatic and paradigmatic relationships hold between like elements. There is a syntagmatic relationship between *watching* and *parrots* because both *watching* and *parrots* are words. We would not talk about a syntagmatic relationship between /ʧ/ and *-ing* because the first is an element of sound, the latter is a meaningful word-part; they are not elements from the same level of analysis. Similarly, when we say there is a paradigmatic relationship between *I* and *we*, it is a relationship between elements which can function as the subjects of the verb *like*, not a relationship between the sound element /aɪ/ and the word *we*, because sound elements and words are not comparable entities.

A set of elements in a syntagmatic relationship is a **syntagm** (/ˈsɪntæm/), and a set of elements in a paradigmatic relationship is a **paradigm** (/ˈpærədaɪm/). The word *syntagm* is usually avoided in modern usage, in favour of the word *construction*. A construction is a syntagm which has internal structure and coherence (including in its meaning). Very often a construction has a meaning which goes beyond the meanings of the elements within it. For example, in *I like parrots*, there is the relationship between *I* and *like*, which we might gloss as a relationship between the experiencer of the emotion and the emotion, and also a relationship between *like* and *parrots*, which we might gloss as a relationship between the emotion and the object about which the emotion is felt. Similar meaning relationships are found in *We hate cats*, *You admire the Queen* and so on, and belong to the construction rather than to the words in the construction. The result is that although there is a syntagmatic relationship between *man* and *are* in *The sons and daughters of a man are his children* (the two words occur adjacent to each other in the stream of speech), we would not call *man are* a construction (although it may be part of a larger construction).

The term 'paradigm' is in general usage, but its usage is often limited. Although paradigm can justifiably be used of any substitution class it is most often used of substitution classes within the word. Thus the normal use for the term 'paradigm' is the kind of substitution class illustrated in (12).

(12) walk
      walks
      walked
      walking

This paradigm illustrates two different kinds of word: there is a sense in which all the items in (12) are different words, which we will call **word-forms**, and a contrasting sense in which the paradigm in (12) illustrates different uses of the same word, which we will call a **lexeme**. We standardly write lexemes in small block capitals and word-forms in italics, to distinguish them where the distinction is important. This terminology (and its corresponding notation) allows us to capture the fact that although *walks* and *walked* are different words in the sense that they have different shapes and occur in different syntactic substitution classes (*walked* can occur in *We walked*, but *walks* cannot occur in

*_We walks_), there is another sense in which all of these different forms are representations of the same word, so that you would look them up in the dictionary under the heading _walk_, not under _walks_ or _walked_, for instance. _Walks_ and _walked_ (like _walk_) are different word-forms that belong to the lexeme WALK. In English some verbs have just one word-form in their paradigm (for example, _must_), some have three forms in their paradigm in this sense (for example, _hit, hits_ and _hitting_), some have four (like WALK in (12)), some have five (for example, _throw, throws, threw, thrown, throwing_) and one has eight (_be, am, is, are, was, were, been, being_). On a world scale, that is fairly modest. Many languages have thousands of word-forms for each verb and Archi, a language of the Caucasus, is reported to have 1.5 million word-forms for every verbal lexeme.

Although the term 'paradigm' is often used for this one very narrow kind of paradigm, that does not prevent there being other kinds of paradigm. One type that is currently controversial is the **derivational paradigm**, where we see different lexemes linked by paradigms of forms within the word. Some examples are given in (13).

(13) a. deceive
      deception
      deceptive
   b. employ
      employer
      employee
   c. proceed
      process
      processual
   d. theory
      theorist
      theorise

Although the examples in (13) show individual sets of words, these series are often generalised over several **word families**, in the sense that (13d), for example, is just one word family whose overall pattern is also illustrated by _fantasy, fantasist, fantasise_. And sometimes, the existence of the paradigm seems to provoke its use in new members of the construction, as illustrated in (14).

(14) a. Like the world is divided into stomp_ers_ and stomp_ees_ and he's a stomp_ee_. (Stephen Dobyns (1998), _Saratoga Strongbox_, New York: Viking, p. 46; italics in the original)
   b. What it needed was to match solicitor with solicitee. (Michael Thomas (1983), _Hard Money_, New York: Viking, p. 191)

    c. The bellower was Harmon Crundall – and the bellowee the mysterious Mrs Smith. (Joan Hess (1986), *Murder at the Murder at the Mimosa Inn*, New York: St. Martin's Press, p. 41)

    d. The stab*ber* might want to stay friends but not the stab*bee*. (Richard Layman (2001), *Night in the Lonesome October*, London: Headline, p. 29; italics in the original)

    e. I found myself more therapist with Julie than therapee. (Robert B. Parker (2000), *Perish Twice*, London: Murray, p. 26)

Examples like those in (14) appear to show the value of the notion of a derivational paradigm: the paradigm supports extensions to the paradigm in places where the relevant words are not (or have not been) established parts of the language. In other words, the paradigm supports the **productivity** of the pattern, its extension to new words. There are other examples which show why some linguists are reluctant to see the derivational paradigm as particularly helpful. Consider the example in (15).

(15)   deceive   receive   conceive   conceive
                                         (a child)   (an idea)
       deceit   receipt   concept
       deception   reception   conception   conception
       deceptive   receptive   conceptual

In (15) we find that the overall paradigm that we can establish with *deceive* and *receive* does not extend completely to *conceive*, that two meanings of *conceive* seem to be members of different paradigms, and that the meanings of the relevant forms are not always parallel. Not only is the paradigm apparently not reliable, it can be difficult to tell what the boundaries of such a paradigm might be: are *receivable* and *conceivable* part of the same paradigm or not (and if so, why is only one of them used as a noun)?

Another place where we use paradigms and substitution classes is in dividing the words of the language into classes for the purposes of grammatical description. These classes of words are called word-classes or, in a rather older terminology, **parts of speech**, and in principle they are paradigms of words.

Consider, for example, a sentence such as *The parrot is pretty*. In place of *parrot* we can substitute a whole series of words such as *book, cat, flower, girl, house, ladybird, monument, statue* and so on. In the place of *pretty* we can substitute *delightful, fierce, grey, incredible, large, ugly, unimaginative* and so on. Each of these substitution classes, or paradigms of words, is a class which can also fit into other slots. For example, *parrot, book, cat* and so on could also fit into the sentences *I can see the parrot*, *Why do you want a parrot?*, *A parrot eats insects* and so on. If we generalise over all of these possible environments, we end up with a huge list of possible words, some of which are excluded from individual sentences by virtue of their meaning, but which are nonetheless members of the class because of the way they fit into other comparable slots. So even if it would not make sense to say *I accidentally killed the monument* to parallel *I accidentally killed the parrot*, we know from the examples above that *monument* and *parrot* do belong to the same substitution class in many instances. To make these super-substitution classes easy to refer to, we give them names, usually (in English) names inherited from the Latin grammarians. The class including *parrot* we call the class of nouns (this word comes indirectly from Latin *nomen* 'name', because nouns in many cases are the names of sets of things); the class including *pretty* we call adjectives (because they are so often added to nouns – from Latin *adjectio* 'I add'). The slots that these words fit into include not only syntactic slots such as the ones illustrated above, but slots in words (nouns can typically be made plural in English, can have endings such as *-ish*, *-y* and *-al* added to them; adjectives can often be compared – *prettier*, *prettiest* – or can have *-ise* or *-ify* added to them).

There is not a limited and finite set of word-classes. There are always word-classes within word-classes. So, for example, there is a limited number of nouns that can be said to purr and that can be substituted for *kitten* in *The kitten purred*. *Kitten* is part of the huge set of nouns, but it also a member of this much smaller word-class which does not have a generally accepted name because we do not need it very often for grammatical description: we could always call it the class of purry nouns. We also find that authorities argue about the legitimacy of some word-classes, and that different word-classes are used at different periods of history as ideas of what is important in defining the word-class varies. It is also the case that the word-classes are not necessarily the same in all languages: in some languages the class of adjectives is very small or subsumed in some larger class.

Nevertheless, there is a set of word-classes which can apply to English and which most authorities agree upon. The classes set out in Table 1.1 are not exhaustive, and the substitution slots illustrated are also examples rather than exhaustive.

Rather than view word-classes as a super-class of substitution classes, we could view them as **canonical** classes. In a canonical class, there are some members which fit all the available criteria for being a member, and some which fit fewer. On this view, *nice* is a more canonical adjective than *afraid*, because *nice* can be used before a noun (attributively)

Table 1.1 Word-classes as substitution classes

	parrot	woman	hatred	knowledge	advisable	pretty	afraid	former	pretend	prefer	deny	be	soon	quickly	then	rather	she	him	ours	the	these	my
the __ is	✓	✓	✓	✓	X	X	X	✓	X	X	X	X	X	X	X	X	X	X	X	X	X	X
can be plural	✓	✓	✓	X	X	X	X	X	X	X	X	X	X	X	X	X	X	X	X	X	✓	X
I recognise the __	✓	✓	✓	✓	X	X	X	✓	X	X	X	X	X	X	X	X	X	X	X	X	X	X
can have *-er/-est*	X	X	X	X	X	✓	X	X	X	X	X	X	✓	X	X	X	X	X	X	X	X	X
can have *-ness*	X	X	X	X	✓	✓	X	X	X	X	X	X	X	X	X	X	X	X	X	X	X	X
the __ (noun)	✓	✓	X	✓	✓	✓	X	✓	✓	X	X	X	X	X	✓	X	✓	X	X	X	X	X
the (noun) is ___	X	X	X	X	✓	✓	✓	X	✓	X	X	X	✓	X	✓	X	X	✓	✓	X	X	X
takes *-s* and *-ing*	✓	X	X	X	X	X	X	X	✓	✓	✓	X	X	X	X	X	X	X	X	X	X	X
												(is!)										
I can __ the (noun)	✓	X	X	X	X	X	X	X	X	X	✓	✓	X	X	X	X	X	X	X	X	X	X
we will __ (verb)	X	X	X	X	X	X	X	X	X	X	X	✓	✓	✓	✓	✓	X	X	X	X	X	X
I did it __	X	X	X	X	X	X	X	X	X	X	X	X	X	✓	✓	X	X	X	X	X	X	X
it is ___ (adjective)	X	X	X	X	X	X	X	X	X	X	X	X	✓	✓	✓	✓	X	X	X	X	X	X
__ can do that or *I saw __*	X	X	✓	✓	X	X	X	X	X	X	X	X	X	X	X	X	✓	✓	✓	X	✓	X
__ red things	X	X	X	X	X	✓	X	✓	✓	X	X	X	X	X	X	X	X	X	X	✓	✓	✓

as in *a nice person* and **predicatively**, as in *That person is nice* while *afraid* cannot be used attributively: **the afraid child*. In terms of nouns, *boy* is a better noun than *insect*, is a better noun than *tree*, is a better noun than *freedom* because human beings are more central to human experience than inanimate objects, and because *freedom* isn't even an object that can be touched or moved, and so on. The English language forces us to treat *freedom* just like any other noun, but it is further from the ideal noun than *boy* is.

Probably the least helpful way of defining word-classes is in terms of their meanings. It is traditional to define a noun as 'the name of a person or thing' and to define a verb as 'a doing word', but it is not clear that *freedom*, *insensitivity* or *belief* is the name of a thing, and *seem* is not obviously a 'doing word', even though it is a verb. Having said that, there are those who defend 'notional' definitions of word-classes, especially because they are not subject to language-dependent formal criteria, such as the form of the *-ing* suffix in the word *seeming*.

1.5 The dictionary

The term 'dictionary' is usually restricted to real-world dictionaries that appear in print and on-line. Dictionaries provide a list of words of whatever language they deal with – in our case, English – and then give a certain amount of information about each of them. Dictionaries tend to have two functions, which may, on occasions, conflict with each other: to describe the language as it is, and to provide an influence for establishing and maintaining the standard form of the language. Clearly, the second function is not to the fore with dialect dictionaries (except insofar as they usually list words which are excluded from the standard), nor in dictionaries of slang and the like, but is often considered to be a function by readers or users of the dictionary, even if it is not the primary motivation of the makers of the dictionary.

To illustrate this point, consider the reaction to the entry for *ain't* in *Webster's Third New International Dictionary* of 1961. The dictionary said of *ain't*:

> Though disapproved by many and more common in less educated speech, used orally in most parts of the U[nited] S[tates] by many cultivated speakers, esp. in the phrase ain't I.

In saying this, the dictionary makers believed they were giving a statement of the way in which *ain't* was used in the English of the United States at the period. In other words, they had a **descriptive** goal. And most of the commentators who recognised the descriptive intent considered that the writers had achieved that descriptive goal. Non-specialist reviewers, however, found this statement offensive. Reviewers wanted the dictionary to tell them that anyone who used *ain't* was, by that very fact, not cultivated ('Cultivated, our foot', scoffed one reviewer). They also objected to a number of other words that were included in the dictionary and not marked as being errors (or just vulgar). These include *boo-boo, drain* (in the sense 'to exhaust a person'), *finalise, greasy spoon, night clothes, no-show, orientate.* I suspect that none of these would cause a raised eyebrow today. (See Sledd and Ebbitt 1962 for examples and discussion.) People who want dictionaries to tell us how we should use language are said to have a **prescriptive** goal.

The distinction between a descriptive and a prescriptive (or **normative**) approach to language has far wider implications than this single, extreme, example might suggest. Crystal (1984) gives entertaining coverage of a number of linguistic issues that were exercising the British public at the period at which he was writing; most of them are probably still relevant to many people. They involve things such as whether it is 'correct' to stress *kilometre* on the first or on the second syllable, what the difference is between *stationary* and *stationery*, whether it is acceptable to use *they* to refer to a single person, when you should use *shall* and when *will.* These are partly matters of vocabulary, but they also involve pronunciation, spelling and grammar. The descriptive versus prescriptive divide covers all of these. The real difference between the two is whether we think there is a 'right' answer to questions of linguistic usage. If we assume that one of *KIlometre* and *kiLOmetre* is right (and the other, therefore, wrong), we assume that there is a unique solution to this question of English usage. We assume that it is a question like *Should you drive on the right or on the left in England?* where there is a single solution laid down by law. We assume it is not like *Should I wear jeans to the party tonight?* where the answer may depend on your age, the dress code for the party, how good you think you look in jeans, whether you prefer to be underdressed or overdressed for any occasion, what else you have to wear, the kind of party that is involved, where the party is being held and so on. Language questions are more often like the jeans question, and less often like the driving-side question. Whatever answer the person you have asked gives you, there will be somebody else, apparently equally authoritative, who will give you a different answer. The moment a dictionary provides only one answer, it becomes de facto an arbiter of usage for anyone who consults it, and thus functions to help define (what its writers consider to be) the standard version of the language.

Linguists often get a bad reputation among the general public for saying that there is more than one answer to such questions. Linguists are much happier saying that one thing is preferred by the young, another by older speakers, or that one thing is well established but another is starting to be heard, that women tend to prefer one thing and men another, or that North Americans tend to say one thing, Britons another. Often, linguists and lay people might be able to agree that something is not standard, is dialectal usage, is used only in technical language, is poetic and so on. But the underlying distinction between saying what happens and saying what should happen (according to some ill-defined norm) remains. Rather than continue to illustrate this dispute, here we need only acknowledge that dictionaries can have these two incompatible goals, and that sometimes one is more to the fore, sometimes another.

Over time, a set of expectations for a dictionary has grown up, and most dictionaries provide comparable information, within the limits of their format. Here, we will consider some of those pieces of information, and where they might support the notional standard.

First of all, dictionaries provide evidence of the existence of a word. The fact that a word is listed in a dictionary at all is taken to prove that there is such a word. This can be misleading in two ways. From time to time, dictionaries list words erroneously, and the word has no existence outside the dictionary. The *OED* gives a list of such **spurious words** including *banket* ('a term in bricklaying'), *David's staff* ('a navigational instrument') and *sardel*, variously supposed to be a fish (the sardine) or a precious stone. Dictionaries far more often fail to list perfectly good words. This is inevitable. No dictionary can list every word of English, and shorter dictionaries list fewer than larger dictionaries. In the very nature of things, there will be some words whose existence is acknowledged in large dictionaries that do not make it into small dictionaries. One of the problems with on-line dictionaries is that the user has no idea of the extent of the word-list in the dictionary, and so cannot tell whether it is worth looking for the desired word in a different, larger, dictionary, if it is not given in that particular source.

Dictionaries list the spelling of a word. Most dictionaries list a single spelling, occasionally two (for example, for *judgement/judgment*). The *OED* lists many spellings, representing spellings at various stages of the development of English, but uses the expected modern spelling for the **headword** (the heading under which the word is discussed). The spelling is important for print dictionaries, because the headwords are ordered according to the spelling. Having said that, 'alphabetical order' is not necessarily obvious. It can be enlightening to put the sets of words like the following in what you consider to be alphabetical order, and then check the order in which they occur in a number of dictionaries: *hatch, hatchery, hatchback, hatchet, hatching, hatbox, hatter, hat trick*.

Many dictionaries provide a pronunciation. Some of them have abbreviatory systems which allow them to give alternative pronunciations in a single transcription (for example, pronunciations with or without the /r/ sound at the end of *prefer*). Dictionaries of pronunciation (for example, Upton et al. 2001; Wells 2008) typically give rather more options, though *Webster's Third New International Dictionary* is said to give twenty-five pronunciations for *berserk* (which is more than either Upton et al. 2001 or Wells 2008). While more and more dictionaries use a transcription system based on the International Phonetic Alphabet, many use their own respelling system. In either case, you will need to be able to interpret the system to use this information in the dictionary.

Dictionaries also provide a meaning, or several meanings, for each word. We can term each of the meanings under a single heading a **polyseme** (see further Section 4.7.1). The number of polysemes provided for a given word is largely a function of the size of the dictionary. Some of the polysemes provided will be largely predictable: for example, the use of *head* to denote part of the human body or part of an animal's body may not need to be given as a separate polyseme. Others are unpredictable, such as the *head* in a tape-recorder being the magnetic part that converts analogue sound to a record on the tape or vice versa. The style of the definition is one of the key decisions facing lexicographers. Should the definition always reflect the word-class of the headword (nouns being defined by other nouns, adjectives by other adjectives and so on), should the definition be a single word or phrase, or is a whole sentence required, is the definition of a plant species by its Latin name sufficient, should all the definitions use a restricted vocabulary, or can they use any words (even ones not in the dictionary) and so on? Very often the style of the definition in a dictionary will be a reason for the reader to like or dislike the particular dictionary, depending on the taste of the reader or the purpose for which the reader requires the dictionary (solvers of cryptic crosswords and learners of English as a foreign language are likely to have different demands, for instance).

Dictionaries usually provide a certain amount of grammatical information. This may be fairly minimal: that *cross* can be a noun or a verb, for example, or that *walk* can be a transitive or an intransitive verb. Other dictionaries, especially dictionaries for foreign learners, give much more grammatical information. The *Longman Dictionary of Contemporary English* (2009), for instance, gives typical subjects and/or direct objects of the verb *cross* with different meanings, and tells you which prepositions to use with the different meanings.

Most dictionaries provide some examples of usage. Sometimes these are just MWEs of various kinds (see Section 1.3), sometimes these are sentences to illustrate grammatical patterns (either from real usage or made up by the lexicographer), sometimes they are examples to illustrate the overall way (including style) in which the word is used. The use of citations from literature to illustrate good usage was made popular by Dr Johnson in the eighteenth century; these days, illustrations from less literary sources are rather more common.

Many dictionaries provide a brief section on the **etymology** of the word. The etymology is the history of the word, where it was borrowed from, when it was first used, what words from other languages derive historically from the same source and so on. Although the word *etymology* comes from a Greek root meaning 'true', and at one time some scholars thought that in providing an etymology they were providing the 'true meaning' of the word, the etymology should never be considered to represent the meaning of the word. For example, the word *innocent* derives etymologically from Latin elements meaning 'not harmful', but *innocent* today does not mean 'harmless' but 'having little experience, not guilty'.

1.6 The lexicon

The **lexicon** is what linguists call the dictionary that is assumed to be in people's heads, or the linguist's best approximation to that. That is, it is fundamentally a psychological entity, and correspondingly, its contents cannot be observed directly, but must be deduced from speakers' and hearers' behaviour. There are two fundamental approaches to the lexicon. The first is that, in the slogan, the lexicon is the home of the lawless (Di Sciullo and Williams 1987): that is, the lexicon contains whatever cannot be predicted by general rule. The second, wider, approach sees the lexicon as not only containing the lawless, but also containing anything to do with the structure of words, whether it is lawless or not.

Among the most fundamentally lawless things is that *cat* means 'cat' (and so on, for thousands of fundamental elements). There is nothing in the form *cat* that indicates that it must mean 'cat', so that is an unpredictable fact. It is so unpredictable that we are surprised when it turns out that the word for 'dog' in the Australian aboriginal language Mbabaram is actually *dog* (and that the word is not borrowed from English). We do not expect the same meaning to be carried by the same form in widely different languages. While not all dictionaries list prefixes and suffixes separately from the words in which they occur (though some do), it seems likely that the lexicon must list not only the fundamental words, like *cat*, that do not contain any prefixes or suffixes, but also the prefixes and suffixes, or at least those which can be used in the creation of new words (that is, those **affixes** which are productive). The usual statement on this is that the lexicon must contain a list of the **morphemes** of the relevant language (where a morpheme is the smallest meaningful unit in the language – including affixes). At the present time, the notion of morpheme is theoretically disputed, which makes it difficult to be sure just what must be included here. Nevertheless, to the extent that we recognise recurrent meaningful chunks within words, we assume them to be listed in the lexicon.

Sometimes, though, words must be in the lexicon even if they contain meaningful elements within them. There are various pieces of evidence that point to this. Derwing (1973: 124) cites the evidence of his three-year-old daughter being delighted when she discovered that *orange juice* had something to do with *oranges*: she had managed to use both words without linking them. A psycholinguistic experiment by Wheeler and Schumsky (1980) found that some speakers did not relate *citizenship* to *citizen* or *baker* to *bake*. Most speakers do not see *foul* as related to *filth* in the same way that *long* is related to *length* (though, in this case, the *-th* suffix is not productive). And in general terms, where a derivative is more frequent than its base it is not clear that speakers break it up into smaller bits: so we probably do not automatically relate *government* to *govern*, even if we relate *confinement* to *confine*, because *government* is heard much more often than *govern* (Hay 2003). This means that for some words, we have two routes to understanding them: we can 'look them up' in our lexicons, or we can work out what they mean on the basis of the elements that make them up. Models of the lexicon which permit such a procedure are called **dual-route models**.

We must assume, then, that we have in our lexicons a list of all the fundamental, unanalysable, words, other meaningful elements (morphemes, if we allow for the presence of such a unit), and also a number of words which, etymologically, are made up of several meaningful elements. However meaningful the elements of *blackmail* were to the person who first used the word, they are not helpful to people today in understanding the word.

This raises the question of how these words are listed in the lexicon. Alphabetical order cannot be a relevant factor – there are far too many people, even today, who speak English but cannot read or write English for this to be the answer. That does not mean that literate speakers of English are not also influenced by spellings, just that spelling is not the fundamental organisational principle of the lexicon. Rather, it seems that there are multiple links between items in the lexicon, some of them dependent upon the form of the word (the sounds it is made up of) and some of them dependent upon meaning.

It used to be thought that readers translated what they saw on the page into a phonological representation in order to link it to a meaning. Now it is far less clear that things are as simple as this. For instance, when we look at pathological cases, we find that some patients are able to understand a written text but not name the words they are reading, or understand a spoken word without being able to link the meaning to a spelling. This suggests that although there is a link between pronunciation and spelling, those two are linked independently to representations of meaning in the brain (Allport and Funnell 1981). We must conclude that spelling is important for literate people as well as pronunciation, and to some extent independent of it.

When we recognise spoken words, we obviously use the pronunciation, and we use the elements within the word in the order in which we hear them. If we hear /gʌ/ we seem to get our brains fired up ready to hear *gubbins* or *guppy* or *gust* or any other relevant word. If we next hear /t/ we do not know whether the word will be *gut* or *gutta-percha* or *gutter* or *guttural* and all these options remain open. If we next hear /ə/ we can rule out *gut* (assuming the /ə/ is part of the same word), and if that is the end of the word we have *gutter*. When we get to the point where no other word will fit what we have heard, we reach the **recognition point**, and we do not need to bother with any further information, because it is redundant. This means that it is easier to recognise *redundant* from /rɪˈdʌ/ than from /dənt/ (Marslen-Wilson and Zwitserlood 1989). This is how we can tell so quickly that *cown* is not a word of (our) English. If we know some 60,000 lexemes (which is the kind of figure that is often provided; see, for example, Aitchison 2003: 8), some of which have several word-forms associated with them, and we could check them off at, say, 60 per second, it would still take us over 1,000 seconds to make sure we have no word in *cown* in our vocabularies. But if we have been checking each sound-element as we hear it, and cutting down the number of options at each step, we already know by the end of the word that we have nothing matching that string in our lexicons.

When we produce words, as opposed to recognising them, we cannot start with the sounds, we must start with the meanings (unless somebody tells you to list as many words as you can starting with /b/). It seems we work in much the same way: we activate a whole lot of words in the relevant part of our vocabulary, and then make a choice between the activated words. For example, if we want to say something about a cow, we may activate a whole lot of words for farm animals (*donkey*, *sheep*, *horse*, *goat* and so on) and from that list choose the word *cow*. At some stage, and it is not entirely clear what that stage is, we assign a pronunciation to the word we have chosen. Sometimes, though, we make a mistake, and we might say *We have to milk the bulls*, because both *cow* and *bull* have been activated in our brains, and we have grabbed the phonological representation for the wrong one. If you talk to someone about electricity, and then make them read something that includes the phrase *sham dock*, they might very well say *damn shock*, because of the prior activation of words associated with electricity (Aitchison 2003: 218); and the phenomenon of the Freudian slip depends upon some subject area being readily activated in the brain, and brought out inadvertently, whether because of a word related in meaning or a word related in pronunciation.

There are multiple ways in which words can be linked semantically. As was just suggested, words for farm animals may be linked by our experience of the entities they denote being linked. Words can be linked by meaning (at least in some contexts) more or less the same thing: *remedy*, *rectify* and *restore*, for instance. They may be linked by being opposites: *happy* and *sad*, *black* and *white*. They can be linked because they often occur together: *keep* and *calm*, *round* and *table*. Words can be linked by being part of the same classification: *tulip* and *rose* (both flowers), *Tyne* and *Severn* (both rivers), *cod* and *whiting* (both fish) and so on. Words can be linked by having the same form but different meanings: *cricket* (the game) and *cricket* (the insect), *guy* (a rope) and *guy* (a person), *potter* (a maker of pots) and *potter* (to undertake small tasks with no haste). We shall deal with such relationships as these in a later section (see Section 4.7.1). For the present, note that these various types of relationship are not necessarily mutually exclusive: *ewe* and *ram* are both farm animals, both types of sheep and opposites in terms of adult sex.

As well as providing some information on meaning, the lexicon must provide some grammatical information. Just how much such information must be there and how it is stored are controversial topics, but some of the information is not predictable from general principles, and is probably therefore listed in the lexicon because it is lawless. Word-class is one such piece of information. There are those who argue that word-class is determined by the syntactic tree into which the word is placed, but somehow the speaker needs to know that *dog* and *cat* will both fit into trees as nouns, but while *dog* will fit into a tree as a verb (*He seems to dog my footsteps everywhere I go*), *cat* – for most speakers of modern English – will not. Equally, while *up* can be a verb (*The doctor upped the dose*) or possibly an adjective (*the up train*), *through* cannot be a verb, and *beyond* cannot be either. Since there is no generality here, it would seem that it is lexical information. More generally, the lexicon must

Table 1.2 Grammatical patterns with some verbs

	She ___d that I should leave	*She ___d me to leave*	*She ___d my departure*	*She ___d my leaving*	*She ___d leaving*	*She ___d me that I should leave*
advise	✓	✓	✓	?	✓	✓
counsel	X	✓	X	X	X	?
exhort	X	✓	X	X	X	X
propose	✓	X	✓	?✓	≠	X
recommend	✓	X	✓	✓	✓	X
suggest	✓	X	?	?✓	✓	X
tell	X	✓	X	X	X	✓
urge	✓	✓	✓	X	✓	X

provide information on the constructions the word can occur in. This will include such usage as transitive and intransitive in verbs (if you can *shoulder a burden*, why can't you *back a coat* or *finger a ring* – especially as you can *back a horse* and *finger a perpetrator of a crime?*), but also much more complex constructions. Consider the set of words and the patterns in which they can occur freely shown in Table 1.2, where the verbs all have to do with communicating something. To the extent that such information is not predictable, it must be in the lexicon.

Some words mean different things when they appear in different contexts. The obvious example is *dry*, which can be used to modify *politician, throat, towel, weather, wine* or *wit*, with a different meaning in each case. Even if some of these meanings arise from perfectly normal extensions of an original meaning, they have become established and, to a large extent, unpredictable. In other cases, even the fact that particular words tend to go together is unpredictable. It does not seem to be predictable that we say *warm welcome* but *friendly wave*, that we have a *vernal equinox* or a *spring equinox* but only *spring flowers*, that you *hide* your eyes but *conceal* your thoughts. When such collocations are unpredictable and linked to the individual words involved, they must be in the lexicon.

The various kinds of MWE discussed in Section 1.3 must also be part of the lexicon. Since such things are either known or not known, when they are known, they must be in the lexicon.

The word *turquoise* is probably used more by women than by men (though *cyan* may be used more by men); the word *doggy* is probably used more by children or to young children than among adults; the term of address *bro* used to be used (and possibly still is) more among some ethnic groups than others; the word *discombobulate* is not entirely serious; the word *ardour* is formal or literary; the word *micturition* is used scientifically or medically. Some of these things are, to a certain extent at least, predictable: words with the *-y* suffix tend to be used more by and for children, but not all of them – *Chevy* (from *Chevrolet*) is not a word children use; *discombobulate* shows its made-up nature by containing unrecognisable elements. Nevertheless, just when a particular word is used is not something that can be determined from basic principles. It can even change over time. The expression *more than somewhat* started life as a joke, but has become serious. Although it is not entirely clear just what information people gather about such words, or what categories they work with, some information on usage must be listed in the lexicon.

All of the material that has been discussed above is the 'lawless' material: things that cannot be predicted by general principles or deduced from other aspects of the words involved. But in the more inclusive view of the lexicon, everything that has to do with the construction of words is there, whether it is predictable or not. According to this view, the terms 'lexical' ('to do with the structure of the lexicon') and 'lexical' ('to do with the structure of words') can be seen as synonymous – or at least, a lot closer to the synonymous than would be the case under the alternative view.

Part of the justification for this view is that the way in which words are made up is not equivalent to the way in which sentences are made up. In a sentence like (16), for instance, the meaning of the sentence can be deduced from the meanings of the words in the sentence and the syntactic structure of the sentence.

(16)   The dog barked loudly at the postman.

If we know what *dog, bark, loudly* and *postman* mean, and we know that *the dog* is the subject of the verb *bark*, we can work out the meaning of the sentence from basic principles. In such cases, the semantics of the sentence is said to be compositional. But if we look at words like *marriage* and *carriage*, we cannot tell from the elements that make up the words and their structure that *marriage* means a legal relationship while *carriage* means a vehicle (in both cases there are other meanings, but these are the most likely ones). Neither can we predict from general principles of English that the noun from *marry* will be *marriage* rather than *marriment* (compare *embodiment*), *marriance* (compare *dalliance, defiance*), *marrial* (compare *burial*) or *marry* (compare *worry*). Furthermore, we cannot predict that if we have *marriage* and *carriage* we will not have *tarriage* from *tarry* or *worriage* from *worry*. Unpredictable meanings and gaps in the paradigm are said to make what goes on in word-formation very different from what goes on in syntax.

Words like *marriage* and *carriage* exemplify **derivational morphology**, the creation of new lexemes. **Inflectional morphology**, the creation of new word-forms of known lexemes, is rather different. Given a verb such as *sing*, it is entirely predictable what *sings* means and where it will occur. Moreover, every non-modal verb has a form with a final -*s*, and it always means precisely the same thing. It would be possible to treat this final -*s* form as being a part of syntax without any problem. The difficulty here lies in how far we can push this. *Sing*, like all other non-modal verbs, also has an -*ing* form, *singing*, but *sing* does not have an -*ed* form, *singed*: rather we find *sang* fulfilling the same role. Still, there is a form in the appropriate slot in the paradigm, even if the form itself is not entirely predictable: why is it *sing* and *sang* but *swing* and *swung*? What about adding -*ly* to adjectives to give things like *commonly*? Here there are some adjectives which do not follow the expected pattern: the adverb from *fast* is *fast*, for instance, and the adverb from *hard* is not *hardly*, which means something else. With plurals there are some nouns which do not have a plural (*knowledge*, for example), some which do not have a singular (*mumps*, for example) and some which have an unpredictable plural (*genera* as the plural of *genus*, for example).

All theories of the lexicon, whether they wish to include word-building in the lexicon or not, whether they want to distinguish between inflection and derivation or not, and whatever the structure of the theory, have to deal with questions like these. How the problem is dealt with may change, but the general nature of the problem does not.

1.7 Summary

In this chapter, we have seen that the notion of word is difficult to define, and that there are elements that are longer than words, which nevertheless share many of the features of words. We have also looked at traditional dictionaries, and talked about the kind of content that is likely to be found there, and then contrasted that with the lexicon, the dictionary that belongs in people's heads, showing how many of the things in the dictionary are also in the lexicon, but that the two do not always match each other.

Exercises

1. Choose any category of MWEs and find another five examples which fit in the category.
2. Find any printed dictionary (preferably one with which you are familiar) and work out what the structure of the dictionary entry

is. What information does it give, what does it not give? How much grammatical information does it give? How does it mark different parts of the entry? How does it deal with MWEs – does it deal with all of them in the same way, or does it distinguish between types?

3. Find five words which you would consider literary or poetic, and five which you would consider colloquial or familiar. If you have access to any large corpora, check the environments in which your words occur. Is your feeling supported by the evidence?

4. Can you think of any prescriptive rules that you have been taught at home or in school? Why do you think you were taught these rules? Did the overt teaching change your behaviour, and if so, how?

5. Can you find, or do you know, any words which have more than one correct spelling? How many can you list (or better, how many can a group of you list)? Are any of these spellings indicative of geographical location? What does all this tell you about the degree to which spelling is fixed by prescription in English?

6. Re-read the section on dictionaries above (Section 1.5) and then, without consulting a dictionary, write dictionary entries for the words *chair*, *drive* and *late*. Explain what decisions you have taken in drafting your entries, and why you took them. Finally, compare your entries with ones from published dictionaries. Are the differences due to ignorance on your part, or to something else? If you were to write a dictionary, what would you learn from this experience?

7. Do you agree with all the ticks and crosses in Table 1.1? Can you improve upon any of the environments proposed in the table?

8. Do you agree with the data presented in Table 1.2? Are there other relevant environments? Are there generalisations which make some of the information predictable?

Recommendations for reading

On the notion of word from a cross-linguistic perspective, see Bauer (2000), Dixon and Aikhenvald (2002) and Hippisley (2015). On MWEs, see Moon (2015). On dictionaries in general, see Mugglestone (2011). On formulaic language in general, see Wray (2012).

2 Making new words

2.1 Introduction

We can divide words into two major categories. On the one hand, we have the words whose meaning we cannot predict at all, we just have to know what they mean. The example of *cat* was given above. There is nothing in *cat* to tell us that it means 'feline quadruped' rather than, say, 'coniferous tree'. We have to know what *cat* means. On the other hand, a word like *friendliness* provides us with some clues as to why it should mean what it means. We still have to know that *friend* means 'friend', but the *-li* and the *-ness*, although they have fairly abstract meanings, tell us that we are dealing with an abstract noun derived from an adjective. The meaning of a word like *cat* is **arbitrary**; the meaning of a word like *friendliness* is partly **motivated**.

In this chapter we are concerned with partly motivated words, and how they are, can be, or have been created in English. In order to create a word, it is typically the case that some procedure is carried out on some other word. In *friendliness*, that procedure is the addition of suffixes. We will see other procedures later in the chapter. We call the original word on which the procedure is carried out the **base** of the new word. Some words like *friendly* have one base, while others like *clocktower* have more than one. *Friend* is the base for the creation of *friendly*, *friendly* is the base for the creation of *friendliness*. Any process which can be used to create new words is said to be productive (as we have already seen in Chapter 1).

2.2 Blends

Consider the English word *hangry*. It is used to describe a fractious child (or indeed, adult) who is simultaneously hungry and angry. It is formed by taking the words *hungry* and *angry* and telescoping them together, omitting some of the phonological or orthographical structure, to give *hangry*. We could write this as in (1).

(1)   hungry + angry > hangry

In this formulation, we see some of the relevant factors in the formation of such words, which Humpty Dumpty in *Through the Looking-Glass* (Carroll 1872) called **portmanteau words** but which today are more often called **blends**. Occasionally the label **telescope words** is used. The first point to notice is that the blend takes the first part of one word (in our example, the *h* from *hungry*) and the last part of the second word (in our example, all of the word *angry*), and makes a new word out of them. This immediately gives rise to questions of how much of each word is taken. In a word like *hangry*, which is made up of two adjectives and means the combination of the two, we have to ask how we know which of the two words to put first. Are there general rules, or is it an ad hoc decision in individual cases? In the case of *hungry* and *angry*, the two base words are phonologically and orthographically rather similar (they share <ngry>, or its phonological counterpart, and the vowels written <a> and <u> sound rather similar). How far is this a requirement for a blend?

Next consider the word *motel*. Just as we wrote the formula for *hangry* in (1), we can write a parallel formula for *motel*, as in (2).

(2)   motor + hotel > motel

This example raises some different questions. The first is, whether there is any reason for saying that one or the other <o> has been deleted. (As far as I know, there is no such reason; it was a random choice.) This time, some material has been deleted from both words (independent of whether the <o> is assigned to *motor* or to *hotel*). Does this make a different type from the *hangry* type? More to the point, *motor* and *hotel* are not two equally balanced words which contribute equally to the meaning. Here *motor* tells us what kind of *hotel*, while *hungry* did not tell us what kind of *angry*. In other words, while *motor* and *hotel* are syntagmatically related words, *hungry* and *angry* are paradigmatically related words (see Section 1.4). This is clearly a different type. Some authorities do not see the *motel* type as blends, but as some other structure; others see them all as blends, just different subtypes, sometimes called paradigmatic and syntagmatic, sometimes called **headed** (the *motel* type, which is a type of hotel) and **coordinative** (the *hangry* type, where the meaning of the blend is the meaning of *hungry* and *angry* together). Here, this second path will be taken, but you should feel free to object, especially if you can find some way in which their semantic structure predicts their behaviour. Any section of a blend which is derived from a word but has some part of the word removed is called a **splinter**. In *motel* it may not be clear whether the splinters are *mo* and *tel* or *m* and *otel* or *mot* and *el*. When splinters are repeated (as in *hotel, motel, boatel*) some people call them **combining forms**, but this term is more usually used for a different kind of word (see Sections 2.4.1, 3.4.2).

Table 2.1 provides a list of examples of blends in English. The examples are not entirely random, but neither are they systematic in any way; they are simply examples from a number of different sources. On the basis of these examples, we can look at some of the constraints on forming blends.

The first thing to notice in Table 2.1 is that there are rather more coordinative blends (marked with a 'c') than there are headed blends (marked with an 'h'). This is typical of blends in English, and if anything, Table 2.1 exaggerates the proportion of headed blends. One of the main uses of coordinative blends in English is to show hybrids, crosses between two things or interbreeding (see, for example, (xxxvi, xli, xlii)).

When it comes to the constraints that apply to blends (which you may prefer to view as the rules for making blends), none of them is absolute. Constraints hold unless there is a good reason for ignoring them. It will be shown below that many of the constraints have exceptions, especially when constraints come into conflict.

The first constraint, then, is that the blend should be no longer than the longer of the two bases that make up the blend. We can measure length here in number of syllables. The exception to this rule is shown in (xii). There are various versions of this word (all the northern hemisphere mid-winter festivals viewed as a single holiday) – some include a splinter for the word *solstice*, for instance – but they are all longer than the longest base, *Hanukkah*. This seems to be a function of trying to put so many elements into the word, and yet keep the bases recognisable. Note that it is also the only example given here of more than two bases being involved in a blend. Such cases are rare, but this example is by no means unique in this regard. Typically, the longest base is the second element in a blend, but note the exception in (x), where the order found allows the overlap in the /f/ sound. Part of what is happening here is that we recognise the beginnings of words more easily than the ends (see Section 1.6). This means that the splinter that shows the beginning of a base can be shorter than the splinter showing the end of a base.

The other side of this is that we tend to retain more material from the second base in the blend, and this usually means maintaining the **stress** pattern from the second base as well. *Posilutely* (xxix) retains the stress from *absolutely*, not the initial stress from *positively*, for example. In *glamping* (xxii), the stress from *camping* is retained, even though it is the shorter base – unless you think that this blend was formed with

Table 2.1 Examples of blends in English

	Blend	First base	Second base	Coordinative/ headed
i.	advertorial	advert(isement)	editorial	c
ii.	ambisextrous	sex	ambidextrous	h
iii.	anecdotage	anecdote	dotage	h
iv.	backronym	back	acronym	h
v.	barococo	baroque	rococo	c
vi.	blingshevik	bling	bolshevik	h
vii.	brasshole	brass	asshole	c
viii.	brunch	breakfast	lunch	c
ix.	Californicate	California	fornicate	h
x.	catastrofuck	catastrophe	fuck(-up)(?)	c
xi.	celebutard	celebrity	retard	c
xii.	christmahanakwanzika	Christmas	Hanukkah, Kwanzaa	c
xiii.	consumertariat	consumer	proletariat	c
xiv.	corpsicle	corpse	popsicle	c
xv.	cutbow	cutthroat (trout)	rainbow (trout)	c
xvi.	dadolescence	dad	adolescence	h
xvii.	dolphinarium	dolphin	aquarium	h
xviii.	edutainment	education	entertainment	c
xix.	feebate	fee	rebate	c
xx.	femoir	female	memoir	h
xxi.	giganaire	gigabyte	millionaire	h
xxii.	glamping	glamorous	camping	h
xxiii.	glitterati	glitter	literati	h
xxiv.	greige	grey	beige	c
xxv.	infotainment	information	entertainment	c
xxvi.	mathlete	math(s)	athlete	h
xxvii.	nun-pocalypse	nun	apocalypse	h
xxviii.	palimony	pal	alimony	h
xxix.	posilutely	positively	absolutely	c
xxx.	powernoia	power	paranoia	c
xxxi.	robocopter	robot	helicopter	c
xxxii.	sadpocalypse	sad(ness)	apocalypse	h
xxxiii.	sexting	sex	texting	h
xxxiv.	sheeple	sheep	people	c
xxxv.	slumitecture	slum	architecture	h
xxxvi.	snirt	snow	dirt	c
xxxvii.	spork	spoon	fork	c
xxxviii.	stagflation	stagnation	inflation	c
xxxix.	staycation	stay	vacation	c
xl.	techsplorer	technology	explorer	h
xli.	thuggon	thug	moron	c

Table 2.1 (*cont.*)

	Blend	First base	Second base	Coordinative/ headed
xlii.	tigon	tiger	lion	c
xliii.	trafficator	traffic	indicator	h
xliv.	webisode	web	episode	h
xlv.	weekaversary	week	anniversary	h

glam or *glamour* as the first base. Examples (x, xi) provide exceptions. In cases like *infotainment* (xxv), we assume that the stress comes from *entertainment* – although the stress pattern would be the same if it came from *information* – because we link the stress pattern with the segmental material it occurs with.

Blends do not always show phonological (or orthographic) overlap between the two bases (consider, for example, *nun-pocalypse* 'a film in which many nuns get killed' (xxvii)), but it seems to be a preferred option if it is possible. Example (x) has already been cited as an example where this seems to be a factor in the order of the elements. In *ambi-sextrous* (ii), inserting one base into the middle of another, rather than keeping them side-by-side, is the only way of allowing appropriate overlap. Note, incidentally, that sometimes phonology seems to be more important than orthography in the make-up of the blend, sometimes the orthography is important. In *weekaversary* (xlv), the letter <a> is used to represent /ə/, even though the base anniversary has an <i> (pronounced either /ɪ/ or /ə/). In instances like *greige* (xxiv) and *staycation* (xxxix), the orthography seems to be used to support the recognisability of one of the elements, where there is phonological overlap. In *femoir* (xx) (if pronounced /femwɑː/), the <e> spelling might belong to the first base, but the /e/ pronunciation must belong to the second.

The order of the elements is determined by the meaning for headed blends, but for coordinative blends the order has to be worked out. In a case like *brunch* (viii), the order of the two seems to reflect the order of the two meals named by the bases. In *tigon* (xlii), the order of the dam and the sire is important, since in *tigon* the tiger is the sire, while in *liger* the tiger is the dam. In *greige* (xxiv), the order might be determined by the fact that the alternative order would give rise to *bay*, which is already a (different, if related) colour. But perhaps more importantly, the bases would not both be recognisable in *bay*, while they do remain recognisable in *greige*. The same would be true for *sheeple* (xxxiv), where *peep* would look like an abbreviation of *people*, and not like a blend at all. In *staycation* (xxxix) the order seems to be determined by the maximal overlap between the two bases. In cases where mono-syllables are blended, it seems that a consonant cluster is better on the first element, since it gives a better clue to the identity of the first base than a single consonant (or none at all) would do. *Snirt* (xxxvi) is more easily recognisable than *dow*, *spork* (xxxvii) is more easily recognisable than *foon*. In *robocopter*, the fact that *robo* is already found as a splinter in words like *robocraft*, *robocide* is probably a supporting factor. In more general terms, it seems to be helpful if the first base can be represented by a whole syllable (and failing that, by the entire onset of the syllable), while the second splinter, if it starts with a vowel, cuts off the onset to a syllable. It would be very unusual to find a blend made out of, say, *stone* and *wood*, having a form with just the <s> from *stone* (that is, having the form *swood*), or a blend from *wood* and *stone* losing just the <s> from *stone* (and having the form *wootone*).

Although not all possible questions about the nature of blends have been traversed here, sufficient has been said to illustrate that making a blend is not an easy business. There are many factors that have to be considered if a good blend is to be produced, and sometimes people fail to make good blends. Consider *celebutard* (xi). It is not clear where the <u> comes from. The form *celebritard* would seem to be a better solution to the problem. Since *celebutante* (from *celebrity* and *debutante*) is also found, it is possible that the <u> has been assigned to the wrong element from the other blend, but that is just speculation. It could be an error. The form in (xii) also seems odd: where does the <i> come from (is it a representation of /ə/ in *hanukkah*) and why does the splinter from *Kwanzaa* fit inside the *hanukkah* element? Because blends like these are not easy, they are special. A good blend draws attention to itself: it is eye-catching, often humorous. Blends are words for special occasions, not for everyday wear, and a good blend must be treasured. In the next sections, ways of making new words that are less difficult and more suited to daily use will be considered.

2.3 Compounds

2.3.1 Basic noun + noun compounding

One way to simplify the production and recognition of new words is not to abbreviate them, but simply to juxtapose two words. Words made by juxtaposing two other words are called compounds. Compounds seem to be easy for English speakers to learn – children learn how to make their own compounds very early – but they are difficult to describe satisfactorily.

You are already familiar with hundreds of compounds. Some examples are given in (3). The examples in (3) are all nouns, made up of nouns, because these are the most easily available compounds in English, although we can recognise various subtypes. We will look at compounds from other word-classes afterwards.

(3)   a. arm-chair, boarding pass, boathouse, coffee cup, computer table, fairy tale, landmark, library book, motorway, power cord, railway, rain-forest, tea-cake, washing powder, windmill

      b. bus-driver, child-minder, debt-collector, deerstalker, English teacher, fire-fighter, lawn-mower, space heater

      c. egg head, hatchback, rug rat, waxwing

      d. boy wonder, child bride, fridge-freezer, singer-songwriter, Southland-Otago, washer-drier

The difference between the words in (3a) and (3d) is the same as the difference between the *hangry* and the *motel* types of blend: an *arm-chair* is a type of chair (the construction has a head in its final base), while *fridge-freezer* is something which is both a fridge and a freezer, so the two are coordinated. The examples in (3b) are like those in (3a) in that a *bus-driver* is a *driver*, but they have rather more constrained meanings. We will look at this in detail in just a few moments. Those in (3c) are sometimes said not to have a head because a *hatchback* is not a back, but a car with a particular sort of back (perceived as being like a hatch). A *rug rat* is not a rat, but something perceived as being rat-like.

Compounds like those in (3a) are called **endocentric compounds**. They make up the largest set of English compounds, but it is not always clear where the borders of such compounds lie. To distinguish them from those in (3b), they are sometimes called **primary compounds** or **root compounds**, neither of which is a particularly helpful piece of terminology. Those in (3b) have a plethora of names: they can be called **secondary compounds**, **verbal-nexus compounds**, **verb-centred compounds** or **synthetic compounds**. The last of these terms will be adopted here, but that is only because it seems to be the most frequent of these labels. Those in (3c) are sometimes called **exocentric compounds**, *centre* being an older term for a head, and the idea is that the head of, say, *waxwing* is not inside the compound, but outside it, in an understood element *bird*. And those in (3d) are called **coordinative compounds**, again with alternative terms like **coordinate**, **copulative** and **dvandva**.

The difference between primary endocentric compounds and synthetic compounds is a matter of how free the interpretation of the compound is. The interpretation of primary compounds is relatively free, in the sense that there does not seem to be a fixed semantic relationship between the two bases in the compound. Consider the examples in (4).

(4)   a. blockhouse, bunkhouse, country house, hen house, summer house, tree house
       b. tree diagram, tree farm, tree frog, tree house, tree line

In the examples in (4) we see a range of different semantic relationships holding between the elements: a *bunkhouse* contains bunks, but a *country house* does not contain countries; hens live in a *henhouse*, but trees do not normally grow in a *tree house*; a *tree frog* lives in a tree, but *a tree diagram* resembles a tree; in the case of *tree line* it is difficult to specify precisely what the relationship is. In (4a) we can see that the semantic relationship is not entirely predictable from the second base; in (4b) we see that it is not entirely predictable from the first base, although other examples parallel to *tree frog* are easier to find that other examples parallel to *tree diagram*, so there are some relationships which particular bases prefer.

By way of contrast, the meaning of *bus-driver* is pretty much determined by its elements: it has to mean 'a person or thing which drives a bus'; it cannot mean 'a driver who lives in a bus' or 'a driver who resembles a bus'. This is the sense in which the meanings of words in (3b) are more tightly constrained than the meanings of the words in (3a).

Having said that, the borderline between the two types is difficult to maintain. *Bus-driving* seems to be like *bus-driver*, constrained in its meaning. The same seems to be true of *university administration*, which means 'administration of a/the university'. But although *city administration* could mean 'administration of a/the city', in *city administration of parks* it means 'administration by the city'. So is *police protection* a primary compound if it means that police protect someone, but a synthetic compound if it means that somebody protects the police? How do we want to classify words that require a preposition in their gloss? An *apartment dweller* cannot dwell an apartment (it is not grammatical); they must dwell in an apartment. That may seem to be like *bus-driver*, or it may not. By the time we get to *Sunday driver*, things are less clear. *Sunday* specifies temporal location, we could gloss it as 'on Sunday', but the verb *drive* does not require a temporal location in the way that it requires a direct object: while *She drives for the company* would be a possible utterance (and *company driver* a possible compound), we would feel justified in asking what she drives, but rather less in asking when she drives. And *town crier* is even harder to deal with: it is not even clear how we should gloss it. Should we paraphrase it as 'somebody cries in the town', 'somebody cries for the town', or something else (*cry* is probably no longer current in the relevant sense anyway)? Most scholars exclude instances like *Sunday driver* and *police protection* (the police do the protecting) from the set of synthetic compounds, but many include not only *bus driver* and *bus-driving* but *apartment dweller* and *apartment dwelling*. There is a slippery slope between the various examples, and just where the boundaries of the type lie is not necessarily clear.

The distinction between examples such as those in (3a) and (3c) is even less clear. First, consider a sentence like (5).

(5)   The hand was working in the field.

In this sentence, traditional rhetoric would tell us that the word *hand* is understood as a figure of speech, specifically **synecdoche** /sɪˈnekdəki/. It does not mean 'a hand', but names a part of the thing that it does mean, namely a person. Synecdoche is sometimes called *pars pro toto* ('the part for the whole'), and is sometimes viewed as a type of **metonymy**. We will look at synecdoche and metonymy in more detail later (see Sections 4.7.3, 4.7.4). Now consider (6).

(6)   The farm-hand was working in the field.

If we take the position that what we have in (3c) is a special class of compound, then we have to say that *farm-hand* in (6) is an exocentric compound. But we also have available the same explanation that we used in relation to (5), namely that *farm-hand* is simply a case of synecdoche. This means we have two explanations for the same element, and this is contrary to a fundamental principle of philosophy called Ockham's razor. For our purposes here, we can gloss this as 'Having one postulate to explain a situation is to be preferred over having two to cover the same function'. So exocentric compounds could be reinterpreted as compounds (endocentric compounds) which are interpreted in terms of some figure of speech (in *farm-hand* it is synecdoche, in *rug rat* it is **metaphor**). The whole notion of exocentric compound is theoretically suspect.

Even if it were not, it is difficult to apply. Consider the example of *monkey puzzle*, which is the English name for the araucaria tree, which is also known as the *monkey-puzzle tree*. In relation to *waxwing*, it was said above that the assumption is that there is a head, *bird*, which is deleted, leaving the exocentric form *waxwing*. If the same is true of *monkey-puzzle tree*, deleting *tree* should leave us with the exocentric *monkey puzzle*. But a *monkey puzzle* is a *puzzle* (if *puzzle* is a noun), at least for the putative monkey. That is, a *monkey puzzle* is a type of puzzle, and this is enough to say that the compound is endocentric and not exocentric. There is another possible analysis: perhaps *puzzle* is a verb, *monkey* is the direct object of the verb, and this is a word which patterns like *prick-tease* (not a very common pattern in English), another exocentric pattern. Overall, then, it is hard to know how we tell whether *monkey puzzle* is endocentric or exocentric. The same is true with something like *tea-house*. Is a *tea-house* a kind of house? If you think that a house is any building, then it is, and *tea-house* is endocentric. If you think it is specifically a building in which humans live (and perhaps, by extension, where animals live), then *tea-house* is not a house, and *tea-house* is exocentric. There are many examples of this kind. Correspondingly, there are many examples where the distinction between endocentric and exocentric compounds is not clear.

2.3.2 Understanding and making new compounds

Because endocentric compounds like those in (4) show a number of different semantic relationships between the two bases involved, a great deal of theorising has taken place over the years trying to work out how speakers and hearers calculate the meanings of new compounds. Old, familiar compounds may simply be learned. We may simply know that a *boat house* has boats in the house but a *tree house* is a house in the tree. But how do we know which of these relationships (if either) will hold in the next compound ending in *house* that we come across? Is there a limited number of possible relationships which we can list, can the relationships be calculated from the lexemes involved, or do we have to guess from the context?

There does not seem to be limited number of listable relationships. The example of *tree line* has already been used to illustrate this point. We might not be sure how to gloss *tree line*: perhaps, 'the apparent line on a mountain-side formed by the trees that grow highest up the mountain; the division between that part of the mountain-side with trees, and that part without trees'. Even if you can formulate that more economically, it seems unlikely that this is one of a fixed number of relationships with which the English language works – it seems far too specific. Or consider the example of *spaghetti western*. The relationship here is something like 'a western (cowboy movie) made in a country whose inhabitants are supposed typically to eat a lot of spaghetti'.

These examples also show that you cannot necessarily deduce the relationship from the lexemes involved. With *spaghetti* we might expect to find something like *spaghetti meal, spaghetti dish, spaghetti recipe*, but *spaghetti* does not have some pre-established relationship to westerns. So how do we come to understand such forms?

Consider the compound *concrete poem*. You may not have come across it before, but even so, you can probably see it as related to *concrete poetry*, and thus as an example of concrete poetry (just as a poem is an example of poetry). You do not have to have a specific meaning in your head to get this understanding, you simply have to recognise the parallel to something else. Similarly, you may not know the compound *cocktail belt*, but in a sentence like *They have just moved out to a new house in the cocktail belt*, you can draw parallels with *commuter belt* or *stockbroker belt* to get a reading where the belt is an area round the city where cocktails are prevalent. Having come across *spaghetti western*, you can probably understand *goulash communism* (used of Hungary in the 1970s and 1980s) to mean 'the kind of communism practised in Hungary – a place where people are supposed to eat a lot of goulash'. Very often we get large number of parallel examples along these lines. Consider the examples with *cake* in (7). (These are examples which are just on the border of constructions which linguists will agree are compounds, some claiming they are just noun phrases, but the basic principle applies.)

(7)   almond cake, chocolate cake, fruit cake, lemon cake, walnut cake

In (7) we find a set of examples where the first base denotes a critical ingredient which distinguishes this cake from others. It is not the major ingredient (flour and sugar are likely to be more fundamental), just the distinctive ingredient. We can also find other series with *cake*, those in (8), for instance.

(8)   birthday cake, Christmas cake, wedding cake

Here it seems that the lexemes involved do distinguish the series in (7) from the series in (8): we do not celebrate lemons, and wedding is not an ingredient for a cake, and we could easily guess which series *prune cake* and *graduation cake* would fit into. The two series in (7) and (8) do not exhaust the possible patterns. We also find examples like those in (9).

(9)   beef cake, cup cake, layer cake, pancake

To interpret these we might have to look to other patterns with *cup* and so on. New words on these patterns are likely to be slightly harder to understand, because these patterns are not as usual. We would probably have to rule out the expected patterns in (7) and (8) before interpreting new words that patterned like these.

What all these compounds share, and what we could see as being the meaning of the compound construction, is that the first base indicates a distinctive subtype of whatever is denoted by the second base, or, more precisely, what is perceived as being distinctive at the time of coining.

That is, the compound denotes a **hyponym** (see Section 4.4.3) of the second base in the compound, and the first base denotes something which makes clear what subtype of base is involved. Although we can see a host of semantic relationships holding between the bases, these are not part of the linguistic structure of the compounds, and all that matters to speakers and listeners is whether the relationship in one word is like the relationship in another or not.

2.3.3 Adjective + noun compounds

Most linguists allow for a set of adjective + noun compounds in English, although some demur. These are compounds like those in (10).

(10) a. blackbird, deep end, flatbread, highway, hothouse, lowland, sweetcorn, wetsuit, whiteboard
      b. hightop, red head, roughneck, softball, whitethorn

The difference between the examples in (10a) and those in (10b) is the difference between endocentric and exocentric that we have already seen in Section 2.3.1, and the same problems for the categories exist here as were discussed above, so that *hothouse* may not be properly categorised in (10).

The examples in (10) share the features that the first base provides a classification of the second base, rather than an absolute description, with the result that the first base may be negated without contradiction (*That blackbird is brown* is a perfectly reasonable sentence), the adjective cannot be submodified by *so*, *very* and so on, or made comparative or superlative (*the hottest house* would no longer necessarily be a hothouse), and they carry stress on the first base.

The examples in (10) show a very restricted set of adjectives, largely monosyllabic and basic, usually Germanic in origin. This is apparently just coincidence, since there are similar constructions with longer (and foreign) adjectives, that share the features of the forms in (10) but are never written as single words: these are forms such as *dental treatment*, *dramatic society*, *primary school* or *solar system*.

On the other hand, there are words which share the same semantic and syntactic features which are not stressed on the first base. Some examples are given in (11).

(11) hard disc, heavy water, light railway, red cabbage, red squirrel, soft lens

The main difference between items like those in (11) and those in (10) seems to be frequency (sometimes, former frequency). There are items which appear to vacillate or be undergoing change. I have heard *bluewhale* and *colddrink* with stress on the first base, and although neither of these seems to be a widespread pronunciation, there seems to be no reason why they should not become common. This raises the question of whether the words in (11) are compounds, too. Almost nobody would accept this proposal, and so the fragility of the concept of 'compound' is illustrated.

2.3.4 Other kinds of compounds

The extent to which there are other kinds of compounds in English is in dispute. There are a number of constructions which look like compounds (in that they are made up of two elements, each of which is a lexeme), which can be classified as endocentric or exocentric, which can be classified as coordinative or **subordinative**, but where, for one reason or another, there is some uncertainty as to whether they really count as compounds. Again, this shows that there is some uncertainty about the nature of compounds.

We can begin with possible compounds that act as adjectives. Some types are presented in (12).

(12) a. grass-green, ice-cold, sky-blue
       b. brand-new, house-proud,
       c. piss-poor, shit-hot, stone dead
       d. bald-headed, blue-eyed, green-eyed, long-legged
       e. new-born, true-bred
       f. fail-safe
       g. bitter-sweet, blue-green, light green, literary-philosophical
       h. blue-skies, stop-go, three-week

The examples in (12a) would probably be classified as compounds, but note that they are stressed on the second base, unlike typical noun compounds. How English deals with such adjectives is slightly odd. *Sky-blue* is a well-established word, but despite the expression *as cool as a cucumber, cucumber-cool* (which seems to have a similar semantic structure) is not an established expression. You can be *as hungry as a horse* or *as hungry as a hunter*, but probably not *horse-hungry* or *hunter-hungry*. That is, there is limited productivity in this pattern which is not easily explicable. This, too, seems to be rather different from what happens with noun compounds.

The examples in (12b) show endocentric expression with varying semantic relationships between the elements, reminiscent of what happens with noun compounds.

The examples in (12c) seem to have semantics like the examples in (12a), but the noun seems to act as an intensifier, rather than as a genuine point of comparison. Shit is not all that hot (and *shit-hot* has nothing to do with temperature). Some examples might sit on the borderline: if we say someone is *snot-dumb*, do we think of the stupidity of snot, or just think of it as an intensifier? Such constructions seem to be more frequent in other Germanic languages (where they have been called **elative compounds**) than they are in English, but we do have a few.

The examples in (12d) are often called compounds, but they appear to have the structure [[blue-eye]d], so that the compound is not made up, at the first level of analysis, by two words. These are sometimes seen as equivalent to exocentric noun compounds like *redcap* ('a person who has a red cap') because they denote 'having blue eyes', but they are rather different in that there is nothing really missing in *blue-eyed*, as there might be in *redcap* – depending on how we wish to interpret such examples. *Green-eyed* ('jealous') is included in the list as a reminder that compounds (of all kinds, but also here) can also be interpreted figuratively.

The example in (12e) shows two adjectives in a subordinate relationship: the *new* modifies the *born*. We might expect to find an adverb in place of *new* in *new-born*.

The example in (12f) appears to have a verb in modifying position, but the interpretation is open to question, and there are very few – if any – parallel examples: is a *fail safe mechanism* 'a mechanism which is safe if it fails', or 'a mechanism which fails to a safe state'? Or does it mean 'a mechanism which is so safe that it will not fail'? How you gloss the word might influence your idea of the relationship.

The examples in (12g) are coordinative. *Light green* might fit better in the set in (12e), there is some dispute about this in the literature. Note that *blue-green* shows a compromise between blue and green, whereas *bitter-sweet* shows the presence of both the bitter and the sweet. Such variability is relatively common in coordinative structures, so is perhaps not worrying, but it indicates that the coordinate category is not straightforward. Some authors deny that any expressions involving coordination can be compounds, because they see coordination as a syntactic process.

Finally, the expressions in (12h) are items which usually appear in attributive position (before the noun they modify), as in *blue-skies research*, *stop-go policies*, *three-week holiday* and so on, but this is the only sign that they might be adjectives. Their internal head is not an adjective, and they cannot be compared or graded, and so on, behaviour which is typical of adjectives. We might want to say that we have a head noun modified by a noun phrase or by some kind of coordinative structure (in the case of *stop-go*). Just where the boundaries of the category of adjective go is problematic in English, and this is just another example of where the boundaries are hard to draw.

If we look at potential compound verbs, we find examples like those in (13).

(13) a. baby-sit, dive-bomb, drink-drive, stage-manage
      b. handcuff, honeymoon, mastermind, snowball
      c. air-quote, custom-produce, high-tail, pistol-whip
      d. download, outsource, oversew, up-skill
      e. blow-dry, freeze-dry, stir-fry

The examples in (13a) are instances of **back-formation**. They are not created by adding, for example, *baby* to *sit*, but by deleting the *-er* in *baby-sitter* (perhaps the *-ing* in *baby-sitting*, perhaps both). Although they end up looking like compounds, they are not formed by a process of compounding.

The examples in (13b) are all derived from the homophonous nouns. If you *handcuff* someone, you do it because you put *handcuffs* on them, and the noun is primary. This formation type is called **conversion**, and will be discussed at greater length later (see Sections 2.5.3, 6.5.11). Again, these examples are not formed by compounding, though they look like compounds and are used as verbs.

The examples in (13c) are less clear. These might be genuine compounds, formed by compounding, but you might not agree with that analysis. In any case, such compound verbs are relatively rare in English.

The examples in (13d) are the best examples of compound verbs. They are formed with a particle and a verb, often with a particle that has lost the literal sense that the same form would have as a preposition. They also raise the question of whether we should include phrasal verbs like *fall out* ('argue'), *look up* (the answer), *put about* (in a ship), *see through* ('persevere') as compound verbs. In English, where these verbs are typically written as two orthographic words, and where they two words can be interrupted (*look it up*, for example), these are usually considered to be syntactic constructions, while in other Germanic languages, where the base forms of the corresponding verbs are usually written as single words, they are thought of as single lexemes.

Finally, the examples in (13e) are often cited as examples of coordinative verb compounds. There is some dispute about this, though. Does *stir-fry* mean 'to stir and to fry' (coordinative reading), or does it mean 'to fry by stirring' (subordinative reading)? A clearer example, like *drop-kick*, is probably derived by conversion from the corresponding noun.

It is not clear whether prepositions like *into, onto* (one orthographic word) and *because of, except for, off of* (US English) are compounds or simply the result of the common collocation of two prepositions in use.

2.3.5 Summarising

Altogether, we can see that there are many constructions which might be considered compounds, but that the category is a slippery one, with boundaries that are unclear. Moreover, we see that the subtypes of compound are not necessarily easily distinguishable from each other, even such apparently basic distinctions as coordinative versus subordinative. There have been many attempts to sort this problem out and to provide a robust categorisation of compounds, but there always seem to be examples which are hard to classify or which are marginal to the idea of the compound. This may be because of the nature of compounding: in its nature it can be argued to be partly a matter of word-formation and partly a matter of syntax, although most specialists prefer to see it as one or the other. The notion of compound can be useful, especially in the clear-cut cases, but it has to be remembered that there are many disputed areas.

2.4 Derivation

Although compounds provide an easier method of word-formation than blends, because fewer operations are required, compounding is not the only possible way of simplifying the process of creating words. In blends, as we saw, one of the calculations that has to be made is where to cut off each of the base words. A way to make this easier would be to have a recurrent word-part which always has the same meaning, and which can be added transparently to other words or word-parts to make new words. This is what we find with derivation. The word-parts involved are prefixes and suffixes which create new lexemes; they cannot stand alone as words, and they attach, respectively, before or after the base they belong with. We have already seen how suffixes can be used specifically to contrast with each other, in example (14) in Chapter 1. In more general usage, affixes (things which are either prefixes or suffixes) create paradigms of words with parallel meanings.

In English, prefixes and suffixes seem to have rather different functions in most cases. Prefixes provide information restricting the application of the base, in much the same way that the first bases in compounds do. Suffixes, on the whole, determine the word-class of the new lexeme (the **derivative**), and in some cases add their own specific meanings, which tend to look rather head-like, just like the second elements in compounds. Because affixes attach to bases (which are usually, but not always, words), derivation and compounding are not of equal value, and we find no coordinative derivatives.

2.4.1 Prefixes

It is an unpredictable fact about English that all prefixes create new lexemes, and none of them are inflectional. Prefixes are rather more promiscuous than suffixes: they tend not to be terribly fussy about the word-class of the base they attach to. Although they have a range of meanings, their meanings tend to be fairly well constrained.

There are several types of information that prefixes tend to give. These are illustrated in (14) and discussed below.

(14) a. negatives: abnormal, atypical, dishonest, ignoble, inelegant, maladjusted, non-absorbent, unkind, untie
    b. location in place: afterdeck, antechamber, by-stander, circum-navigate, cis-Atlantic, endo-skeleton, exo-biology, forearm, mid-Channel, premolar, subparagraph, surcoat, underbody
    c. location in time: afterbirth, antedate, ex-wife, foresee, inter-menstrual, mid-Cambrian, perinatal, post-war, pre-select
    d. size and number: megabyte, microsecond, millilitre, mini-cab, semicircle, supermarket, unicycle
    e. intensifying: hypersensitive, mega-star, super-absorbent, ueber-rich, ultra-clean
    f. downtoning or denying: anti-hero, hyposensitivity, pseudo-science, quasi-slavery, non-person
    g. for and against: anti-British, counter-bid, pro-democracy
    h. a mixed residue: arch-deacon, cooperate, metarule, neo-liberalism, proto-Germanic, re-capture
    j. verbalising: bewitch, defrock, disarm, encode, unearth

A. NEGATIVES

Negative prefixes can be seen as forming opposites from their bases. The notion of opposite, though, is not easy, as it can mean many different things (see also Section 4.4.2). *Unkind* and *inelegant* provide a scale going from *kind* to *unkind*, or *elegant* to *inelegant*, and there are intermediate steps on the way. The prefix *non-*, in contrast, divides the world into two classes, those denoted by the base and those denoted by the prefix plus base. Anything which is not *absorbent* is *non-absorbent*, and vice versa. Again differently, something that is *maladjusted* is poorly adjusted, rather than not adjusted at all. When added to nouns and verbs, these prefixes have rather different meanings. An *unperson* is someone who is a person, but does not fully qualify as a person for some reason (being ignored by society, for instance). If you *untie* something, you reverse the process of tying it.

Unlike most prefixed words, most of these words are not hyponyms of their bases (see Section 4.4.3): if you are unkind you are, by definition, not kind; *unkind* is not one type of *kind*.

It is not always clear which prefix should be used on a given base, even if they both mean the same thing. Some people use *untypical* rather than *atypical*, and note that the noun corresponding to *unjust* is *injustice*, and corresponding to *unequal* we have *inequality*.

Note that the prefix *in-*, in particular, is subject to **allomorphy**. In allomorphy, the same underlying element arises with different forms, depending on the context in which it is found. With the prefix *in-*, we find *intolerant, inoperative,* but *imprecise, illiterate* and *irrelevant*. That is, in spelling the <n> becomes <m> before a consonant made with both lips, becomes <l> before another <l> and <r> before another <r>. In pronunciation, only one [l] sound is pronounced in *illiterate*, so the prefix is really pronounced /ɪ/, and the same is true of the prefix written <ir>. If you listen carefully, and think about what is happening to your tongue and lips, you will also discover that in pronunciation, things are even more complex. In a word like *infallible*, the <n> may be pronounced with the top teeth touching the bottom lip as well as (or instead of) with the tongue touching behind the front teeth. In *inconclusive*, the <n> may represent the sound at the end of *sing* (/ŋ/) rather than the sound at the end of *sin*. And in *injudicious*, the <n> may be pronounced with much more of the tongue touching the roof of the mouth than is the case in *inoperable*. Many affixes show allomorphy. The prefix *a-* in *atypical, asemantic* occurs as *an-* in *anechoic, anhydrous*. You can find many more similar cases.

B. LOCATION IN TIME AND SPACE

Most of the prefixes that are used for location in place are also used for location in time. There are very few which do not get both uses: *cis-* appears to be exclusively use for spatial location, and *ex-* (in the sense 'former') is, of course, only used for temporal location. There is a much wider range of prefixes than has been illustrated in (14), some of them very rare, many of them added mostly to bases that are not in themselves words of English but are derived from the classical languages, Latin and Greek. With elements like *by-* (in *by-stander*) and *under-* (in *underbody*) we can legitimately ask whether these are words, and thus whether words created using them are compounds rather than derivatives. They pattern with other prefixes, but if they have precisely the same meaning as the relevant preposition rather than a specialised meaning, there is a good argument for treating them as compound elements.

Notice that an example like *post-war* is exocentric in that its apparent head is a noun (*war*), but *post-war* is used as an adjective or an adverb. There are many such forms in English, and there is no easy way to determine how they should be assigned to word-classes.

C. SIZE AND NUMBER AND INTENSIFICATION

Some of the prefixes that can be used to show location can also be used to show (usually large) size. The obvious example is *super-*, which shows location in *superstructure*, but size in *supermarket*, and intensification in *super-absorbent*. Another similar case is provided by *extra-*, which is used spatially in *extra-terrestrial* but to show intensification in *extra-special*. Many of the markers of size, such as *micro-*, *mega-*, have technical meanings showing number, and informal usage showing relative size. Some such forms, such as *mini* and *mega*, even get turned into words in their own right, and so, again, we find instances where we might not be sure whether we are dealing with a compound or a derivative. Many of the prefixes showing number are Latin or Greek, and are rarely used attached to English words. We recognise them in words such as *centipede*, *hexagon* and *tripod*, but they are fully analysable only in a few words like *pentangle* and *tricycle*. We can include here prefixes such as *ambi-*, *hemi-*, *multi-*, *omni-*, *pan-*, *poly-* which also show relative frequency, but which might be seen as showing intensity in some uses, as perhaps in *omnipotent* or *panpharmicon*.

D. DOWNTONING OR DENYING

The word *unperson* has already been cited as a case of negation, and here we have *non-person* which can mean the same thing. In general terms, the prefixes dealt with here deal with showing degrees of belonging to the category of the base, to the extreme case of not belonging at all. At that point, we can view the category as being negated.

E. MOST OTHER PREFIXES

After these major categories, we are left with rather less important categories, although individual affixes within the categories may be common. The prefix *re-*, for instance, is a common prefix, but is in a category by itself (unless you think that it shows structure in time). There is little to say about these from a theoretical point of view.

Do note, however, that there is a large class of elements which sometimes behave as though they were prefixes, but which are usually called combining forms. They are mostly learned, often medical or scientific, and usually borrowed from Greek or Latin. Some examples are given in (15). Others have been smuggled in to other lists in (14), masquerading as prefixes. Although these items attach to words (and do so in the examples in (15)), they also attach to other combining forms making compound-like items, usually termed neo-classical compounds, illustrated in (16). Neo-classical compounds will be dealt with in Section 3.4.2.

(15)   aero-dynamics, electro-plate, hydro-electricity, neuro-surgeon, photo-electric, psycho-therapy, socio-linguistics, television, thermo-nuclear

(16)   electrolysis, hydrogen, neuralgia, photograph, psychogony, sociology, telepath

F. THE VERBALISING PREFIXES

The verbalising prefixes illustrated in (14j) are unusual in English. As was said above, in general terms, the word-class of a word created by an affix is determined by a suffix or, if there are no suffixes, by the base word. With the examples in (14j), however, we find words which are not verbs made into verbs by prefixes. Many of these, but not all of them, are negating prefixes. The prefix *be-* is now no longer in use for the creation of new words, but there are many words like *bewitch* which still show an old pattern. The existence of these words creates problems for the theorising of derivation in English, because they are exceptional.

2.4.2 Suffixes

Not only do suffixes typically determine the word-class of the word in which they occur, they typically have meanings which are quite difficult to pin down. Sometimes we find suffixes with an apparent range of meanings; sometimes we find meanings which are shared by a range of suffixes. Although we seldom notice this when we are speaking or reading, the result is quite a confused system.

In what follows, we will begin by looking at semantic categories of suffixes (just as we did with prefixes), before looking at some other features of their behaviour.

A. SUFFIXES DENOTING PEOPLE

In (17) there is a list of words which denote people, and these words all end in suffixes which seem to carry some of the load of making the words mean what they mean. If the words as wholes denote people, then it is also partly because the suffixes involved typically create nouns (occasionally we find examples which are less clear).

(17) a. advisor, collaborator, dancer, driver, lover, teacher
      b. accompanist, cyclist, harpist, pacifist, purist, receptionist
      c. accountant, attendant, defendant, descendant, inhabitant
      d. addressee, arrestee, dedicatee, employee

Each of the suffixes illustrated in (17) has its own peculiarities, and we will look at each in turn.

The basic function of the suffix *-er* (sometimes *-or*) is to show the person who carries out the action of the verb, as in the examples in (17a). The precise division of labour between *-er* and *-or* is not completely fixed, and some people write *supervisor* and some *superviser*. If there is a legal term, it usually takes *-or*, and sometimes the only difference between an *-er* word and the corresponding *-or* word is that the *-or* version is specifically legal. In only one case does the difference in spelling seem to lead to real contrast in modern English: a *sailor* is person and a *sailer* is a ship. However, this division is a nineteenth-century innovation, and seems to have been artificially imposed. Otherwise, although some spellings are preferred with some readings, there does not appear to be real contrast.

In its function of marking agents, the suffix *-er* is added to bases which are verbs. But *-er* is also added to bases which are nouns – where *-or* is rare (*backbencher, cricketer, falconer, trumpeter*), adjectives (*commoner*), numbers (*fiver, forty-niner*), or prepositions (*outsider*). It has a whole range of possible meanings, depending on how narrowly you want to define a 'meaning' of the suffix. Examples are given in (18). You may wish to argue about some of these categories (feel free to invent your own set), and you may not know how many of these are 'the same' suffix *-er*, or whether there are several homophonous suffixes.

(18) a. animal agent: pointer, retriever, warbler, woodpecker
      b. instrument: amplifier, blender, computer, freezer, revolver, stapler
      c. patient: boiler ('boiling fowl'), keeper ('a thing worth keeping'), loaner, milker ('a cow')
      d. location: diner, sleeper
      e. inhabitant: Aucklander, Berliner, Icelander, Londoner, New Yorker
      f. clothing: jumper, slipper, sneaker, sweater
      g. origin: northwester

    h. meal: dinner, supper
    i. ship: clipper, cruiser, destroyer
    j. miscellaneous: goer, liner, Peeler, three-wheeler

Some forms may have two or more meanings. A *sleeper* may be a person, a carriage in a train, the train itself, a kind of earring, a piece of clothing, something used to keep the rails of a railway a fixed distance apart and so on. A *keeper* may keep animals in a zoo or be something you want to keep. A *dish-washer* can be a person or a machine; *computers* and *typewriters* were once people.

The suffix *-er* may occasionally have an irregular form or meaning, or demand an irregular form in its base. Some examples are *collier, furrier, glazier, vintner*. The deletion of *-y* pronounced /i/ before *-er* as in *philosopher* and *sorcerer* seems to be regular. The meaning of *prayer* is irregular, as is that of *lover* (except in synthetic compounds like *dog-lover*) in that it presumes a sexual relationship. The meaning of *batter* (for cooking), *blazer* (the garment) and *washer* (the circle of metal) cannot now be analysed in terms of the base and an *-er* suffix.

The suffix *-ist* in (17b) differs from *-er* in that it is most often used on bases which are nouns. There are several different shades of meaning, which we might group together under 'person associated with'. Examples are given in (19), although the categories presented may overlap and are not exhaustive.

(19) a. habitual association: cyclist, nudist, stylist
      b. professional association: harpist, physicist, receptionist
      c. practitioner of an -ism: atheist, communist, fascist, idealist, purist
      d. practitioner of an -ology: biologist, psychologist, sociologist
      e. prejudiced person: misogynist, racist, sexist

The suffix *-ant* in (17c) seems to prefer bases which are verbs, but the words are often more bureaucratic or professional than corresponding words in *-er* (if both are in use): a *descender* is a part of a letter of the alphabet going below the line, while a *descendant* is a person holding a particular legal or biological status. Like *-er*, *-ant* sometimes forms nouns which are not people (consider *ascendant, coolant, dominant, pendant, propellant, repellant* among many others). The most striking thing about *-ant*, though, is that it also forms adjectives – rather more easily than it forms nouns. Sometimes a form in *-ant* can be either an adjective or a noun (*a consultant psychologist* or just *a consultant*), sometimes only an adjective (*abundant, elegant, reliant*) and sometimes only a noun (*contestant, defendant, propellant*).

Words that use the suffix *-ee*, as in the examples in (17d), denote a human non-volitional participant in an action. There are a few words in technical subjects like linguistics and computer science which have non-human *-ee* words, but in general use, only human nouns are found: even if you own a dog or a car, it would be very odd to call it your *ownee*. Because the participant is non-volitional, this usually means that the derived noun denotes the direct object or the indirect object of the verb in the base: an *employee* is someone you employ, a *payee* is someone to whom you make a payment. Occasionally, the *-ee* noun can be the subject of the verb: a *standee* (originally US, but now in wider usage) is a person who is forced to stand in public transport because there are no seats; a *retiree* is presumably seen as having no influence on moving to the state of being retired. In a few cases, the *-ee* word is based on a corresponding *-er* word, even if there is no verb in the base: a *biographee*, an *executionee*.

B. SUFFIXES SPECIFYING GENDER

There are two major suffixes specifying gender in English, *-ess* and *-ette*. Because both of these suffixes treat the male as the norm and specify the female, they are widely seen as creating sexist labels, and are considered disparaging. Most actresses in the present century prefer to see themselves as actors, and *waitperson* seems to have replaced *waitress* (and *waiter*) in many contexts. But not all of the words created by these suffixes are on a par. *Undergraduette* seems indisputably disparaging; *lioness* could be simply descriptive; *mayoress* is ambiguous, between the wife of a mayor and a female who holds the position of mayor; *mistress* has become totally divorced from *master* (and, arguably, is used in a far more disparaging way). The suffix *-(tr)ix*, as in *aviatrix*, *executrix*, *testatrix*, forms very formal female nouns. When it is used today, it can also be disparaging.

C. SUFFIXES DENOTING COLLECTIONS

The suffixes *-ery* and, to a lesser extent, *-age* can be used to show collections of items, as in *greenery, jewellery, joinery, acreage, signage*. Both can also be used to show locations, as in *distillery, nunnery, nursery, orphanage, parsonage*. Both suffixes also have other meanings (see also below in this section), one of which for *-age* is 'sum of money paid for ~', as in *cellarage, postage, wharfage*.

D. SUFFIXES CREATING ACTION NOMINALISATIONS

There is a large set of suffixes which produces what are often termed **action nominalisations**, nouns which mean 'act or process of performing the action mentioned in the verb from which the noun derives'. Some of these suffixes also have other functions. We will need to look at the meanings of these suffixes in more detail, but some of the relevant suffixes are illustrated in (20).

(20)　a.　-age: blockage, leakage, marriage, slippage
　　　　b.　-al: arrival, denial, disposal, recital
　　　　c.　-ance: ascendance, clearance, compliance, hindrance
　　　　d.　-ancy: ascendancy, expectancy, occupancy
　　　　e.　-ation: justification, organisation, reformation
　　　　f.　-ence: abhorrence, coherence, recurrence
　　　　g.　-ing: living, providing, seeing
　　　　h.　-ion: commission, construction, profession, suspension
　　　　i.　-ment: abasement, entrapment, management, statement
　　　　j.　-ter: laughter
　　　　k.　-ure: closure, erasure, fixture, pressure
　　　　l.　-ency: dependency, sufficiency, tendency

It is usually taken that *-ion* and *-ation* are variants of the same suffix, although it is not altogether clear whether their occurrence is predictable. The same is true with *-ance/-ancy* and *-ence/-ency*. Which vowel is found depends largely on Latin rather than on English factors, and whether the *-y* is or is not present often seems random, with both forms being attested for some bases. The suffix *-ing* is very common, being available for any non-modal verb, while *-ter* seems to be limited to *laughter* (and perhaps *slaughter*). Apart from *-ation* (after *-ise* or after *-ify*) and *-ing*, these are of minimal productivity, although sometimes an unexpected suffix is used to draw a semantic distinction, so that *committal*, *commitment* and *commission* can be distinguished by their meanings.

The label 'action nominalisation' for these forms is a sort of default label. Many of these suffixes have (or can have) very precise meanings on particular bases, meanings which are not easily covered by 'action'. Some examples are given in (21). The range of **readings** (which is perhaps to be preferred to the term 'meaning' here, when the context can determine how the word is understood) is large, but not unlimited, and difficult to specify clearly. The readings seem to be pragmatic interpretations of the nominalisation in context, some of which become fixed as the name for a particular phenomenon, or which become fixed as having one reading in preference to others.

(21)　*carriage* is usually a vehicle
　　　　government is usually an institution
　　　　marriage can be a celebration

mixture is usually a physical object
painting is often a physical object
recital is usually an event
transmission can be part of a car engine
trial is often a legal process

E. SUFFIXES MAKING VERBS

There are four major suffixes making verbs, two of which are still in general use. Examples are given in (22).

(22) a. -ate: activate, administrate, hyphenate, liquidate, rusticate
  b. -en: blacken, harden, redden, widen; hasten, hearten
  c. en- . . . -en: embolden, enliven
  d. -ify: humidify, purify, syllabify, versify
  e. -ise: equalise, passivise, terrorise, womanise

The suffix *-ate* is most often found on bases that are not English words, but are Latin elements. When used on English words, it may be attached to nouns, adjectives or verbs, though *administrate* may come from *administration*, rather than vice versa.

The suffix *-en* is a Germanic form, which has functions beyond those illustrated here. It attaches to adjectives (in particular) or nouns (less regularly), in both cases preferring to attach to words that end in a phonetic stop or a fricative. This seem to be why we have *lengthen* and *strengthen*, rather than **longen* and **strongen*, which would break this rule. Nevertheless, you may be able to find counter-examples. In a very few cases we find *en-* before the base and *-en* after the base. We also find *en-* as a prefix making verbs (see Section 2.4.1), but it never seems to contrast with the repeated *en-*. . .*-en*, in contrast to what happens with the suffix illustrated in *liven* (which usually co-occurs with *up*) and *enliven*, which are not **synonyms**.

The suffixes *-ify* and *-ise* seem to mean the same thing (although it is a complex matter to specify exactly what the relevant meaning(s) might be), and most of the time are in complementary distribution: you cannot have **humidise* or **versise*, and neither can you have **equalify* or **womanify*. These are the only two of these suffixes which can still be used freely to make new words.

F. SUFFIXES MAKING ADJECTIVES

We can divide suffixes making adjectives into two main groups. Those that are merely **transpositional** (that is, their job is simply to make something into an adjective, with as little addition to the meaning as possible), and those that carry their own meaning, the most frequent of which is 'resembling ~' or 'approximating to ~' whatever is the base. Some examples of transpositional adjectives are provided in (23).

(23) a. -al: adenoidal, parental, professorial, scribal, sexual
      b. -an: African, mammalian, suburban
      c. -ant: defiant, expectant, observant
      d. -ar: cellular, columnar, molecular, peninsular, polar
      e. -ary: budgetary, customary, urinary
      f. -ic: acidic, encyclopedic, syllabic
      g. -ical: alphabetical, liturgical, typical
      h. -ile: erectile, infantile
      i. -ine: alpine, crystalline, vulturine
      j. -ous: hazardous, lecherous, scandalous, zealous

There are a number of comments to be made about these as a group, as well as some comments on individual suffixes.

First of all, and most trivially, there are various spelling changes that are made at the boundary of base and affix. Most of these are regular, and no further comment will be made about them. Less trivially, there are frequent changes to the pronunciation made as a result of affixation. Sometimes some part of the base is cut off, sometimes some material is added (the elements that are added may be called **extenders**), sometimes the stress pattern of the base is changed, sometimes a vowel in the base is changed. Some of these changes are regular, many of them are irregular and not predictable. There is no apparent reason in the system of English, for example, which explains why it should be *professorial* (with an extender) but *doctoral* (with no extender). All of the suffixes in (23) are foreign to English. Although examples have been given here where the suffixes attach to English words, the same suffixes are (in some cases more often) used to attach to foreign bases which may not be recognisable as words of English. Some of the suffixes prefer bases which are nouns, some prefer bases which are verbs. In some cases the adjectives choose a specific meaning of the base, and do not apply to all meanings or uses of the base: you can *erect a tent*, but a tent that you can do this to is not **an erectile tent*.

The distinction between *-al*, *-ial* and *-ual* is unpredictable in English, though note that *habitual* and *habituate* both share the extra *-u-*, and *uxorial* and *uxorious* both share the *-i-*, which implies that there may be historical reasons for the markers. The same is true of *-al* and *-ar*. In Latin, these are alternative forms of the same suffix, and in English their occurrence is mostly determined by the base they attach to: a base containing /l/ is unlikely to take *-al*. On the other hand, the coexistence of *familial* and *familiar*, *laminal* and *laminar*, *lineal* and *linear*, shows that the rule is not completely fixed for English.

The relationship between *-ic* and *-ical* is complex; it is not even clear that they should be listed as separate affixes. In many cases, either is possible without any difference in meaning: *herpetologic* and *herpetological* may both be possible in the same contexts. In other cases, such as *syntactic* and *syntactical*, one is preferred (at least by professionals) but the other may also be found. In a few cases, there is, or is widely said to be, a semantic difference between the two: *economic* has to do with the *economy*, while *economical* has to do with saving money; *classic* is of something which is excellent of its kind, while *classical* refers to the period of ancient Greek and Roman supremacy (or things which mimic that) – in this case, both have other uses as well.

Adjectives which specifically mean 'having a resemblance to ~' are illustrated in (24). Some of these suffixes also have different uses, usually transpositional uses, like the adjectives in (23).

(24) a. -esque: Byronesque, picturesque, statuesque
     b. -ish: foolish, reddish, thirty-ish, waspish
     c. -like: child-like, lady-like, spring-like
     d. -ly: friendly, godly, manly
     e. -y: croaky, sketchy, starchy, stodgy

Of the suffixes illustrated in (24), *-esque* is the most specialised, meaning 'in the style of ~' when attached to proper nouns (and it is rare in other uses). The suffixes *-ish* and *-y* are very easy to use, and can occur in new words. Note that *-ish* attaches easily to adjectives and numbers as well as to nouns. It is not clear whether we should call *-like* a suffix or a word (in which case, *child-like* would be a compound, not a derivative); it is included here because it has the same meaning as things which are clearly suffixes. The existence of several suffixes with the same fundamental meaning allows for the different suffixes to be used to distinguish finer shades of meaning. *Manly* is a positive description, while *mannish*, especially if used of females, may be rather disparaging; *childish* is definitely a bad thing to be, but *child-like* is much more neutral in tone; *workmanly* and *workman-like* are both positive things to say.

Some suffixes with other meanings are illustrated in (25). The list is not exhaustive.

(25) a. -able: expendable, marriageable, payable, retrievable
     b. -en: drunken, golden, wooden
     c. -ern: eastern, northern
     d. -free: carefree, fat-free, sugar-free

  e. -ful: careful, hopeful, insightful
  f. -ible: accessible, digestible, responsible, sensible
  g. -less: careless, hopeless, priceless

Note that *-able* (25a) is usually added to verbs, with the meaning 'able to be ~ed', but that it is sometimes added to nouns and it does not always have the same meaning. The suffix *-ible* (25f), in contrast, is often added to nouns. It is usually added to verbs which are Latin in origin, and so is more formal than *-able*. Note that while *-less* often gives a word whose meaning is the opposite of an adjective in *-ful*, this is not always true. The difference between *-less* and *-free* is often that where the suffix *-free* is used it implies that it is a good thing for the material in the base to be missing. On the phonology of *-en*, see the comments on examples in (22) above.

G. MAKING ADVERBS

The major way of making adverbs is with the suffix *-ly*, which we will look at in some detail. There are other affixes that are used to make adverbs, though, and some of them are illustrated in (26).

(26) a. a-: abed, afire, around, asleep
      b. -s: besides, betimes, sometimes, upstairs
      c. -ward(s): downward(s), homeward(s), toward(s), westward(s)
      d. -ways: edgeways, endways, lengthways, sideways
      e. -wise: clockwise, contrariwise, likewise, widthwise

Many of the items in (26) can also be used as adjectives, on occasion as prepositions or conjunctions. None of them is particularly productive in creating adverbs, but new forms are found occasionally with several of them. The suffixes *-ways* and *-wise* sometimes seem as though they are variants of each other (*lengthwise, lengthways* with the same meaning), but they are not automatically interchangeable.

The suffix *-ly* provides us with a puzzle. It is very productive. If you find a new adjective that you have never heard before, the chances are high that you can create an adverb in *-ly* from it. At the same time, there are places where you cannot.

There are a number of cases where the adverb has the same form as the adjective, and a number more where the adverb can use *-ly* or can have the same form as the adjective. For example, *fast* can be an adverb or an adjective (*She drives a fast car, She drives fast*), but *slow* can have an *-ly* form (*He drives slow, He drives slowly*).

Speakers usually avoid adding adverbial *-ly* to adjectives that end in *-ly*, but there is some variation. Adjectives that end in the suffix *-ly* can sometimes take an extra -*ly* (She smiled *friendlily*, He strolled *leisurelily along the front*), but such things are usually avoided; adjectives denoting periods of time that end in -*ly* do not take adverbial -*ly*: *New stock arriving daily* (**dailily*), *We will send your payment weekly* (**weeklily*). Adjectives that end in -*ly* because -*y* has been added to a base in -*l* or whose base happens to end in -*ly* used to take -*ly*, but these days do so only rarely: *jollily, oilily, sillily, wobblily* are now odd. The adjective bases for these words cannot be used as adverbs, as the *friendly* and *daily* types can be.

Some adjectives, when used colloquially to modify and intensify an adjective, do not take -*ly*: *She's dead smart, This looks real stupid, That's pretty clever, That curry is fucking hot, It's fair impossible* (note that *fairly* impossible would be a downtoner, not an intensifier).

In some instances, the apparent adverbial form derived by -*ly* from an adjective does not have the expected meaning: *barely, deadly, hardly, lately, scarcely* are not related semantically to their apparent bases.

Perhaps the biggest puzzle is whether adverbs and adjectives are a single word-class or two distinct word-classes. The latter viewpoint has been adopted here, and is traditional, but the question is highly contested in the literature. In most cases, which form will arise in a particular context is fully predictable, and only occasionally do the two contrast on a superficial level (then usually with different syntactic structure). Compare *I left the house quietly* and *I left the house quiet*, for example. In colloquial spoken English, it seems to be more and more common that -*ly* is omitted from adverbs, which suggests that many speakers do not distinguish adverbs from adjectives in a consistent way.

2.5 Words without affixes

There are several patterns of words in English where the process of creating the words does not involve affixes. Most of these processes are not productive, but some are. The others are left-overs from earlier periods in the history of English. These left-overs will be dealt with first, and the productive patterns will follow.

2.5.1 Words with internal changes

There are several patterns where one word is apparently derived from another by a change of one of the phonological elements in the word. This phonological element may be a consonant, a vowel, or a stress pattern. The terminology surrounding these cases is not consistent, but they can be grouped together by saying that they all involve **internal modification**.

Examples with a change of consonant are illustrated in (27).

(27) a. believe   belief
         house /haʊz/   house /haʊs/
         mouth /maʊð/   mouth /maʊθ/
         prove   proof
         relieve   relief
         sheathe   sheath
         use /juːz/   use /juːs/
         wreathe   wreath
     b. descend   descent
         extend   extent
         gild   gilt
         intend   intent
     c. expand   expanse
         offend   offence
         pretend   pretence
         respond   response

What the various patterns in (27) share is that there is a voiced final consonant sound in the verb, and a corresponding voiceless consonant sound in the noun. They differ in the details. In (27a) the sounds are fricatives, mainly /ð/ ~ /θ/ and /v/ ~ /f/. The alternation of /z/ and /s/ is rare. This pattern is an English pattern in origin, arising because when the fricatives were intervocalic they were voiced. When the final vowel was lost, the voiced fricatives remained voiced, and a contrast between voiced and voiceless fricatives arose. The other patterns are mainly borrowed from Latin, and are not particularly reliable in English. This kind of internal modification is sometimes called **consonant mutation**.

Examples of changes in vowels are provided in (28). Such vowel change can also be termed **vowel mutation**, **ablaut** or **apophony**. In the clearest instances, the vowel difference is the only difference, but there are rather more instances where the vowel change is accompanied by affixation (as in (28d)).

(28) a. fell   fall
         lay   lie
         set   sit
     b. fill   full
         shoot   shot
         sing   song
     c. bathe /beɪð/   bath /bɑːθ/

       choose /ʧuːz/   choice /ʧɔɪs/
       glaze /gleɪz/   glass /glɑːs/
  d. assume   assumption
      conceive   conception
      opaque   opacity
      school   scholar

In (28a) we find examples of the difference between transitive (or causative) and intransitive verbs being marked by vowel change. In (28b) we have the difference between verb and either adjective or noun being marked. In (28c) we have both vowel change and consonant change simultaneously, and as in (27), the verb has the voiced final consonant. In (28d) we find apophony arising from patterns in the classical languages and borrowed with the words into English.

Examples of changes in stress are illustrated in (29).

(29) a. digést   dígest
        extráct   éxtract
        impórt   ímport
        permít   pérmit
        protést   prótest
        transfér   tránsfer
    b. frequént   fréquent
    c. áffricàte   áffricate
        coórdinàte coórdinate
        ímplemènt   ímplement
        próphesỳ   próphesy
        númeràte   númerate
        apprópriàte apprópriate

In the examples in (29), the verb is stressed later than the noun or adjective. In (29c) this later stress is a later **secondary stress** (that is, subsidiary stress) on the final syllable; elsewhere, it is a matter of second syllable main stress for verbs and first-syllable main stress for nouns or adjectives. The verb–noun pairs in (29a) are marginally productive: new members join the set of about 100 such pairs in English, old ones fall out of use. The example in (29b) may be unique – others which used to behave this way are rare or not known these days. Even *frequent* is often heard in the media pronounced with first-syllable stress on the verb.

Change of stress also often correlates with suffixation (and to a lesser extent with prefixation), so that we find examples such as those in (30), which are symptomatic of a very large set of similar forms in English.

(30) áuction   àuctionéer
      élement   eleméntary
      fámous   ínfamous
      Japán   Jàpanése
      párent   paréntal
      prefér   préferable
      sólid   solídify
      théatre   theátrical

Stress in such cases can usually be worked out if sufficient principles are known, but there is always a core of irreducibly irregular forms. Given that words like *preferable* (also *comparable*) are currently changing their stress, from a conservative first-syllable stress to a more modern second-syllable stress, definitive answers on the position of stress in such examples are not always possible.

2.5.2 Reduplication

Reduplication is repetition of a phonological element (a consonant sound, a syllable and so on) for morphological reasons. Complete reduplication is rather rare in English, and is found most often in children's language (examples like *choo choo, quack quack*), but there is a lot of reduplication where the vowels in the reduplicated element are fixed (or extremely restricted). Some examples are provided in (31).

(31) a. chitchat
          dilly-dally
          pitter-patter
          tittle-tattle
      b. flip-flop
          ping-pong
          sing-song
          wishy-washy

The two patterns of vowel change illustrated in (31), /ɪ/ ~ /æ/ and /ɪ/ ~ /ɒ/, are the commonest patterns of vowel alternation in such structures in English. In the examples given in (31), the /ɪ/ is clearly the reduplicated element, and the other vowel is part of the base, but it is not always possible to tell, as in *riff-raff, shilly-shally*.

A slightly more complex pattern of reduplication is that illustrated in (32).

(32) blankety blank
      clickety clack

clickety click
clippety clop
flippety flop
hippety hop
hoppity hop
lickety split

Here there is sometimes the same pattern of vowel change in the first syllable that we have already seen, sometimes the first syllable of the base is retained, and the suffix-like *-ety* is added to the reduplicated element.

There is also reduplication motivated by rhyme: the two elements involved are identical except for the onset to the first syllable. This usually gives rise to at least one nonsense element (occasionally two), although there are some cases where the result looks like a normal compound that just happens to have rhyming elements (in (33b) below). The initial consonant of the derived form does not appear to be predictable (which is surprising), though labial consonants such as /p/ and /w/ seem to be over-represented.

(33) a. boogie-woogie
         easy peasy
         higgledy-piggledy
         hocus-pocus
         humdrum
         hurly-burly
     b. cop-shop
         culture vulture
         hotshot
         sin bin

2.5.3 Conversion

We can define conversion as the derivation of one word from another without any change of form at all.

In this section, conversion will be introduced briefly, but not dealt with in great detail: that will be left for Section 6.5.11, because conversion turns out to be something of a puzzle in English. One of the reasons that it is odd is that cross-linguistically, change of derivational status without any marking is very unusual, but it is common in English.

In (34) we find examples where words with the same spelling (and the same pronunciation) can be either nouns or verbs.

(34) control, dream, drive, guide, love, package, pressure, remark, return, surrender

In the examples in (35) we have cases where an adjective and a noun have the same form.

(35) blue, friendly, glossy, intellectual, mobile, superlative, tonic

In some of the instances in (35) you may want to say that there is a suffix which can create either adjectives or nouns (though it is seldom the case that both noun and adjective uses are available for every word with the suffix); in others, you may prefer to say that the noun comes from the adjective or vice versa; in a few, you may not be able to say whether the noun gives rise to the adjective or the other way round, and you may prefer a different analysis altogether.

The existence of adjective and adverbs with the same form has already been commented upon (Section 2.4.2). Such examples can also be included here, as in the invented examples in (36).

(36) *Adjective*   *Adverb*
      a fast car   she drove fast
      a friendly wave   she smiled friendly
      a hard cheese   he hit me hard
      a quarterly payment   we pay quarterly
      a real pleasure   real stupid
      a round stone   we drove round
      his late father   he arrived late

Much more detail on the borderline between conversion and something syntactic or figurative will be dealt with in Section 6.5.11.

2.5.4 Making words by deleting material

There are two major ways of making words by deletion to be discussed here; a third, blending, has already been discussed in Section 2.2.

The first of these is clipping. In **clipping** a word has material removed from it to make it shorter. The material may be removed from the beginning, the middle or the end of the word, sometimes more than one of these. The resultant word means the same thing as the base, but is less formal, more colloquial, sometimes trivialising or humorous. Some examples are provided in (37).

(37) a. doc < doctor, exam < examination, jumbo < jumbo jet, photo < photograph, pub < public house, telly < television
      b. bus < omnibus, phone < telephone, plane < aeroplane/airplane

    c. flu < influenza, fridge < refrigerator, gator < alligator, shrink < headshrinker

In (37a) we find the most common pattern, with the beginning of the base retained. We can call this **back-clipping**. In (37b) it is the last part of the base which is retained, and these are sometimes called instances of **foreclipping**. In (37c) it is the middle of the base which is retained. The term **ambiclipping** is available here, though it is rarely used (perhaps because the type is relatively rare). As is shown in the examples in (37), the base of a clipping can be a non-compound word or a compound or a whole phrase.

At some level, the borderline between clipping and **alphabetisms** becomes obscure (see Section 2.5.5).

Clipping can also be used to form pet-names or **hypocoristics** such as *Chris* (< *Christopher, Christine*), *Laurie* (< *Laurence, Lorraine*), *Pat* (< *Patrick, Patricia*), *Sam* (< *Samuel, Samantha*). Here, as in other clippings, the clippings may be **embellished** with a form which could be described as an affix. Particularly with names, the phonology of the base may be changed, sometimes in unpredictable ways. Some examples are given in (38).

(38) a. *-o* on names: Johnno < Jonathan

      b. *-o* on nouns: garbo < garbage collector, muso < musician, journo < journalist (all mainly Australian)

      c. *-s* and *-ers*: Honkers < Hong Kong, preggers < pregnant, rugger < rugby

      d. *-s* on names: Babs < Barbara, Debs < Deborah

      e. *y* (or *-ie*) on names: Annie < Anne, Bobby < Robert, Sally < Sarah, Willy < William

      f. *y* (or *-ie*) on nouns: bookie < bookmaker, homie < home boy, pollie < politician

      g. *-zz* for *-r-* on names: Gazza < Garry, Shazza < Sharon, Tezza < Terry, Theresa

The other type of deletion process is called back-formation. In back-formation something which is or looks like an affix is deleted, and then the base is used as a new word. The fascinating thing about this is that it tends to vanish with time: we might (or might not) be aware that to *surveille* comes from *surveillance* rather than the other way round (it is a relatively recent example of back-formation), but we are unlikely to be aware that *edit* comes from *editor*, rather than the other way round – the process of forming *edit* has disappeared, and we are left with a perfectly normal pair of verb and agent noun. In a few instances, though, the irregularity of the back-formation remains visible. If we form to *contracept* from *contraception*, there is a false analogy: *receive* gives *reception*, *perceive* gives *perception*; if there is a verb corresponding to *contraception*, we would expect it to be **contraceive*. If it is not, we have visible evidence of the way in which the new verb was formed.

2.5.5 Alphabetisms

We might question whether alphabetisms are really new words, or simply new ways of making MWEs manageable. We have two types of alphabetism (word-like items based on spellings). One is **initialisms** where the first letter of each word in the base MWE is pronounced in isolation. For example, *Federal Bureau of Investigation* gives *FBI* pronounced /ef bi: aɪ/, and we don't have to know what the Russian base is to remember *KGB* (/keɪ dʒi: bi:/).

In the other type of alphabetism, called an **acronym**, the letters of the base provide a sequence which can be pronounced as a normal word. For example, *UNICEF* is pronounced /juːnɪsef/, in accordance with the usual rules of pronouncing the letters in English words, and you may know something about the organisation, even if you cannot recall that it stands for *United Nations International Children's Emergency Fund*. Sometimes, a suitable word is first created, and then the phrase on which it supposedly based is invented. This is sometimes called a **backronym**. *MADD* (*Mothers Against Drunk Driving*) seems to be a likely example.

In some words it may not be clear whether the form is an acronym or an initialism, and both pronunciations may be heard. *FAQ* (< *frequently asked question*) is an initialism if pronounced /ef eɪ kjuː/ but an acronym if pronounced /fæk/. *Massachusetts Institute of Technology*, *MIT*, is pronounced as an initialism and not as an acronym, though there is no apparent reason why. Neither is it clear why it is *the FBI* but just *MIT*. With an example like *email* (< *electronic mail*) it may not be clear whether the initial <e> is an alphabetism or an extreme form of clipping.

2.6 Inflection

By definition, inflection is the kind of morphology that produces word-forms of lexemes. In many languages, this definition is perfectly satisfactory, and provides quite a clear division between inflection and derivation. English is not one of those languages. In English there are some very clear examples, and then some contested examples. In languages where the distinction is clear-cut, inflection is regular in form and meaning, must apply everywhere it can, and reflects the syntactic structure of the construction within which it occurs. In English, these criteria do not always align. There is another way of providing a definition, and that is ostensively: that is, we can just say this category and this one are inflectional. This is what many scholars resort to in English (and they usually agree). Here we will take that generally accepted set of categories, look briefly at how they work, and if they do not fit the criteria easily, show why.

2.6.1 Inflection on verbs

Perhaps the most obviously inflectional ending in English is the *-s* which marks the third person singular of the present tense, as in *collapses, consecrates, prefers*. This always has the same meaning (although it would actually be preferable to term the present tense the 'non-past' tense, since it can also be used for future time, as in *The plane arrives at two this afternoon*), has a predictable form, applies to any non-modal verb, and helps indicate what the subject of the verb is (a syntactic function). The **modal verbs**, which do not take this form, also lack an *-ing* form and can precede the subject in a question. The list is *can, could, may, might, must, ought (to), shall, should, will, would* and, for some speakers or in some constructions, *dare* and *need*. In some varieties of English, we could add *better* to the list (as in *You better watch out*). We do not find forms like **You are musting go*, we do not find forms like **She oughts to go to bed*, and we do find things like *Can I come to the party?*, although we do not find, in contemporary English, expressions like **Know you the answer?* with verbs that are not modals.

Not only is the meaning of this form regular, its form is also regular. In phonological terms, if the base ends in one of the consonants /ʧ, ʤ, ʃ, ʒ, s, z/ then the suffix will be /ɪz/ (/əz/ for some speakers); if the base ends a voiceless consonant which is not one of those just listed, the affix takes the form /s/; and otherwise, the affix takes the form /z/. *Collapse* ends in /s/, so in *collapses* we add /ɪz/, *consecrate* ends in /t/, which is voiceless, so *consecrates* has an affix /s/, and *prefer* ends in a vowel in Standard Southern British English, and in /r/ for those varieties that can have /r/ at the ends of words (rhotic varieties), and so *prefers* contains a suffix /z/. We can rewrite this in spelling terms, so that following the consonants <s, z, sh, ch> we add <es>, and otherwise we add <s>. Note that this means that the final <s> is sometimes pronounced /s/ and sometimes pronounced /z/. Relevant examples are *fusses, buzzes, pushes, watches, judges, selects, refers, sees*. There are just four irregular forms: *is, has, does, says* (when it is pronounced /sez/). In cases like *quiz*, *quizzes*, the doubling of the <z> is a regular part of English spelling, parallel to the doubling of <t> *patted* (see further Section 5.2).

The major part of the discussion of English verb inflection centres on the past tense and past participles (these are the forms that we find in *She finished the book* and *She has finished the book*, respectively). We have to keep these two forms distinct, because we get examples like *She ate the fish* and *She has eaten the fish*, where the two have different forms. In the vast majority of cases, the past tense and the past participle have the same form in English, and it is mainly where the past participle ends in /n/ that there is a difference.

In the regular case, the past tense and past participle end in <ed>, pronounced /ɪd/ immediately following /t/ or /d/ (*wanted, handed*), pronounced /t/ immediately following any other voiceless consonant (*worked*) and pronounced /d/ everywhere else (*preferred, called, screwed*). It is the irregular forms which cause the problems, because they are not easily classified, not, in general terms, predictable, and sometimes subject to change or dialectal variation. Some examples of different patterns in standard English are provided in (39), although the list of types is not exhaustive.

(39)	be	was/were	been
	come	came	come
	do	did	done
	draw	drew	drawn
	feed	fed	fed
	have	had	had
	hit	hit	hit
	keep	kept	kept
	learn	learnt	learnt
	ride	rode	ridden
	say	said	said
	see	saw	seen
	speak	spoke	spoken
	stand	stood	stood
	swim	swam	swum
	swing	swung	swung
	think	thought	thought
	throw	threw	thrown
	wake	woke	woken
	win	won	won

Note that only one verb still has a singular/plural distinction in the past tense (*be*), although this was the norm in Old English. Note further that it is not always clear whether a verb will behave like *swim* or like *swing*. In non-standard English, the second pattern more or less takes over from the first, and even in standard English a verb like *shrink* may be found in either pattern. Finally, note that nobody seems to be very sure what the past participle of the verb *stride* is. J. K. Rowling in the Harry Potter books usually uses *strode*, but most people avoid the issue if they can. For most people, none of *He has strided, He has strode* or *He has stridden* sounds right. Similarly, there is a lot of variation as to what the past tense of *shit* is, exacerbated by the fact that the verb is taboo, and so relatively rarely heard in public usage.

Some verbs change with time. *Strive-strove-striven* is currently being replaced with *strive-strived-strived*. For many years, the distinction between *hang-hanged-hanged* and *hang-hung-hung* has been vanishing, with the irregular form winning out, and being used for 'to execute by hanging' as well as in the more general sense. *Cleave* (originally two distinct verbs, one meaning 'stick together' one meaning 'split apart') used to be irregular, but is now usually regular, if used at all, with *cleft* and *cloven* appearing only as adjectival forms in fixed expressions like *cleft palate* and *cloven hoof.* The form *bade* (/bæd/ or /beɪd/) seems to be vanishing in favour of *bid*, but the verb is no longer common (and the *bid* heard at auctions and the card-game bridge is probably a separate verb).

There is some regional variation. In American English, the past participle of *get* is either *gotten* or *got* (depending on the meaning), and that usage is spreading to other areas. In Britain, for a couple of hundred years, the past participle of *get* has been *got*, and the past participle of *forget* has been *forgotten.* The past participle of *forget* is usually *forgot* in the USA. A relatively recent American innovation is *dove* as the past participle of *dive.* For people who used *dove, dived* sounds like baby-talk, as if someone had used *eated.* For people who use *dived, dove* sounds like a joke, like *thunk* for the past participle of *think.* The use of *drug* as the past tense (and sometimes past participle) of *drag* is also an American innovation that is spreading. *Snuck* as the past tense of *sneak* is similar. Scottish and New Zealand varieties of English sometimes have *bet* as the past tense (sometimes also the past participle) of *beat.* There are other American forms such as *spit* as the past tense of *spit* (*spat* in British English), and *hid* as the past participle of *hide* (*hidden* in British English).

There is also social variation, with *come, done* and *seen*, for example, being widely used as past tense forms in non-standard usage around the world.

Such factors make the inflection for past tense and past participle extremely complex, and extremely fascinating, areas. They also mean that it is very difficult to summarise what is going on in this area.

Just occasionally there are traces of the **subjunctive** in English (a minor usage in English, with various meanings, set out below). In the present tense this is shown by the lack of a third person singular -*s* (or, perhaps a better description, the use of the base form of the verb with third person singular), especially in sentences like *God save the Queen!*, a wish, or like *I request that he be brought before the court.* This latter usage is expanding in present-day English, under the influence of American English; this use of the subjunctive looked as though it might die out for a while, and was replaced by a modal, for example *I request that he should be brought before the court.* In the past tense, the form of the subjective has long been the same as the past tense, so that it is invisible except with the verb to *be.* The use of *were* in *If I were you* is a subjunctive form (so it implies that I am not you). This is often replaced by a simple past tense: *If I was you.*

Since there is no overt inflection for the infinitive or for the imperative in English, the last potential verbal inflection is the -*ing* form. This has regular form (it is always -*ing*, although there are some people who regularly or irregularly pronounce it /ɪn/), it always means the same thing (whatever that meaning is), and it can be applied to any verb that is not a modal. That seems enough to make it inflectional. Also, in the most basic uses, it remains verbal. This is shown in sentences like *I was finishing my tea, when she came in* and *Sitting in the corner of the room, I could see everyone from my chair*, where two distinct uses are illustrated. But -*ing* forms can sometimes be adjectival (*a very interesting question*) and sometimes nominal (*the building has fallen down*), and changing things from one word-class to another is typical of derivation rather than of inflection.

2.6.2 Inflection on nouns

We could make a case that there is no inflection on nouns. Both types of marking of nouns that are usually thought of as inflectional have been claimed to be something else.

The one that is most likely inflection is plural marking. The regular markers of the plural are precisely the same as the markers of the third person singular on verbs, except that -*s* doubling does not always take place before them: the verb is *busses*, the noun is *buses* (with *gas* the situation is less clear, and *gasses* can be seen for both). There are, though, many irregular patterns, illustrated briefly in (40).

(40) a. foot, feet; goose, geese; louse, lice; man, men; mouse, mice; tooth, teeth; woman, women
      b. calf, calves; dwarf, dwarfs ~ dwarves; knife, knives; wolf, wolves

    c. mouth, mouths /maʊðz/
    d. ox, oxen
    e. child, children
    f. brother, brethren
    g. deer, deer; fish, fish ~ fishes; sheep, sheep
    h. criterion, criteria; phenomenon, phenomena
    i. crisis, crises /kraɪsiːz/; emphasis, emphases; parenthesis, parentheses
    j. alumnus, alumni; cactus, cacti; stimulus, stimuli
    k. bacterium, bacteria; erratum, errata; stratum, strata
    l. am(o)eba, am(o)ebae; formula, formulae; vertebra, vertebrae
    m. appendix, appendices; index, indices; matrix, matrices
    n. bureau, bureaux; milieu, milieux; plateau, plateaux
    o. chassis, chassis; corps, corps
    p. cherub, cherubim; kibbutz, kibbutzim
    q. soprano, soprani; tempo, tempi; virtuoso, virtuosi
    r. corpus, corpora; genus, genera; larynx, larynges; species, species

The examples in (40a) provide a full list of the words that make their plural by **umlaut** or vowel-change. Occasionally some of these nouns get a regular plural, especially as a joke or in figurative uses. Uses of other words with umlaut plurals are always jokes (for example, *spice* as the plural of *spouse*), except for *mongeese* from *mongoose*, which has nothing to do with *goose*.

The examples in (40b–c) show cases where the final fricative of the singular becomes voiced in the plural. There is only one word which does this with /s/ becoming /z/, and that is *house, houses*. Even that is not invariable: there are many Scottish and American varieties where *house* has become regularised, so that the plural is /haʊsɪz/. There are many more examples where /f/ becomes /v/ in the plural, and this is nearly always shown in the spelling. Because this happens with nouns that are met frequently, the noun *giraffe* has been added to the list by some speakers in recent years, but it never has its plural written with <v>. Because there is often no difference in the spelling of /θ/ and /ð/, speakers do not always know which nouns that end in /θ/ have a plural in /ð/, and there is quite a lot of variation. *Path* is one of the most likely to have a /ð/ in the plural.

The examples in (40d–f) have various plurals ending in -*n*, often with vowel changes at the same time. *Brethren* is the plural of *brother* only in a religious sense, and these days not always even then. Occasionally *sistren* can be heard, with similar connotations.

The examples in (40g) do not mark the plural at all. *Deers* is occasionally heard, *sheeps* is extremely rare, and *fish* is more common than *fishes*, but it is not quite clear what the difference between the two is (assuming that there is a consistent difference). Other animals, birds and fish that are hunted for economic purposes can join the list of words having unmarked plurals. Again the usage is variable. *Trout* and *salmon* are more likely to have an unmarked plural than *sardine* and *anchovy*, with *herring* somewhere in the middle. *Duck* can be the plural of *duck* when the birds are wild and being hunted, but they are almost certainly *ducks* in the farmyard. *Quail*, on the other hand, very often has an unmarked plural. *Elk* and *moose* seem to prefer the form with no marking, as does *mink*. All these cases have a regular plural when the plural means 'different types of ~'. Another set of words which fits slightly oddly in this category is the set of words showing people of various nationalities or origins. These include particularly words that end in *-ese*, and include *Chinese, Japanese, Portuguese, Swiss, Viennese*. Speakers are often uncomfortable with such words in the singular, and prefer to use them with a definite article when they are making a generalisation: *The Japanese eat a lot of sushi* feels better than *I saw two Japanese coming out of their embassy*, and that is better than *I saw a Japanese wearing traditional dress today*.

All the other types in (40) are foreign **borrowings**, and this is slightly odd because it is unusual (though not impossible) to borrow foreign inflections. In nearly all' of these cases, it is possible to use regular English plural marking, but the foreign plural is often fixed in professional or technical usage. Those in (40h–i) are borrowed from Greek. English speakers have great problems with the pattern in (40h), not always knowing which is the singular and which the plural, or how to form a plural. The examples in (40j–m) are all Latin. While most of these are unlikely to be extended to new words, the pattern ending in *-us* can be. Toyota thinks that the plural of *Prius* is *Prii*; it is less clear what the plural of *Lexus* should be. We often hear *octopi*, even though the *-pus* at the end of *octopus* is the Greek word for 'foot', and not a Latin ending at all. There are also many words which could take these Latin patterns, but which usually do not. Words like *bonus, campus, circus, genius, arena, diploma, panorama, album* and *museum* take regular English plurals, and do not follow the Latin patterns. Moreover, the Latin endings can show variable pronunciation (see some discussion in Section 5.4). So final *-i* is sometimes /iː/ and sometimes /aɪ/. The *-ae* is sometimes pronounced /aɪ/, sometimes /iː/ and in *vertebrae*, is usually pronounced /eɪ/.

The examples in (40n–o) illustrate French patterns, and here the spelling is different from the pronunciation, and different from the modern French. Final -*x* in these words is pronounced /z/, and the plurals of the nouns in (40o) are pronounced as though they were regular plurals.

The pattern in (40p) is Hebrew, and affects very few nouns. The pattern in (40q) is Italian, and is often misleading. As a genuine plural, the pattern is used only in the technical fields of music, art history and cookery, and a regular English plural is more common among non-specialists. A few words with Italian plurals (*spaghetti, zucchini, panini*) are used as singulars in English – uncountable nouns in the names for pasta, but countable nouns with *panini* and *zucchini* (in some places, the term *courgette* is preferred, which avoids the issue). The patterns in (40r) are irregular as far as English is concerned; others could be added to this set.

This is all very confusing, not least because it demands etymological knowledge on the part of speakers who want to use the system appropriately. It becomes worse in that sometimes different plurals indicate different meanings of the base – at least for some speakers. Some examples are given in (41).

(41)	appendixes	in medicine	appendices	in a book
	brothers	'family members'	brethren	'monks'
	cherubs	'sweet children'	cherubim	'angels'
	indexes	in a book	indices	in mathematics, medicine
	stigmas	'disgraces'	stigmata	'marks on the body of Christ'
	youths /θs/	'young ages'	youths /ðz/	'young men'

Where expressions consisting of two orthographic words that act as an MWE take a plural, the general rule is that the head element takes the marking, but there are different types and variation even within types. Some examples are provided in (42).

(42)	forget-me-not, girl friend, houseboat	these are standard usage, and take a final plural marker
	gentleman farmer, woman doctor	both elements marked for plural, but only when the first element takes an irregular plural (**adults sons*)
	mother-in-law	prescriptively, *mothers-in-law*, but *mother-in-laws* is also heard; less common expressions of this kind – like *lady-in-waiting* – are more likely to take plural marking on the first element
	lay-by, take-off	*lay-bys, take-offs*

attorney general,   *attorneys general, governors general* is
governor general   etymologically accurate, but *attorney generals*
                     etc. is often heard

The other side of all this is that sometimes an apparent plural marker is not associated with a plural meaning and/or plural grammar. *Phonetics* is grammatically singular (*Phonetics is/ *are the study of the sounds of speech*), but this -*s* can be seen as a distinct (derivational) suffix. Some other examples are given in (43). Some of these typically take an expression such as *a pair of* ~ or *a set of* ~, which suggests a plural, others just do not have a singular form, and some of them typically take singular agreement (like the example with *phonetics* above).

(43) a. adjectival bases: goods, news
      b. body parts as the source of emotions: brains, guts
      c. clothes to fit the legs: shorts, tights, trousers
      d. diseases: measles, mumps, shingles
      e. games: bowls, draughts, ninepins
      f. instruments for the eyes: binoculars, glasses
      g. miscellaneous other types: amends, banns, customs, lodgings, (good) looks, premises, tropics
      h. other instruments with two parts: scissors, shears, tongs, pliers, scales

Equally, some nouns that act as plurals do not have plural form. Some examples are listed in (44).

(44) cattle, people, police, swine, vermin

With all these variables, and all these exceptions, it is not surprising that there are areas where speakers do not agree, or where usage, even in individuals, may vary. When they first appeared on the scene, the plural of *mouse* for a computer was often *mouses*, now it is more usually *mice*. People may not know (or may not agree) on what the plural of *tenderfoot* or *cloverleaf* is. Some people say *forums*, others say *fora*. *Media*, originally the plural of *medium*, is now often used as a singular noun.

Next we turn to **genitive** or possessive marking. If we call it genitive marking, it sounds as though we see this as inflectional; possessive marking may not have the same implication. The problem is that, if it is inflection, we expect to find the marking only on nouns, while in modern English there are some, rather rare but colloquially normal, constructions where the possessive marker is found on the end of noun phrases. These are instances such as those in (45).

(45) the girl you saw me with's mother
the Queen of England's fortune [it is the Queen's fortune, not
England's]
the woman I was admiring's dress

Examples like these make the -'s possessive marking look like a **clitic** (a particle that cannot stand alone that is attached to a phrase) rather than a suffix. This does not prevent some authorities referring to it as the **Saxon genitive**, reflecting its origin rather than a full range of its modern usages. A second problem here is that there is an alternative way of marking possession, doing so syntactically. *The cat's tail* and *The tail of the cat* can mean precisely the same thing. They do not always do so. There is only one definite article in *The cat's tail*, and it could be attached to *cat* or to *tail*. If we use *The cat's eye* (meaning the reflective marker in a roadway), then *the* refers to *eye*, because there is no specific cat involved. If, on the other hand, we say *I watched the cat carefully, and the cat's eye remained firmly fixed on the mouse, the* refers to *cat*, and not to *eye*. In other words, *The cat's tail* can mean 'the tail of a cat' or 'the tail of the cat', but the same ambiguity is not present with the *of*-genitive.

Some nouns prefer the Saxon genitive, some prefer the syntactic alternative, but there is no hard-and-fast rule about which is used. With possessors who are people (including names), the Saxon genitive is more usual: *Paul's book* is more usual than *The book of Paul* (they may even mean different things). With inanimate or abstract possessors, the use of *of* is more likely: *the root of the tree* is probably more likely than *the tree's root, The victims of flu* is more likely than *Flu's victims*.

So far, it has been made to sound as though these various forms always show possession, but that is not true. Consider the examples in (46), which provide only a few of the possible meanings.

(46)	's *example*	*of example*	*meaning*
	a winter's day	the first day of Christmas	time
	wolf's bane	a day of rest	purpose
	an hour's wait	a lump of dough	partitive
	New York's Empire State Building	the sea of Galilee	place
	St Michael's Mount	the Vale of York	named after

The form of the possessive marker provides problems in writing, but that is mainly because of pronouns rather than nouns. In the singular, the phonology of the possessive marker is the same as the phonology of the regular plural marker, but there are no exceptions: the possessive of *man* is *man's*, the possessive of *child* is *child's*, the possessive of *wolf* is *wolf's*, the possessive of *quiz* (if it is ever used) is *quiz's* /kwɪzɪz/ and so on. The possessive plural is slightly more complicated. Where there is an irregular plural that does not end in /s/ or /z/, the possessive is formed phonologically in exactly the same way as the possessive in the singular: the possessive of *men* is *men's*, the possessive of *teeth* (if it is ever used) is *teeth's*, the possessive of *children* is *children's*. Where the plural of the noun ends in /s/ or /z/, phonologically there is no change for the plural possessive. The plural possessive *girls'* sounds just like the plural *girls*, which sounds just like the singular possessive *girl's*. That is why nobody knows how to spell *girl's school/girls school/girls' school*. A way to reformulate this in orthographic terms is: to make the possessive, add <'s>; if this gives a sequence of <s's> where the first <s> shows the plural, delete the last <s>.

The problems here arise largely with non-possessive uses of the apostrophe. Although it used to be good English to write an apostrophe in a few plurals (things like *&'s*, *1990's*, *A+'s*, *if's* and even, at one stage, words ending in a vowel letter other than <e>, such as *guru's*) nowadays it is much rarer, and apostrophes are omitted if at all possible. *Lamb's* must be a possessive, not a plural. Apostrophes are also sometimes used to indicate missing letters. *It's* can mean 'it [i]s' or 'it [ha]s' (with the missing letters in square brackets). *Its* is a pronoun showing possessive, but pronouns never contain apostrophes: like *his* and *hers*, with no apostrophes, the possessive pronoun must be *its*.

There is split usage with names that end in /s/ or /z/, like *Archimedes*, *James*, *Jesus*, *Matthews*. Sometimes they are made possessive by adding <'s> (pronounced /ɪz/), and sometimes simply by adding an apostrophe (not pronounced at all). Although some language-users used to distinguish between classical names (like *Archimedes*) and modern names (like *James*), the fundamental rule these days seems to be to write what you would say, and either version is found.

2.6.3 Inflection on adjectives

Again, we might query whether there is any inflection on adjectives, although the general consensus is that there is. We have already met one contentious example: the use of *-ly* to turn an adjective into an adverb. That will be ignored here. The other possible category, the one usually accepted, is the marking of comparison: the **comparative** and **superlative** forms. In principle, these apply only to adjectives which are gradable: you can have different degrees of bigness, so *bigger* and *biggest* are possible, but you cannot have different degrees of being pregnant, so that *pregnanter* and *pregnantest* (or *more pregnant* and *most pregnant*) are odd. In practice, of course, speakers are more flexible than this implies, and expressions like *She is more French than the French*, *He looked deader than roadkill*, *This is the most unique experience I've ever had* are heard quite frequently.

These examples illustrate one of the major problems with the comparative and superlative: they can be marked with suffixes (*-er* and *-est*), or syntactically, with the words *more* and *most*. There are a handful of irregular forms (*good, better, best, bad, worse, worst, much, more, most* and a few others), and in *longer, stronger, younger* the <g> is pronounced as /g/, not simply as /ŋ/ as in *singer*. Nobody can explain when speakers use the suffixes and when they use *more* and *most*. It seems that multiple factors influence which is used (see Section 6.3). Even very general rules such as 'three-syllable words take *more* and *most*' are proved insufficient by *curiouser and curiouser* (though it is worth noting that when Alice says this, we are told that she 'was so much surprised that for the moment she quite forgot how to speak good English'), and *unhappier* and other such forms, as well as by other less frequent forms, which might be considered errors or jokes, as in (47).

(47) a. I think he's probably one of the most unluckiest people in the world. (Sheila Quigley (2011), *Nowhere Man*, Houghton-le-Spring: Burgess Books, p. 199)

      b. "A substantial sum?"
         "The substantialler the better." (Grace Burrowes (2017), *Too Scot to Handle*, New York and Boston: Forever, p. 156)

2.6.4 Other patterns

There are some other patterns which are sometimes viewed as inflectional, which deserve brief mention.

The most important of these is that adverbs can inflect for comparison, like adjectives. Again, the suffixes *-er* and *-est* are used, and the words *more* and *most*. The suffixes are never used with adverbs ending in *-ly*, so that the forms in (48) are the expected ones.

(48) a. He told her to run faster.
      b. He told her to run more quickly.

Although pronouns do not show clear patterns of base and suffix, there are some patterns which arise historically from inflectional behaviour, and might still be considered inflectional. The final *-m* in *him, them, whom*, originally a dative case marker, can be seen as a marker of oblique case (where **oblique** is the name given to the case that is not the nominative). Similarly, the final /z/ in *his, hers, yours, ours, theirs, whose* can be seen as a possessive marker, though historically the <r> is the genitive case marker, where it exists. More complex patterns are illustrated in (49). Speakers today do not analyse these words (in some cases, do not use them at all), and are generally unaware of their potential analysis.

(49) here   hither   hence
      there   thither   thence   this   that   these   those
      where   whither   whence

Note that in *there, thither, thence*, the initial <th> has to be understood as **distal** ('near you', 'away from me'), but in *this* and *these* the same analysis cannot be made, because these are **proximal** ('near me'). While it might be possible to view the final /z/ in *these* and *those* as plural, the vowel changes between singular and plural here are unpredictable.

2.7 Summary

In this chapter we have considered the many ways of building new words in English. Some of the words built by these processes are new lexemes, but if they are built using inflectional morphology, then the new words are word-forms of already-known lexemes. We have seen that there are important border disputes, not only between inflection and derivation, but also between the various word-formation processes. There are also theoretical disputes as to how these processes work or should be described. The conclusion must be that, although we know how most of the processes operate on a fairly superficial level, we cannot provide an optimum description without better theory, nor a really good theory without better descriptions.

Exercises

1. Find ten compound words that do not share a first element and do not share a second element. What types of compounds have you found?

2. Look up words for hybrid animals on the internet (you may find articles on hybrids in general, or sites that consider hybrids of, for example, dogs). Are there preferences for what kinds of formations are used to name hybrid animals?

3. Find ten words that make their plural by changing an <f> to a <ve> (for example, *wolf, wolves*). Using a reverse dictionary (for example, Lehnert 1971), find some exocentric compounds that end in these

elements. How are these compounds made plural? Check in several sources. Do your sources agree? Are there any generalisations?

4. Consider the way in which the verbs listed below make their past tense and past participle. Do different grammars or dictionaries agree on what the forms of the verbs are? Can you predict which sources will list which forms?

> bid, burn, cleave, dive, dream, hide, spell, spit, thrive

The following questions demand access to native speakers of English, or require you to be a native speaker. Do not attempt them unless you can meet these expectations.

5. Do speakers stress *blue whale* in the way they stress *blackbird* or the way they stress *red squirrel*? Try with a number of adjective + noun structures, including *black currant, cold drink, hot drink, red currant*. Are exocentric compounds more consistent? Try *big top, bluebeard, redhead*. Find your own examples to test.

6. In a group, find out which words ending in -*th* have /θ/ in the plural form and which have /ð/. How far does the group agree? How far are individuals secure in their judgements? Do different meanings of the words give rise to different pronunciations? You should consider at least the following words:

> death, lath, moth, mouth, oath, path, sheath, truth, wreath, youth

7. Can you find other patterns of verb to add to the list in (39)? Can you find verbs which might use more than one pattern?

8. Ask your parents and grandparents (or people of their generation) about the words in (41). Do they use the plurals in the same way as your peers, or are there differences?

9. Find ten more examples like those in (29a) where verbs and nouns differ in stress. Do your classmates agree on which words behave in this way? Can you find pairs in a dictionary which behave differently from the way in which you use them?

10. Nobody knows precisely when the plural of *fish* is *fish* and when it is *fishes*. Can you find any particular domain or environment that is likely to call forth *fishes*?

Recommendations for reading

The most complete coverage of material in the area covered by this chapter is Bauer et al. (2013). Adams (1973, 2001), Bauer (1983) and Plag (2003) provide textbook coverage. Adams is particularly good on providing examples, Bauer's book is theoretically out-dated, but covers important points, and Plag's is more of a how-to guide. For more detail on inflectional morphology, see Quirk et al. (1985) and Huddleston and Pullum (2002). On the meanings associated with the suffixes *-ise* and *-ify*, see Plag (1999). On embellishment, see Bauer and Huddleston (2002). On the question of whether adjectives and adverbs belong to a single class or two, see the competing analyses in Payne et al. (2010) and Giegerich (2012).

3 The development of the vocabulary

3.1 A potted history of English words

English is a Germanic language, related to modern Dutch and German, and less closely to Danish, Norwegian, Swedish and Icelandic. The Germanic languages are a branch of the Indo-European language family, and speakers of the earliest form of Indo-European that we might call Germanic originally lived on the Baltic coast of modern-day Germany and Poland.

But the Germanic speakers were late arrivals in England. Until the fourth century CE, the inhabitants of England spoke a variety of Celtic, related to modern Welsh and Gaelic. It was Celtic speakers whose territory had been invaded in the Roman invasion of Britain in the first century CE. From the fourth century onwards, Germanic speakers started landing in England. The myth of Hengist and Horsa tells us that the first Germanic speakers were invited in by the Celts as security guards in an unstable environment; this may well be founded in truth. In any case, when the Germanic speakers started to arrive in earnest, they settled first in the east (East Anglia is named for the Angles, one of the peoples who settled from this period onwards), and gradually moved westwards.

It is not understood why the Germanic language pushed out the earlier Celtic language. It seems unlikely that speakers of Celtic were killed rather than assimilated, but there are very few traces left in English of Celtic words from this period. Some of them are *brock* ('badger'), *combe*, *druid* and *dun* (the colour). The word *cross* also seems to be Celtic, rather than directly derived from Latin *crux*.

Some names are Celtic, too: *Thames* and *Severn*, for example. The name *Avon* derives from the Celtic word meaning 'river', so that *River Avon* is, historically speaking, something of a tautology.

Although there is relatively little trace of any Celtic language in modern English, there are traces of Latin from the same period, because

Christianity came from Rome in the sixth century CE. Words like *abbot, alms, angel, fennel, lily, mass, minster, nun, plant, temple, verse, wine* seem to have come into England at about this time, illustrating not only narrowly religious terminology, but the influence of the religious life.

By the eighth century CE the language of the Germanic people was general throughout most of England. It used to be called Anglo-Saxon after the Angles and Saxons, two of the invading peoples, but today it is more usually called Old English. Old English was spoken throughout most of England, but not in Cornwall, and not in Wales. There were several distinct, but inter-comprehensible dialects of Old English. Old English was a highly inflected language, in some ways more like modern German and modern Icelandic than like modern English.

> Ðā wæs æfter manigum dagum þæt sē cyning cōm tō þæm ēalande, and hēt him ūte setl gewyrcean.
>
> (Then it was after many days that the king came to the island and commanded (them) to make him a seat in the open air.)

Towards the end of the eighth century CE, the linguistic status quo was challenged by the arrival of the Vikings ('the people from the bays'), who sacked the monastery at Lindisfarne, Northumberland, in 793 CE. The Vikings were Scandinavians, and brought with them their own Germanic languages. There were two fundamental groups of Vikings who settled in Britain over the next century or so: the Danes, who settled on the eastern seaboard of England, and the Norwegians, who settled in Dublin, the Isle of Man and north-west Britain.

It is not entirely clear how much the Viking invaders could understand the English and vice versa. For the most part, the Vikings adopted the English language, but they added to it a number of clearly Scandinavian words, some of which persist to the present day. These include *bank, birth, crawl, dirt, egg, fellow, get, give, scowl, skin, sky, take, tight, weak*. In a few instances we have both the Scandinavian word and the English word, both from the same Germanic source, now differentiated by dialect or by meaning: *church, ditch* and *shirt* are English, corresponding to Scandinavian *kirk, dike* and *skirt*, respectively. Most surprisingly, the Scandinavians gave us the pronouns *they, them* and *their*, the words *both* and *same*, and the third person singular *-s* suffix on the end of a word like *takes*. The fact that so many common words of English are Scandinavian loans speaks to the long coexistence of the two languages. You can more or less plot where the Scandinavians settled by looking at a map of England for place names ending in *-by*, like *Whitby, Kirkby, Lazonby, Maltby*. The *by* element meant something like 'settlement', related to the Scandinavian word for 'inhabit'. *By* is still the modern Danish word for a town.

Relations between the English in the south and the Scandinavians in the north were often fraught, but at the end of the ninth century CE, King Alfred (famous for burning the cakes) negotiated a settlement with the Danes, such that the land north of a line from London to Chester became the Danelaw, subject to Danish rule, and the English ruled south of that line. Even that did not mean that relationships were not troubled from time to time, but there were overt attempts at conciliation.

In 1042 CE, Edward the Confessor became king of the English. His title of 'Confessor' reflects his perceived piety. Originally, he intended to remain celibate, but he married in 1051, though he never had any children to whom he could pass on the crown. By the time he died in January 1066, he had personally promised the kingship to at least two people, and others thought they had a good legal case. Harold was crowned to replace Edward, and he had to deal with an attack from the north from a Norwegian claimant to the throne and then, almost immediately afterwards, the famous battle of Hastings in the south, where Harold was killed, and William the Conqueror assumed the throne.

We think of William as being French, but he was the descendant of Vikings, who had been attacking north-western France as long as they had been attacking England. Linguistically, however, he was French, although the French he spoke was not the direct forerunner of modern standard French. The French spoken in England after the Norman conquest is termed 'Anglo-Norman'. The English word *castle* arises from Latin *castellum* via French, but the modern standard French form is *château*. The change of initial [k] to [ʧ] (spelt <ch>) and the loss of the final [l] had already happened in the forerunners of modern French by the time of the conquest, but had not happened in Norman French.

The invasion by William was an entirely different kind of event from the earlier invasion by the Scandinavians. The Scandinavians had settled in the villages, had worked the land alongside the English, and had interacted with the English on a daily basis. The Normans brought in the feudal system, and claimed the land, but left the English working the land and paying tribute to their lords. The Normans also held the high positions in the church. This meant far less interaction with the Germanic-speaking people, especially in the early years, and meant that the Germanic language was left relatively untouched in its fundamentals. Something like 80 per cent of the population spoke only English; less than 10 per cent spoke only French. Some of the French-speakers had to learn English to make sure that the work was carried out as was desired and the tributes collected; some of the upwardly mobile

Germanic speakers had to learn French to communicate upwards; and there was a certain amount of intermarriage. But the two languages were not constantly intermingled. And the change towards the general use of English with a lot of French words came relatively slowly. Henry II (1133–89), although he could understand some English, could not speak it; Henry III (1207–72) was the first of the Norman kings to put out public documents in English, although he surrounded himself with French courtiers; Richard II (1367–1400) spoke English to the peasants during the Peasants' Revolt, although he was said to speak good French (perhaps not surprisingly, since he had been born and brought up in Bordeaux). The fact that the standard of his French was worthy of comment rather than the standard of his English shows how much things had changed in a century.

The Normans brought with them a number of words for the new system and their way of life, such as *baron, clerk, convent, countess, crown, diamond, government, justice, minstrel, miracle, prison, treasure*. Some of these words passed into English fairly early, others took hundreds of years to become fully adopted. One of the results is that there were often French synonyms for English words, and in legal texts both were sometimes used to ensure both full understanding and full coverage. Thus we have expressions like *care and attention, fit and proper, goods and chattels, lord and master, power and might, true and correct, will and testament*. In more general terms, French, Latin and Greek provide innumerable synonyms in English, and these will be considered in Section 3.5.

One of the results of the Norman conquest was that England (but not, at this period, Wales or Scotland) was united, politically and, in time, linguistically. As far as the Norman lords were concerned, whatever people were speaking in England, if it wasn't French, was English. And while there are differences in the language of the various regions at the period which have left traces in modern dialects, it was the language of the Norman capital, London, that came to dominate.

By about 1400, the period when Chaucer was writing, English had once again become the dominant language in England. English of this period is now called Middle English. It is very different from the Old English of the period of King Alfred. Not only had a lot of French been assimilated into English, the morphological complexity of Old English had been considerably simplified. Later in the fifteenth century, Caxton brought printing to England, and discovered that it was hard to know how to print English, because there were dialect words and inconsistent spelling conventions. With the advent of printing, we get the start of a standardisation of English, and the new standard was a southern one.

Caxton, writing in 1490, tells the story of a northern merchant trying to get a meal of eggs in the south of England (note the inconsistent spelling of the words *eggs* and *understood*, as well as the problem with understanding the northern (Scandinavian) form *eggs*).

> And specyally he axyed after eggys. And the good wyf answerde that she coude speke no frenshe. And the merchaunt was angry for he also coude speke no frenshe but wold haue hadde egges and she understode hym not. And thenne at laste a nother sayd that he wolde haue eyren. Then the good wyf sayd that she understood hym we.
> (He specifically asked for eggs. The good woman answered that she couldn't speak French. The merchant was angry, because he couldn't speak French either, but he wanted eggs and she couldn't understand him. And then at last another said that he would like 'eyren'. Then the good woman said she understood him well.)

The standardisation was a long time coming. Shakespeare, a hundred years later, notoriously spelt his own name several ways. Nevertheless, a fair amount of comment on the variety of dialects in England, written over the next century or so, has survived, with attitudes which people from the late twentieth century would have recognised: northern English is ugly and incomprehensible, scarcely a language at all, but just a series of strange noises. Such attitudes support a movement towards notions of correctness and purism in language (and, to some extent, a movement towards descriptivism: we must write down what proper English involves). They laid the foundations for the codification of English that was to follow.

In the meantime, as was happening all over Europe, the classics (the literature of Greece and Rome) were rediscovered. While the classics were admired as paragons of what culture was all about, not only in literature but also in sculpture, at this period there was little reason to continue to use Latin (even less, Greek) in real life. Rather, Latin and Greek resources were called upon to develop and increase the vocabulary of English, so that English, too, could aspire to such glory. And in the Early Modern English period we see that potential being realised in the works of the Elizabethan and Jacobean dramatists, the poetry of people like John Donne, the King James authorised version of the Bible, and the development of science. Isaac Newton's *Principia Mathematica* (first published in 1687) was still published in Latin, but English was beginning to take over as the language of science by that period. Latin and Greek words such as *alibi, arena, basis, bathos, comma, data, dislocate, dogma, focus, larynx, obscene, orchestra, sceptic, series, skeleton,* came into English in the sixteenth and seventeenth centuries.

This flood of classical words, sometimes called 'inkhorn' terms, is made fun of in Shakespeare's *Love's Labour's Lost* (1593):

> He draweth out the thred of his verbositie, finer than the staple of his argument. I abhor such phanaticall phantasims, such insociable and poynt deuise companions, such rackers of ortagriphie, as to speake dout fine, when he should say doubt; det, when he shold pronounce debt; d e b t, not det: he clepeth a Calf, Caufe: halfe, hawfe; neighbour vocatur nebour; neigh abreuiated ne: this is abhominable, which he would call abhominable: it insinuateth me of infamie: ne inteligis domine, to make franticke, lunaticke?
>
> (This is from the First Folio, and has not been entirely understood by the scribe: *infamie* should probably be *insanie*, and the second *abhominable* should probably be *abbominable*.)

Here it is the pronunciation that is in question, but the sheer number of words was a problem as well as how to pronounce them. Thus we find dictionaries being written, so that people could understand these words. One of the earliest is Robert Cawdrey's *Table Alphabeticall* (1604). The full title of this work is *A table alphabeticall conteyning and teaching the true writing, and vnderstanding of hard vsuall English words, borrowed from the Hebrew, Greeke, Latine, or French, &c. With the interpretation thereof by plaine English words, gathered for the benefit & helpe of ladies, gentlewomen, or any other vnskilfull persons. Whereby they may the more easilie and better vnderstand many hard English wordes, vvhich they shall heare or read in scriptures, sermons, or elswhere, and also be made able to vse the same aptly themselues.* This is the start of a lexicographical tradition that leads on to Samuel Johnson's *A Dictionary of the English Language* (1755) and eventually to the *Oxford English Dictionary* (under this title only in the twentieth century).

At the beginning of the seventeenth century, we find the first lasting settlement of English speakers on the North American continent, in 1607. This move was to have an incredibly large influence on the way the English language developed. It also signals the start of the spread of English all round the world through trade and conquest. And as English speakers spread, they find themselves faced with phenomena they have never met before, and they bring back to England words which are used to describe these phenomena. There are innumerable words of this type, and any list can do no more than give a brief introduction to the range of words and the range of sources those words come from. Some non-European examples with their linguistic origins and the dates of first attestation in English are provided in Table 3.1.

Borrowing of foreign words, both European and extra-European, continues to be a major source of new words in English right up to the

Table 3.1 Loan words from around the world

Word	*Source*	*Reaches English through*	*Date and comments*
algebra	Arabic	Latin	1551 (in the mathematical sense)
assassin	Arabic	French	1531 (in the sense 'murderer')
budgerigar	Yuwaalaraay		1847
bungalow	Hindustani		1676
caddy	Malay		1792
caravan	Persian	French	1596
commandeer	South African Dutch		1881
curry	Tamil		1598
haiku	Japanese		1899
igloo	Inuit		1856
kangaroo	Guugu Yimidhirr		1770
kiosk	Turkish or Persian	French	1625
kumquat	Cantonese		1699
marijuana	Nahuatl	Spanish	1874
moose	Eastern Abenaki		1614
potlatch	Nootka	Chinook Jargon	1844
pyjamas	Persian	Urdu	1801
raccoon	Algonquian		1608
safari	Swahili		1859
tank	Gujerati	Portuguese	1634
tea	Amoy Chinese	Malay, Dutch	1660
thug	Hindi		1810
toboggan	Micmac	French	1829
tulip	Turkish		1578
tycoon	Japanese		1857

present day. What changes, to some degree, is the source languages and the topic areas of the words that are borrowed. Some more recent loan words are presented in Table 3.2.

Words have also been borrowed from regional dialects, and moved into standard varieties of English. A few examples of this phenomenon are given in Table 3.3.

As at all periods of history, newly coined compounds and derivatives continue to expand our vocabulary. Such formations are discussed in Chapter 2. What may be worthy of note is the number of relatively minor formation types, which seem to have increased in recent years. In Table 3.4 we have initialisms, where the first letters of the words in a phrase are used as a name; in Table 3.5 we have acronyms, where the initial words of a phrase are pronounced as a new word; in Table 3.6

Table 3.2 Some recent – and predominantly European – loan words

Word	Source	Date
Blitzkrieg	German	1939
bustier	French	1978
fado	Portuguese	1902
geisha	Japanese	1891
Gestalt	German	1992
glasnost	Russian	1981
hygge	Danish	1960
lingerie	French	1835
nacho	Spanish	1948
nosh	Yiddish	1873
ombudsman	Swedish	1872
rodeo	Spanish	1811
spaghetti	Italian	1845
tsunami	Japanese	1897

Table 3.3 Some dialectal terms in standard English

Word	Dialectal source	Meaning	Date
blackmail	Scottish		1530
craic	Irish or Ulster Scots		1972
emmet	Cornish	'tourist'	1975
flummox	Western England		1837
grockle	South-west England	'tourist'	1964
guffaw	Scots		1721
kerfuffle	Scots	'dispute, disorder'	1946
moke	Hampshire, Devon	'donkey'	1839
Scouse	Liverpool	'Liverpudlian'	1960
up the duff	Australian	'pregnant'	1941

we have clippings, where words are shortened; in Table 3.7 we have backformations, where apparent affixes are removed from longer words to make shorter ones. Although these formation types may have been around for a long time, they seem to have been used with greater frequency of recent times, and thus seem to be one of the ways in which the English language has changed in the last century or so.

3.2 Recognising the sources of words

The result of this mixed history is that we can distinguish between five major types of word that, even today, behave rather differently from each other. First we have the original Germanic words, whether they

Table 3.4 Initialisms

Initialism	Standing for	Comment	Date
aka	Also Known As		1948
ATM	Automatic Teller Machine		1975
CID	Criminal Investigation Department		1910
DJ	Disc (Disk) Jockey	Originally US	1946
DVD	Digital Video Disc (Disk)		1993
NB	Nota Bene	'note well'	1651
URL	Uniform Resource Locator		1992

Table 3.5 Acronyms

Acronym	Standing for	Comment	Date
Aids	Acquired Immune Deficiency Syndrome		1982
AWOL	Absent WithOut Leave		1894
FLOTUS	First Lady Of The United States		1983
Nasdaq	National Association of Securities Dealers Automated Quotations		1968
PIN number	Personal Identification Number	Originally US	1976
scuba	Self-Contained Underwater Breathing Apparatus		1952
snafu	Situation Normal All Fouled [euphemism] Up	Originally US military	1941
yuppie	Young Urban Professional + -ie	Often interpreted as 'Young Upwardly mobile Professional'	1984

Table 3.6 Clippings

Clipping	Source	Date
ad	advertisement	1799
bike	bicycle	1880
emo	emotional hardcore	1988
fiche	microfiche	1959
flu	influenza	1839
grad	graduate	1871
mike	microphone	1911
shrink	headshrinker	1966
stash	moustache	1940

Table 3.7 Backformations

Backformation	Source	Date
automate	automated, automation	1954
brainstorm	brainstorming	1945
burgle	burglar	1872
choreograph	choreography	1943
complicit	complicity	1855
edit	editor	1791
extradite	extradition	1864
lech	lecher	1911
second-guess	second-guesser	1941
surveil(le)	surveillance	1960
Tase	Taser	1991

come from Old English or from Scandinavian. All the others come in from outside Germanic (a few come more recently from Germanic languages) and add to the fundamental Germanic base of English. These are usually called loan words, and are said to be borrowed from the relevant languages, although such borrowings are rarely returned, and often develop in English in rather different directions from the way they develop in their home environments. Some prefer to see these words as being stolen or hijacked.

The first group of these loan words is the words that come from French. English has borrowed from French throughout its history, from old words like *castle* to more modern words like *lingerie*. The older words are generally harder to spot as being foreign, because they have become so much a part of English.

The second group of these words comes from Latin. There is a problem here, in that French is derived from Latin, and so most of the French words we have also come from Latin, just at one remove. Linguistically we can often see that the French words have undergone changes between Latin and French, and that English has borrowed the French version. For instance, Latin *populus* gave rise to modern French *peuple* which has got into English as *people*: the loss of the ending -*us* and the vowel change are products of French, not products of Latin. The real Latin words are the inkhorn terms, borrowed directly from Latin (and not always, it must be said, accurately).

The third group of loan words comes from Greek. Many of these have been transmitted to us through Latin or French or both, but their Greek character tends to show through.

The final group is a miscellaneous group of words borrowed from disparate languages all round the world. They do not form a coherent grouping, in the way that the other sets here do, and how well they fit into the system of English depends on how long they have been a part of English, as well as on the spelling system or sound system of the language from which they are taken. For example, *yak* looks foreign, because the normal English spelling would be <yack>, but it sounds like an English word (similar to *back, jack, lack* and so on). *Dzo* (also spelt <zho> and <zo>) looks and sounds foreign because English does not normally have words that begin with <dz> or /dz/ – or even, with other spellings, with /ʒ/. On the other hand, *moose*, which is equally a loan word, looks just like an English word (partly because the original has been written down using an English system) and sounds just like an English word. We can term all such words **exotic** words.

In what follows, we will consider each of these groups, and show how they can be recognised (to the extent that they can be) in terms of their spelling, their pronunciation and their morphological behaviour.

3.2.1 Germanic

The original Germanic words are usually one or two syllables long, and if two, stressed on the first.

Where verbs are concerned, the first-syllable stress can be overruled if the verb contains what was once a prefix. Forms like *a-, be-, for-, re-* and *un-* are relevant prefixes, and sometimes forms that look like prepositions fill the same role, forms like *off-, out-, over-, up-, with-*. This means that the following are typical Germanic verbs: *arise, beget, behold, forget, offset, outshine, overhear, redo, undo, upset, withhold*. Such verbs can also appear as the rightmost element in compounds like *roughcast* and *typecast*.

Verbs with ablaut are Germanic verbs, verbs such as *bear, come, do, fight, keep, rise, wake*. Surprisingly, most of them do not have cognates outside of Germanic. These verbs also tend to have a lot of phrasal verbs built on them. Corresponding to *give* we can find *give in, give up, give out, give over*, and with *get* we find *get on, get up, get out, get off, get down, get in, get through* and so on, many of them with several meanings. There are some phrasal verbs with non-Germanic verbs (*power up, sign in* – both of which are of French origin) but they are much rarer.

Both the fact that these verbs retain ablaut and the fact that they appear in so many phrasal verbs means that they are some of the most common verbs in English (if they were not common, they would lose ablaut, like *cleave* and *strive*, for which some more conservative speakers may still use ablaut forms, but which many modern speakers treat as regular verbs).

Monosyllabic adjectives which take *-er* inflections tend to be Germanic, although there are a few which are early loans from French, such as *grand* and *gross*. These tend to be treated as though they were Germanic. A surprising example is *pink*, the colour, arising in the seventeenth century and of uncertain origin, but not inherited directly from Germanic. It appears to behave as though it were an original English word. These adjectives can occur in adjective + noun compounds, with stress on the adjective, as in *blackbird, highroad, lowland, whitethorn*.

Germanic words are among the most basic words: *man, woman, calf, tree, die, sleep, smile, old, white*. There are, though, occasional surprises: *tank* is a loan from an Indian language; *girl* and *boy*, although they may have Germanic ancestry, do not occur in English until the Middle English period; *joke* is from Latin, although it is spelt like a native word; *sole* (of the foot) is from French.

There are some spellings which usually mark Germanic words (though occasionally, as with *moose*, loan words are spelt according to the norms of native words instead of being borrowed along with a spelling), and this is set out in Table 3.8. In Tables 3.8–3.12, '#' means the fringe of a word, so that '#k' means word-initial <k>, and 'k#' means word-

Table 3.8 Spellings marking Germanic words

Spelling	Specifically when pronounced	Examples	Comments, exceptions, etc.
#dw, #tw		dwell, dwindle, twin, two	Dialectal *dwang* is from Dutch; *tweezers* is apparently from French, but written as though native
#kn	n	knight, know	
#th	ð	there, this	Occurs only in grammatical words
#wh	w, hw	when, why	
#wr		write, wrong	
ch	ʧ	chick, church	Some early French words have /ʧ/ as well: *chase, check, chief*
ck#		back, lack, suck	*check*
ea	e	head	*treasure* and like words are from French
ee	iː	feel, see	When not final, as in *employee, feeble* is from French
gh		night, sigh, though	Italian words like *ghetto* and *spaghetti*; *ghost* is Germanic, but the <h> in the spelling is from Caxton
nk		sink, think	
oo	uː	boot, root	When not final, as in *kangaroo*

Table 3.9 Spellings marking French words

Spelling	Specifically when pronounced	Examples	Comments, exceptions, etc.
ch	ʃ	chamois, chauffeur, chef	
é#, ée#	eɪ	dragée, fiancé(e), protégé(e)	The accent is often omitted in English
eau#		plateau, tableau	
gn	nj	cognac, vignette	*Bologna* is Italian
#j	ʒ	jabot	
ou…e	uː	route	
qu	k	bouquet, boutique, exchequer	
s#	Ø	Beaujolais, chamois, debris	That is, the final <s> is not pronounced at all

final <k>; C means any consonant letter; V means any vowel letter; '/__ X' means 'when it occurs immediately before X', Ø means 'zero', so not pronounced or not marked.

3.2.2 French

Words containing the sound /ʒ/ are often French, especially if the sound comes in initial or final position, as in *jongleur, beige*. There are also some Russian words that fit this criterion: the Russian words usually have initial /ʒ/ spelt <zh>, like *Zhivago*, while in French words it is spelt <j>, like *jabot*. But even words like *treasure* are French, and words like *vision*, though Latin, come through French. Words that make their plural by adding *-x* are French: *tableaux, bijoux*; this could be reduced to a final spelling of <ux> in a plural word. The spelling can be a clue to some French words, and this is set out in Table 3.9.

3.2.3 Latin

One of the best ways to recognise Latin words is by their morphology. Particular suffixes and prefixes tend to indicate a word of Latin origin, especially when the base the affix is attached to is not an English word in its own right. Of course, sometimes these affixes are added to Latin words which have also been borrowed into English, and occasionally native words have these affixes added, but the affixes added to words which are not English more or less guarantees that the words are Latin – although care must be taken as there may be non-suffixes of the same form. Some of the relevant prefixes and suffixes are listed and illustrated in (1) and (2).

Table 3.10 Spellings marking Latin words

Spelling	Specifically when pronounced	Examples
cc		accomplish, succeed
s /__ <i>, /j/	ʃ or ʒ	closure, occlusion, profession

(1)   ad-, anti-, de-, ex-, inter-, multi-, post-, pre-, re-, sub-, super-, supra-, trans-
adhere, adopt; anticipate, antimony; defer, descend; excuse, expel; interregnum, interrupt; multiply, multitude; posterior, posthumous; predicate, preliminary; receive, recipe; subject, submit; supererogatory, superlative; transient, translate

(2)   -ary (-arian), -ible, -ion (-sion, -tion, -ation, -ition, -ution), -ify, -ity, -ive (-ative, -itive), -or, -ous, -um, -us
granary, library; eligible, horrible; union (emulsion, station, natation, volition, solution); pacify, verify; amenity, veracity; captive (durative, transitive); author, monitor; atrocious, conscious; capsicum, museum; rumpus, virus

Note that *octopus* and *polyanthus*, despite ending in *-us*, are Greek. There are also a few spelling rules which indicate Latin words, as set out in Table 3.10.

3.2.4 Greek

The elements of Greek words tend to stick together: if you recognise one Greek element in a word, the chances are that other elements in the word are also Greek. Of course, there are exceptions. *Television* is a word made up of Greek *tele-* ('distant') and Latin *vision*; *asexual* has a Greek prefix and a Latin base; the suffix *-ism*, though Greek, is often borrowed through French, and can attach to many things. But in most cases, if you do not recognise the other part of the word, it is safest to assume that Greek goes with Greek. It doesn't necessarily make sense to talk about prefixes and suffixes here; rather, we can talk about introductory elements and final elements, or, more generally, of combining forms. These will be treated in greater detail in Section 3.4.2, so only a few examples will be given here, and more examples will be given with the later discussion. Some Greek introductory elements are given in in (3), and some final elements are given in (4).

(3)   a- (negative), bio- ('life'), cardi- ('heart'), geo- ('earth'), hyper- ('extreme'), leuk- ('white'), mega- ('large'), neo- ('new'), phil-

Table 3.11 Spellings marking Greek words

Spelling	Specifically when pronounced	Examples	Comments, exceptions, etc.
#bd		bdellium	The only word with this spelling
#pn		pneumonia	
#ps		psalm, psychology	
#pt		pterodactyl, ptomaine	*ptarmigan* is Gaelic, spelt with a <p> because it was falsely assumed to be Greek
#rh		rhombus, rhyme	The name *Rhodri* is Welsh
ch	k	chemistry, chimera	
eu	juː	euphony, neurotic	
Non-final y	aɪ	cyanide, hybrid, thyme	*dyke* and *tyke* are native, as are *dye* and *lye*, *nylon* is invented; *lychee* is Chinese
ph	f	photograph, sylph	*pho* is Vietnamese
sm#		organism, spasm	Words with -*ism* indicate the Greek suffix, which may be attached to elements which are not Greek

('like, love'), pseudo- ('false'), tele- ('distant')
atypical, biopsy, cardiogram, geology, hyperbole, leukaemia, megalith, neophile, philosophy, pseudopod, telegraph

(4)   -genesis ('origin'), -graph ('writing, picture'), -itis ('inflammation'), -mancy ('divination'), -ology ('study'), -phobia ('fear'), -phone ('sound'), -pod ('foot'), -saurus ('lizard'), -tomy ('cut')
pathogenesis, photograph, laryngitis, ornithomancy, theology, gynephobia, xylophone, pseudopod, brontosaurus, mastectomy

There are also various spelling conventions which indicate Greek origin. These are set out in Table 3.11.

3.2.5 Exotic: other loans

Given the wide range of other languages from which English has borrowed or stolen words (sometimes just one or two, sometimes many), there is no necessary expectation that they will conform to a coherent set of spelling patterns. Nevertheless, a number of patterns seem to be used mainly or exclusively with words loaned from such languages. Some of these are set out in Table 3.12. It is also worth pointing out

Table 3.12 Spellings marking exotic words

Spelling	Specifically when pronounced	Examples	Comments, exceptions, etc.
a	ɑː	lava, saga, salami	This is specifically <a> alone, without an <r>. Words that end in <age>, <ade> or <ale> are probably French; <a> pronounced /ɑː/ before /f/, <th> or /s/ is not exotic
ah#		mitzvah, mynah, purdah	*bah* and *hurrah* may be exceptions
Ca#		alpaca, copra, panda	There are many words from Latin with final <a>
Ci#	i	chilli, patchouli, sari	Some words with final <i> are from Latin or Italian
Cu#	uː	seppuku, zebu	Nearly all words ending in <u> are non-Germanic, but many are French
kh	k	ankh, gymkhana, khaki	k+h can occur elsewhere over a boundary as in *black+head*, *jack+hammer*
q without u		Iraq, qanat	
tz		blitz, waltz	These are late Germanic loans
Vk#		muntjak, trek	The V must not be <oo>, <oa>, <ea> or <ee>
z#		fez, topaz	Some words with final <z> are English, but have an unusual formation, such as abbreviation (*biz*) or imitation (*fuzz*), or possibly slang (*jazz*)

that in English a word of only two letters is nearly always a grammatical word: *am, be, do, he, in, is, it, me, on, to* and so on. A full noun, verb or adjective with only two letters is thus a signal that the word is not an ordinary English word. Words like *ka, qi, ti, xi, zo* – many of them showing foreign spelling conventions anyway – are marked as non-English. However, there are exceptions to the general rule, sometimes with words with two spellings such as *do* or *doh* (the musical note), *fa* or *fah* (the musical note), *jo* or *joe*, *pa* or *pah* ('Maori village'), *re* or *ray* (the musical note), sometimes with just a single spelling, notably *go*.

Words which speakers still perceive as exotic tend to avoid English prefixes or suffixes. When they are found with such affixes, they are usually the very common ones: affixes such as *un-*, *-er*, *-ish*, *-ness*, *-y*]$_A$ (that is, *-y* creating an adjective).

3.3 Latin words in English

Latin and Greek words have their own formation types, and recognising the relevant elements may help understand what words containing them mean. In this section, Latin words are considered, in the next, Greek words.

Just like English words, Latin words are made up of a base and an optional prefix and one or more optional suffixes. The difficulty for the English speaker is that, once they get to English, the prefixes and bases do not have fixed meanings, and that that the prefixes and bases do not have fixed forms. As in English, the suffixes, when they are included, determine the word-class of the word as a whole. Many of the suffixes have also become affixes of English, and then behave more transparently, both in terms of forming sequences of affixes, and in terms of allowing native affixes to follow them. We will look at prefixes, bases and suffixes in that order.

3.3.1 Prefixes

Many Latin prefixes have multiple forms depending on the first letter/sound of the base. In Table 3.13, the original Latin meaning of the prefix is also given, although that meaning is often difficult to discern in the English word, so that these are not strictly speaking prefixes in English. Some Latin prefixes are also used in English, and there the meaning may be clear. The set of Latin prefixes in Table 3.13 is not exhaustive, but illustrative.

3.3.2 Bases

There are many elements in English which are Latin bases; sometimes their meaning is easily determinable, sometimes it is not. When these bases are Latin verbs, they often have fixed patterns of derivation based on them. Since, in principle, the whole of the Latin language is available for use, only a small number of common examples can be given.

3.3.3 Suffixes

Latin suffixes are almost all used in English as well, with the same meaning or function. Some examples are given in Table 3.16.

Table 3.13 Latin prefixes

Prefix	Other forms	Latin meaning	Examples	Use in English	Comments
ad-	ac-, af-, al-, an-, ap-, as-, at-	'to, towards'	adhere, accede, affect, allocate, announce, append, assess, attenuate		The double consonant after initial <a> is often (but not always) a clue to the presence of this prefix
con-	col-, com-, cor-	'with, together'	confide, collocate, commerce, correspond	co-agent	
de-		'down, off; undo'	defer	denature	English, French and Latin words can all begin with *de-*, but the 'undo' meaning as in *debug* tends to be English
ex-	e-	'out of, from'	expel, emit	ex-directory, ex-minister	
in-	im-	'not'	indelible, immune	inactive, improper	
in-	im-	'in, on, into'	inject, impel	imperil	A French spelling, *en-*, is often preferred
inter-		'between'	interject	interfold	
post-		'after'	postpone	post-apocalypse	
pre-		'before'	prepare	presuppose	
pro-		'before, forward'	produce	prolong	*pro-* is also a Greek form; in English it has several other meanings, as in *pro-chancellor*
re-		'again, back'	receive	reappoint	The English prefix is /riː/, the Latin one usually /rɪ/ or /rə/
sub-	sup-	'under'	subject, support	sub-tropical	The meaning is often figurative – 'nearly', 'part of'
super-		'above'	supersede	supercharge	The meaning is often figurative – 'greater than', 'larger class'
trans-		'though, across'	transfer	trans-Siberian	

Table 3.14 Latin verbal bases

Base	Other forms	Latin meaning	Examples	Derivatives and comments
cede	ceed, sede, cess	'go'	accede	-cession
ceiv	cept	'take'	perceive	-ception, -ceptive
clud	clos	'shut'	preclude, disclose	-sion
curs	curr	'run'	incur, cursive	-cursion, -cursive
duc	duct	'lead'	abduct, produce, ductile	-duction, -ductive
fac	fec, fic	'make, do'	factor, affect, suffice	-tion, -tive
fer		'carry'	prefer	-erence
grad	gred, gress	'step'	retrograde, digress	-ession
greg		'flock, gather'	congregate	
ject	jac	'throw'	inject	-ection
laps		'fall, expire'	collapse	
mit	mis	'put'	commit	-mission, -missive
mot		'move'	promote	-tion
mut		'change'	commute, mutable	
pel	pul	'push'	compel, repel	-pulsion, -pulsive
tract		'pull, drag'	tractor, contract	-tion
vic	vinc	'conquer'	evict, convince	-iction

Table 3.15 Other Latin bases

Base	Other forms	Latin meaning	Examples
bell		'war'	bellicose
burs		'pouch'	imburse
civ		'city'	civilian
dent	dens	'tooth'	dentist
gem	gemin	'twin'	geminate
lab		'lip'	labial
lac		'milk'	lactate
noc	noct, nox	'night'	nocturnal, equinox
ped		'foot'	pedal
ver		'true'	veracity

3.4 Greek words in English

Like Latin (and English and French) words, Greek words have prefixes and suffixes, some of which have become more widely used in English, attached to non-Greek elements. It is Greek bases which have contributed most to the English vocabulary, though, and they will be dealt with after the prefixes and suffixes.

Table 3.16 Latin suffixes

Suffix	Other forms	Examples from Latin	Examples in English
-al	-ar	aerial	bridal
-ance	-ence, -ancy, -ency	relevance	hindrance
-ible		visible	gullible
-ion	-ation, -ition, -ution, -sion	aggression, vision	botheration
-ous	-os	amorous	righteous
-trix		testatrix	aviatrix

3.4.1 Greek prefixes and suffixes

Some easily recognisable Greek prefixes are set out in Table 3.17.
Some Greek suffixes are presented in Table 3.18.

3.4.2 Greek compounds

A Greek compound is made up of two (occasionally more) bases put
together, just like English compounds. The difference is that in Greek
compounds, it is not allowed for two consonants to occur side by side at
the contact point between the elements (<h> is sometimes classed as a
vowel for these purposes). Accordingly, whenever this situation would
otherwise occur, an <o> is inserted between the elements, creating
combining forms. (When Latin words are used instead of Greek words,
the letter <i> is often inserted, as in *homicide, millipede.*) Most often, a
suffix is then added to the compound. This is sometimes a Greek suffix,
sometimes an English suffix. *Hydrophobia* ('rabies') is made up of a base
hydr, a link *-o-*, and another base *phob*, with the Greek suffix *-ia* ('condition'). *Hydr* means 'water', *phob* means 'fear' and *hydrophobia* literally
means 'the condition of fearing water', since one of the symptoms of
rabies is that the sufferer cannot swallow fluids. Although in principle
any base can be found in first or second position in a compound, in
practice some are more often found in one or the other, or the base (or
combination of base plus suffix) may take on a specific meaning in one
position. Bases which translate as adjectives are usually found in first
position, for example.

As with English compounds, the meaning of the compound as a whole
may be endocentric (the compound denotes a subtype of the second
element), exocentric (the compound denotes something which has features described by the elements in the compound) or coordinative (the
two elements go together to name the denotatum). Some relevant bases
are given in Table 3.19, and some compounds are then analysed. Since

Table 3.17 Greek prefixes

Prefix	Other forms	Greek meaning	Examples	Use in English	Comments
a-	an-	'without, not'	apathy, anonymous	apolitical	The form *an-* occurs before a vowel or <h>, as in *anharmonic*
ana-		'back, again, up'	analysis	anabaptist	
anti-	ant-	'against'	antipathy, anthelion	antibody	The form *ant-* is found before a vowel or <h>
cata-		'back, away, down'	catabasis, catarrh		
di-		'two'	diglossia	disyllabic	
dia-		'through, across'	diameter, diarrhoea	diachronic	
dys-		'badly'	dyspepsia	dyspraxia	
hetero-		'other'	heterodox	heterosexual	
homo-	hom-	'same'	homonym, homophone	homosexual	The form *hom-* occurs before a vowel
hyper-		'over, excessively'	hyperbole	hypersensitive	
hypo-		'under, slightly'	hypothesis	hypothermia	
iso-		'same, equal'	isosceles	isobar	
macro-		'large'	macrocosm	macroeconomics	
meta-		'transcending, changed, across'	metaphor	metaphysics	
micro-		'small'	microcosm	microscope	
para-		'alongside	parallel	paramedic	
peri-		'around, near'	peripatetic, periphery	perinatal	
poly-		'many'	polygamy	polytechnic	
proto-		'first'	protoplasm	prototype	
syn-	sym-	'together, with'	syntax, symposium	synaesthesia	

Table 3.18 Greek suffixes

Suffix	Other forms	Greek meaning	Examples	Use in English	Comments
-ia		'state, condition'	amnesia		
-ic		creates adjectives	tragic	photographic	The suffix -*ic* can come from either Greek or Latin: *classic* is Latin, *tragic* is Greek
-ism		'doctrine'	cynicism	modernism	Many words with this suffix are borrowed into English from French
-ist		'person'	analogist	harpist	
-oid		'having the shape of, like'	android, thyroid	fibroid	
-sis		produces nouns	thesis	hypnosis	

Table 3.19 Greek bases often used in English

Greek base	Meaning	Example
andr	'man'	android
anem	'wind'	anemone
angi	'blood vessel'	angiogram
anth	'flower'	polyanthus
anthrop	'human being'	anthropology
arachn	'spider'	arachnid
arch	'rule'	anarchy
bibl	'book'	bibliography
bio	'life'	biology
cac	'bad'	cacophony
chir	'hand'	chiropody
chrom	'colour'	monochrome
chron	'time'	chronic
cosm	'universe, order'	cosmic
crat	'govern'	democratic
cry	'cold, freeze'	cryonics
cryp	'secret'	decryption
cyan	'blue'	cyanide
dactyl	'finger'	pterodactyl
dendr	'tree'	rhododendron
eccles	'church'	ecclesiastic
emet	'vomit'	emetic
entom	'insect'	entomology

Table 3.19 (*cont.*)

Greek base	Meaning	Example
erg/org/urg	'work'	ergonomic
gam	'marriage'	gamete
gloss, glott	'tongue, speech'	glottal
gram, graph	'write'	photograph
gyn	'woman'	gynaecology
haem, hem, aem	'blood'	haemoglobin
hedon	'pleasure'	hedonistic
hedr	'side'	dodecahedron
heli	'sun'	heliocentric
herp, herpet	'snake'	herpetology
hipp	'horse'	hippopotamus
hydr	'water'	hydrogen
hypno	'sleep'	hypnotise
idio	'same, self'	idiosyncrasy
itis	'inflammation'	tonsillitis
lacrym, lacrim	'tear, weep'	lachrymose
leuk, leuc	'white, colourless'	leukaemia
lith	'stone'	monolith
log	'word, speak, study'	dialogue
meter	'measure'	metric
morph	'shape'	morpheme
narc	'sleep'	narcosis
odon(t)	'tooth'	periodontist
onom, onym	'name'	synonym
ophthalm	'eye'	ophthalmologist
orth	'straight'	orthodox
paleo, palaeo	'old'	Palaeocene
phag	'eat'	anthropophagy
phil	'love'	philosophy
phleb	'vein'	phlebitis
phob	'fear'	claustrophobia
phot	'light'	photograph
phys	'nature'	physics
pod, pus	'foot'	octopus
pseudo	'false'	pseudopod
psych	'mind, spirit'	psychopath
pter	'feather, wing'	pterosaur
pyr	'fire'	pyrotechnics
rhin	'nose'	rhinoceros
rrh, rrhag	'flow'	diarrhoea
saur	'lizard'	dinosaur
scop, scep	'see, view'	telescope

Table 3.19 *(cont.)*

Greek base	*Meaning*	*Example*
soph	'wise, knowledge'	philosophy
tax	'arrange, order'	syntax
tele	'far, distant'	television
theo	'god'	theology
tom, tm	'cut'	atom
xen	'foreign'	xenophobic
xyl	'wood'	xylophone
zo	'animal'	zoology

the whole of the Greek language is available to provide bases, only some of the more common ones are provided here.

These bases can occur with prefixes and suffixes in the expected ways. *Diameter* means 'measure across', *mania* means 'a condition of strong desire', *periodontist* means 'a person who deals with the areas around the teeth', *polyandrous* means 'having many husbands (literally, men)'. Such glosses do not necessarily give an accurate and immediately interpretable insight into the modern word, but they certainly provide very strong clues.

Compounds provide comparable clues. Note that *log* at the beginning of a compound usually means 'word' (*logogram* 'single sign representing a whole word', *logorrhea* 'excessive flow of words), but in *-ology* typically means 'the study of'. Some examples are provided in Table 3.20.

These Greek elements can also be placed next to other English words to provide a different kind of compound. Some examples are given in Table 3.21.

3.5 The use of non-Germanic words in English

In general terms, Germanic words are used for the most basic things: *woman, go, small, then* are such words. Compounds made of Germanic words are equally basic: *herdsman, watercress.* French words are sometimes used for things which may seem equally fundamental, but if there is a choice between a native word and a French word, the French word is likely to be slightly more refined. Latin words are, in general terms, rather more formal words, words which try to impress. Greek words tend to be technical and, especially, scientific (including medical). These differences can often be seen if we put words from these various layers of English vocabulary together to allow comparisons. This is done in Table 3.22. Of course, the individual words have also developed their

Table 3.20 Greek compounds analysed

Compound	First element	Second element	Gloss	Meaning today
anemometer	anem	meter	wind measure	instrument for measuring the wind
anthropophagai	anthrop	phag	human eat	cannibal
arachnophobia	arachn	phob + ia	spider fear	excessive fear of spiders
bibliophile	bibl	phil	book love	person who loves or collects books
chiropodist	chir	pod + ist	hand foot person	specialist in the care of feet
cryptography	crypt	graph + y	secret writing	the study of codes
hippodrome	hipp	drom	horse run	place for horses to race
leukaemia	leuk	(h)aem + ia	white blood	medical condition in which there are too many white blood cells in the blood
ophthalmologist	ophthalm	log + ist	eye study person	eye specialist
philosopher	phil	soph + er	love wise person	a person who studies fundamental problems of knowledge
psychology	psych	log + y	mind study	the study of the mind
rhinitis	rhin	itis	nose inflammation	inflammation of the (lining of the) nose
telephone	tele	phon	distant sound	machine for allowing conversations at a distance
xylophone	xyl	phon	wood sound	musical instrument in which wooden bars are struck to produce musical notes

own particular meanings, or they occur only as elements in the example words, but there is a thread of meaning which recurs in these sets.

3.6 Exotic words in English

Exotic words in English are used to denote objects which, at the time the words were acquired, were unknown in English culture. Very often these words denote flora, fauna, cultural practices, food and the like which were viewed as foreign, or for which no English word was available (sometimes English speakers made up their own words from the

Table 3.21 Compounds with one English and one Greek element

Compound	Greek element	Overall meaning
bioluminescence	bio 'life'	emission of light by living creatures
methodology	log + y 'study'	systems applicable to work in a given scientific area
neo-Darwinism	neo 'new'	the modern version of Darwinism
pseudorandom	pseud 'false'	appearing to be random, but not genuinely so
psycho-linguistics	psych 'mind'	the study of linguistic structures in the mind
theocentric	theo 'god'	focused on god

Table 3.22 Words from various layers of English vocabulary

Germanic	French	Latin	Greek
big	grand, large	ample, colossal	megalith
blossom	flourish, flower	floral	polyanthus
go, walk	amble, march	proceed	peripatetic
kind	genre	genus	genesis
land	country	rural, rustic	bucolic
man	person	human, persona	anthropoid
ox	beef	bovine	boustrophedon
snake		serpent	herpetology
star		stellar	asteroid
tongue	language	lingual	diglossia
town	city	municipality	metropolis
water		aqueduct	hydrate
wife, woman	female	uxorious	gynaecology

resources of English). Verbs and adjectives can also be borrowed, but just as most English words are nouns, so most borrowed words are nouns. Examples have already been given in Table 3.1, and some are provided in (5).

(5)   alcohol, atoll, avocado, capercaillie, chocolate, croissant, dzo (*also* yakow), espadrille, fado, jejune, koala, kowtow, mammoth, orange, paella, spaghetti, stiletto, taboo, tui (*also* parson bird), zero, zither

3.7 Summary

In this chapter various clues have been provided as to how to tell Germanic words from the various kinds of loan words or borrowed words. In the final analysis, a good etymological dictionary is the best way to confirm this information. Information has also been provided on the way in which words of Greek and Latin were constructed (in some cases, still are, although the languages are no longer spoken except in highly specialised contexts), with the intention of making such words more transparent to the reader who may not have special knowledge of these languages. Overall, the reader should have come to an appreciation of the way in which various strands of vocabulary have coalesced into English, to such an extent that although the grammar of English may still be largely Germanic, many people argue that most of the vocabulary is derived from Latin, either directly, or indirectly through French.

Exercises

1. If *phobia* means 'excessive fear of', what do the following words denote, and what other words can you find that use the same first elements?

    agoraphobia, hypnophobia, nyctophobia, pyrophobia, xenophobia

2. The names of dinosaurs are often made up of Greek elements. What do the names of the following imply?

    brontosaurus, iguanodon, pterodactyl, stegosaurus, triceratops

3. Choose ten elements from the list in Table 3.19 and see what words you can find that use them, and how the meaning of the whole word arises. Consider whether the compound is endocentric or not and whether it has a figurative interpretation.

4. Find ten words not mentioned in the chapter that you think must be loan words. Why do you think so? Check them in a dictionary that provides etymology to see if you are right. If you are wrong, what misled you?

5. Find ten verbs using the Latin bases in Table 3.14. Can you translate them literally into English? Would the meaning be comprehensible from the English forms?

6. What would you expect the following words to mean, working from basic principles? What do they mean?

    chrystocracy, hysterectomy, laryngitis, platypus, rhododendron

7. What would you expect the following words of Latin origin to mean, working from basic principles? What do they mean?

    adduction, bilingual, precursor, prelapsarian, transcendental

8. Make an argument either for or against the postulate that all English words are loan words.

9. Using the information provided in this chapter, what can you deduce about the origins of the following words? Check your answers in a dictionary that provides etymological information.

bedeck, gynocratic, jampani, reflection, skulk

Recommendations for reading

The short passage of Old English in Section 3.1 is taken from Bede's *Ecclesiastical History*, as presented by Baugh (1959: 73). The information in this section is distilled from Baugh (1959), Pei (1967), Strang (1970), Lass (1987) and Hogg and Denison (2006). On minor types of word-formation, see Bauer (1983) and Bauer et al. (2013). On Greek and Latin elements in English words, see Denning and Leben (1995) and Stockwell and Minkova (2001). On English spelling in general, and the term 'exotic', see Carney (1994). On loan words more generally, see Poplack (2018).

4 The meanings of words

4.1 Introduction

In this chapter we look at the ways in which the meanings of words work. We look at different aspects of meaning, and the ways words are linked together by meanings which are, in some way, related to each other. The overall message of the chapter is that meaning is not a simple matter, but is due to a network of relationships, so that a part of a word's meaning is determined by just where in the various networks the word fits.

4.2 Denotation and connotation

The word *dog* denotes a canine quadruped. So does the word *cur*. But if you use the word *cur*, you are not only denoting a canine quadruped, you are displaying something of your attitude towards that animal. A *cur* is a dog that you dislike or despise. On the other hand, if you call the same animal a *doggie*, the chances are that you like the animal (you might just be pretending for the sake of a child, but you are definitely implying that it's a nice dog). The **denotation** of a word is the type of entity in the world that it can be used to describe. The **connotation** is the emotional overtone which accompanies the denotation.

Sometimes, the emotional overtone is not carried by the word itself, but by the way you say the word, or the context in which you put it. Calling someone a *student* might be simply descriptive, it might be a sign that you approve of them, or it might be a strong condemnation of the person. This is not connotation. This type of attitude is shown by the particular collocation you might use (*helpful student* versus *damned student*), your intonation, voice quality and other phonetic aspects of the utterance, and it sometimes has to be determined pragmatically from the context. *They're students, so what do you expect* is unlikely to indicate a good opinion of students, for instance. Connotations are more firmly established (and thus unavoidable) implications behind a word. If you can avoid an implication by smiling, that implication is not a connotation.

Connotations are generally fairly simple: liking or disliking, approval or disparagement, trivialising or aggrandising. Sometimes connotations are more subtle. *Nude* (in contrast with *naked*) probably implies either an artistic scenario or pornography. In fact, many pairs of words that mean more or less the same thing are distinguished by different kinds of implicit attitudes, often differences that are very difficult to express, to such an extent that some scholars avoid the term 'connotation' altogether as being too loose a term. Consider *work* and *labour*: in some contexts they may mean the same thing, but *labour* may involve working harder than work does, or doing manual work, rather than cerebral work. These implications are probably not connotations.

Differences due to formality levels or different dialects are not usually included as connotations; there is a different terminology in such cases. But just where the borderline of connotations runs is a matter of dispute.

Sometimes, connotations can be carried by particular affixes. Typically, this is the case with so-called evaluative affixes, such as the *-ie* that gives us *birdie, doggie, sweetie* and the *-ette* that gives us *cosmonette, undergraduette*. These do not necessarily just have one connotation on all occasions, but they call forth extra connotations. The *-ie* on *doggie* makes us think of talking to children, but the same is not true of the *-ie* on *goalie* or the *-ie* on *movie*. Nevertheless, *-ie* is generally (but not inevitably) positive, whether it arises in child language (or child-directed language), in hypocoristics, in endearments, or just on everyday nouns. Non-positive effects of *-ie* can probably be seen in *girlie* and *quickie*. The suffix *-ette*, in contrast, is mainly disparaging (as in the examples above); in words for types of fake material such as *leatherette, satinette, stockinette*, carrying the connotation of low quality seems to be the main function of the affix. The affect may be slightly diluted in words like *kitchenette, sleeperette*, but even then, the idea that these are rather poor-quality kitchens or sleepers persists.

4.3 Lexicon versus encyclopedia

It is far from clear what in our lexica is linguistic and what is information that we hold about the world around us, but which is nothing to do with linguistics. At one end of the scale we find linguists who see the two as widely divergent, at the other we find linguists who think there is no distinction at all.

Consider the word *rabbit*. It might be lexical knowledge that there is a synonym, *bunny*, with very positive connotations. It might equally well be lexical knowledge that *bunny* has been appropriated for a scantily clad young woman acting as a nightclub hostess. It might also be lexical knowledge that a male rabbit is called a *buck* and a female is known as a *doe*, and that the young are called *kits* or *kittens* (although *baby rabbit* is in common usage, too). It might be lexical knowledge that *coney* (also spelt *cony*) is the technical name for the fur of a rabbit. It is less clear whether it is lexical knowledge that rabbits have soft fur and long ears, that they live in burrows, that they breed prolifically, that they eat carrots and dandelion leaves and (for those that remember Beatrix Potter's *Peter Rabbit*) radishes. It is presumably not lexical knowledge that rabbits come in a range of colours, have fur of different lengths and can be kept as pets, though they are also seen as pests.

In general terms, if we can distinguish between lexical information and encyclopedic information, it would seem that the lexical information is what we need for a definition, while the encyclopedic information is what we discover by our experience of the world we live in. The difficulty is that it is hard to draw any such distinction.

First of all, it is not clear that everybody has the same definition of a word like *rabbit*. For a child with a hutch in the garden, rabbits may be defined as soft, cuddly pets, but for farmers they may be defined as pests that need to be shot. Although rabbits are classified as mammals, the long ears may be a far better definition of the animals on an experiential level. Indeed, for many people who do not live in the country, rabbits and hares may be indistinguishable, and both may fall under the heading of *rabbit* – even if the person involved is aware that there is a word *hare* that is used of a similar creature.

As another example, consider the word *kakapo*, which denotes a kind of parrot, one which has the features outlined in (1).

(1)
- the most endangered parrot in the world (there are, at the time of writing, under 150 individuals alive)
- the largest parrot in the world
- the heaviest parrot in the world (weighing up to 4.5 kg)
- the only flightless parrot in the world
- the only nocturnal parrot in the world
- the only parrot in the world to use the lek breeding system, whereby the mail calls females with loud booming sounds
- probably the longest-lived bird in the world, individuals living to be 90

As well as having the unique features listed in (1), the kakapo has other features which are not unique to it: it is mostly green, it lives in

New Zealand. Any one of the features in (1) is sufficient to identify the kakapo uniquely. Its rarity, though, is not a defining feature – at any moment some other parrot species could become more endangered, so that must be encyclopedic information. Of the other factors listed in (1), there is no way to determine what provides lexical information (a definition) and what provides encyclopedic information. Indeed, most definitions from real dictionaries mention its colour and the fact that it is a New Zealand parrot. These things are more useful for real people who want to know about the kakapo, but less useful in providing a unique identifier of the bird. The things which uniquely identify the bird are not necessarily part of our linguistic knowledge. The example shows that the borderline between what is linguistic and what is encyclopedic, if it exists at all, cannot be drawn in any principled way. It might vary from individual to individual. It might not provide enough information to circumscribe the denotation of the word. Even if we think it useful to distinguish between what is in the lexicon and what is in the encyclopedia, it may not be possible to do this in any systematic way.

4.4 Relationships between words

4.4.1 Synonymy

Two words are synonyms (or are synonymous) if, in context, they mean precisely the same thing, if they denote the same entity. So if (2a) and (2b) mean the same thing, if in every condition under which (2a) is true (2b) is also true and vice versa, *chiropodist* and *podiatrist* are synonyms.

(2)   a. I have to visit the chiropodist tomorrow.
        b. I have to visit the podiatrist tomorrow.

The context is important. *Freedom* and *liberty* are often thought of as synonyms, and in some contexts that seems to be true. Consider, for example, the sentences in (3).

(3)   a. We must all have the freedom to elect the government we want.
        b. We must all have the liberty to elect the government we want.

But this does not mean that we can always use *freedom* in precisely the same places that we can use *liberty*, and that it will always mean the same thing. We can, for example, talk about *freedom of expression*, but we do not talk about *liberty of expression*: at least, the collocations are different. In the sentence (4a), replacing *liberty* with *freedom* to give (4b) does not provide an equivalent statement.

(4)   a. He's taking liberties again.
       b. *He's taking freedoms again.

Here it seems to be more than just the collocation involved: *liberty* and *freedom* do not have the same range of meanings. This is typical. We might be able to have *a bucket of water* or *a pail of water* (and for some speakers, at least, they may be entirely equivalent), but we can have *the bucket of a front-end loader* and not *the pail of a front-end loader*; we can have *a bucket seat* in a car, but not a *pail seat*.

So most synonyms are not synonyms in all contexts. We can speculate that this is because it is redundant to have two or more labels for exactly the same thing, but this does not seem to be accurate. There are some things for which we have many words: being drunk is one example. Dying is another. Being outstandingly good yet another. The words (sometimes MWEs like *push up daisies* for 'die') may differ in formality or in regional usage, may be more modern or more conservative and so on, but they are still synonyms, and speakers do not seem to have problems with that.

The difference between synonyms in these areas of vocabulary and synonyms in other areas might be that these are areas where new expressions have a high impact factor. If something outstanding has been *the gear* or *brill* for a number of years, something new is required to make sure that the impact of its outstandingness is maintained. It might have to become *awesome* or *epic*. If we define synonymy such that *epic* and *brill* are not synonymous because they are not maximally impactful at the same period (and extend this to other relevant factors), then it may be that we never actually have synonyms which match perfectly for all possible factors.

Certainly, young children, and even dogs, expect a lack of synonymy. A sheepdog has been trained in Germany to fetch things on oral command. If you tell it to *Fetch the doll*, it fetches the doll. It has a vocabulary of some 200 words. If you put a tyrannosaurus figure among the things it can find, and say *Fetch the tyrannosaurus*, it fetches the tyrannosaurus, even if it has never heard the word before. It assumes that the new label fits a new entity, and not that *tyrannosaurus* is another name for a doll. Given such preferences, any degree of synonymy is something that has to be explained.

Sometimes we are exposed to synonymy that is dialectal: words for the same object may be different in different dialects, and we happen to hear both. Consider the MWE *French fries*, which started out as the American expression for what the British call *chips*. Now both are heard in Britain. *Trousers* used to be the British word for what Americans call *pants*, but now both are heard in Britain. It used to be the case that American men wore *vests* and British men wore *waistcoats* (which used to be pronounced /weskɪt/), now both can be heard in Britain (though *waistcoat* is pronounced /weɪskəʊt/). The original situation was a lack of synonymy: you either knew *vest* or you knew *waistcoat*, but you had only one label for the garment (and in Britain a *vest* was the name for an undershirt). When both labels become available, you have to learn to deal with that. Perhaps you assume that *chips* are hand-cut, while *French fries* are machine-made, and skinnier than chips. Perhaps you assume that *pants* are for women and *trousers* are for men. Perhaps you assume that *vests* are filled with down, while *waistcoats* are made of the same fabric as the suit they belong with. Whatever you assume, it is not necessarily clear that everyone else will make the same assumption; someone else may decide that chips go with fish and French fries go with hamburgers. Your idea of the difference might change as you are exposed to different people using these words in different ways. In this way, things that are first experienced as synonyms may lose their synonymy and become distinguished from each other semantically.

As well as arising from dialect differences, synonyms can arise from slang. Part of the value of the slang is to make the topic of discussion incomprehensible to the outsider. Synonyms for standard language words are thus a benefit. But once the slang becomes understood by outsiders, the outsiders have synonyms (and the insiders may change the slang term, to make it opaque once more). From prison slang we have expressions like *do porridge, do time, do bird* (rhyming slang: *bird lime* = *time*), any of which might be heard in isolation, but which are unlikely to be genuine free choices for individual speakers.

4.4.2 Antonymy

Antonyms are opposites, but this requires a great deal of deconstruction. The central case of **antonymy** is provided by pairs like *happy* and *sad*, *deep* and *shallow*. These pairs are gradable, so that you can be more or less happy than someone else, some bodies of water can be deeper than others, you can be very sad and find water which is quite shallow. To put it another way, *deep* and *shallow*, *happy* and *sad* are different end-points on the same scale, and there is a large middle ground between them. That middle ground is filled by a number of expressions such as *happy* and *sad* modified by any number of downtoners or intensifiers: we find things like *really sad, not unhappy, quite happy, intensely happy* and so on. It is also typically the case that the words at the two ends of the scale are not linguistically equivalent. You can ask *How deep is the water?* without any presupposition that the water is actually deep (and the answer *It's only 2 cm deep* would be perfectly in place); but if you ask *How shallow is the water?*, you imply that you know it is shallow (an answer such as *It's sixty fathoms shallow* would be really odd). Equally, we tend to talk about the *depth* of the water rather than of the *shallowness* of the water, and we have a word *unhappy*, but a word *unsad* seems rather odd (though such instances are found). In such cases we talk about **gradable antonyms**, and we say that *deep* is the **unmarked** member of the pair of *deep* and *shallow*. For some authorities, only these gradable antonyms are called 'antonyms', and any other kind of opposite has different name.

Complementary terms are such as divide a particular field of meaning between them. For example, for things in the relevant domain, if they are not *alive* they are *dead*, and if they are not *dead* they are *alive*. Clearly, this does not apply to, say, stones or knowledge, which is why the 'relevant domain' is important. Other examples of complementarity are *male/female, married/single, pass/fail* (an examination). If one does not apply, the other does.

Complementarity is an extreme form of **incompatibility**. With incompatible terms, the application of one implies the non-application of the others, but there is more than just one other choice. So *My car is black* implies that my car is not red or blue or green, and the use of any of these alternatives would imply that the car was not black. We have a set of paradigmatically related items which mutually exclude each other. There are many such sets. Consider *This mammal is canine, This car is a hatchback, This garment is a shirt*: in each case there is a set of incompatible items in the relevant paradigm.

In all these cases, it is possible to quibble about the borderlines between the categories. We may know people who consider themselves neither fully male nor fully female, we may know someone who is a bachelor or a spinster, but who acts in all but legal respects as though married, and we may consider such a person to be neither married nor single. Incompatibles and complementaries are to that extent normative: they assume a default situation (usually a situation which is or has been seen as the most frequent situation) and they imply it applies everywhere. Speakers are quite adept at manipulating such instances where they do not seem to apply.

Converse terms are pairs of terms which imply a particular point of view, and where each member of the pair implies an alternative point of view. For example, if Kim buys something from Lee, then Lee has sold that same thing to Kim. Whether we call it an instance of buying or an instance of selling depends on the viewpoint we take. Many such cases use the same verb in such cases: *Kim leased the house to Lee, Lee leased the* *house from Kim*; *Kim rented the car to Lee, Lee rented the car from Kim. Teaching* and *learning* is an interesting pair in this regard. *The teacher taught Kim differential equations* and *Kim learnt differential equations from the teacher* can be seen as being converse statements of the same process (and in many languages are linguistically marked as being converse terms). If someone objects that the teacher doing the teaching does not necessarily involve the pupil learning, we can either see the kind of boundary dispute that we have just discussed in relation to complementaries, or we can claim that the teacher has not taught the material unless the pupil has learned it. Note, incidentally, that in some non-standard varieties of English, *learn* is used for both points of view (just as *rent* and *lease* are in standard English).

The opposite of a verb like *to zip* is *to unzip*, that is, the derived verb means to do the opposite or reverse the action of the verb. A verb like *unzip* is called a **reversative**. Although reversatives are often shown by affixes (like *unzip, dismount*) or by adding affixes to adjectival gradable antonyms (for example, *lengthen* vs *shorten*), they can also be found among words which are morphologically simple in English. The verbs *ascend* and *descend* are probably **monomorphemic** (have only one meaningful element) in English, though not in Latin, from where they come; *clean* and *dirty* as verbs are related by conversion to their adjectival bases, and might be thought to be like *lengthen* and *shorten*; *rise* and *fall*, *arrive* and *depart* seem to be relatively secure examples of monomorphemic reversatives.

Although it may not quite qualify as an opposite, membership of a particular category can be denied by saying something like *It's not a real/proper/true X* (where X is some noun). Such expressions can be used either where not belonging to the relevant category is genuine at some level, or where it is figurative. If one were to say of an orca that *It's not a real whale*, the mismatch of category would be genuine, since an orca is a dolphin – even if it is also called a *killer whale*. Here the speaker is rightly stating the incompatibility of *orca* and *whale* (rather than the hyponymy). If, on the other hand, you were to say *Larry is not a proper lamb, he lives in the kitchen*, you are apparently denying Larry's being a lamb, but really denying that Larry meets all the criteria that one would expect a lamb to meet, including living in a field. By the majority of criteria, Larry would, indeed, be classified as a lamb.

4.4.3 Hyponymy

Hyponymy is the relation between a word like *flower* on the one hand and a word like *tulip* on the other. It is crucial here to see this as a relationship between words, not as a relationship between entities in the world. Although the hyponymy between *flower* and *tulip* exists because a tulip is a kind of flower, hyponymy is a linguistic relationship between linguistic items, not a classificatory relationship between actual items. This can be shown by the fact that we sometimes have sets of words without hyponymy, even though there is a classificatory relationship.

Consider the items *table, chair, bed, wardrobe, sofa*. All of these are items of furniture. But the word *furniture* is not a **superordinate** term (some scholars prefer **hypernym** or **hyperonym**, but they sound rather too much like *hyponym* to provide for efficient spoken communication, especially in varieties of English which are non-rhotic) for *chair* (and accordingly, *chair* is not a hyponym of *furniture*, as *tulip* is a hyponym of *flower*). The reason is that *a chair* is not *a furniture*, because *furniture* is a collective noun. Linguistically, we would have to say that a chair is a *piece of furniture*. Other languages have a word like French *meuble* which is a superordinate term; in English, the words *table, chair, bed, wardrobe, sofa* do not have a superordinate.

Hyponymy is most often illustrated with nouns, as in the examples above, but *crimson, scarlet, vermilion* are hyponyms of *red*, and *bake, boil, roast, grill* are hyponyms of *cook*. Note that, although *grill* has the superordinate *cook* in the last example, *grill* also has the superordinate *question* in a different context. Polysemy (see Section 4.7.1) can lead to multiple lines of hyponymy.

It is not always easy to tell whether words are in a relationship of hyponymy or not. Typically, where we have hyponymy, it will be possible to say that the hyponym is a particular kind of the superordinate. So, for instance, we have the examples in (5).

(5)   to grill someone is to question them very thoroughly
       to quiz a class is to question them orally (American usage)
       to interrogate someone is to question them at length and aggressively
       to cross-examine someone is to question them in a particular legal context
       to sweat someone is a slang term for to question them at length

Note that in the examples in (6) we do not have a word that is a superordinate for all vehicles that carry people or for all vehicles that carry goods, and that the expression we have to cover buses and trams is the very technical *PSV* (*public service vehicle*), not an everyday word at all, and an MWE.

(6)   a car is a vehicle that drives on roads and carries a small number of
        passengers
        a tram is a vehicle that runs on rails set in the roads in town and is
        for public transport
        a van is a vehicle that drives on roads and is designed to carry
        small quantities of goods
        a lorry is a vehicle that drives on roads and is designed to carry
        large quantities of goods

(7)   if someone is plump they are pleasingly fat
        if someone is obese they are unhealthily fat
        if someone is stout they are rather fat

With the examples in (7), there comes a point when we have to ask
whether words are hyponyms or synonyms. Is *stout* a synonym of *fat*, just
one with rather more pleasant connotations, or does it really represent
a lesser degree of fatness? Is *corpulent* a synonym of *fat*, but a more polite
word, or is it distinguished in some other way from *fat*? What about
chubby? Does it just collocate with different nouns, or does it mean something different? It is for this reason that it is often difficult to use a thesaurus appropriately. A thesaurus will provide a list of near-synonyms,
but unless you know the connotations, the collocations, and the reason
for any hyponymy, you cannot use the word properly. We would normally say that words that differ only in terms of their formality, style, or
pleasant/unpleasant connotations are synonyms rather than hyponyms,
but the border is a little fuzzy.

In principle, the difference between synonymy and hyponymy is that
if for two words w_1 and w_2, what is true with w_1 is true with w_2 and what
is true with w_2 is true with w_1, you have synonymy; if the implication
goes only one way, you have hyponymy. So if it is true that anyone who
can be described as *corpulent* can also be described as *fat* and that anyone
who can be described as *fat* can also be described as *corpulent* with equal
truth, then the two words are synonyms. However, if is true that anyone
who is *corpulent* is *fat*, but not true than anyone who is *fat* is *corpulent* (or
vice versa), then we have hyponymy. Even this example shows that
things are not necessarily clear-cut, though in the case of *tulip*, it is clear
that everything that is a *tulip* is a *flower*, but not everything that is a *flower*
is a *tulip*.

Hyponyms can occur on multiple levels. We can divide living things
into animals and plants, and then divide animals into, say, mammals,
reptiles and birds, and then divide mammals into carnivores and her-
bivores, and then divide carnivores into dogs and cats, and so on. If our
classification functions properly, then anything that comes under the

label of *dog* (such as *retriever*, *bitch*) can also be described as a *dog*, can also be described as a *carnivore*, can also be described as a *mammal*, can also be described as an *animal*.

More confusingly, there can be incompatible trees of hyponymy. For example, for biologists, a *banana* is a *berry* and a *raspberry* is an *aggregate fruit*, and not a *berry*, and a *tomato* is a *fruit*. For most of us, a *tomato* is a *vegetable* (we would not put it in a fruit salad), a *raspberry* is a *berry* and a *banana* is not. You can sometimes get arguments going between people who think the *potato* is a *vegetable* and those who believe it is not. The examples given here depend upon incompatible definitions of either the superordinate or the hyponym. These examples may not seem particularly serious. But consider another classification of vegetables. Scientifically, *pumpkins*, *courgettes* (or *zucchini*), *marrows* and *cucumbers* are all members of the same family, but they are used so differently that they are probably classified differently in ordinary language, where a *cucumber* could be called a *salad vegetable*, but the others could not. It is not clear how to classify a *pumpkin* in British English, although it is a type of *squash* for Americans. British English has the term *gourd*, and a *pumpkin* may be a *gourd*, but it would be unusual to classify a *courgette* as a *gourd*, because its skin is never used as a container for fluids.

4.4.4 Meronymy

If hyponymy is a relationship determined by 'is-a' (a *tulip* is a *flower*), meronymy is a relationship determined by 'has-a'. *Wing* and *tail fin* are **meronyms** of *aeroplane*, and *aeroplane* is a **holonym** of *wing* and *tail fin* because an aeroplane has a wing (or, perhaps equivalently, the wing is part of an aeroplane). That is to say, meronymy is the relationship between parts and their wholes.

Having said that, there are innumerable problems with meronymy. The first is whether it is really a linguistic relationship. Is it a fact about an aeroplane that it has a part which is a wing, or is it a fact about *aeroplane* that it has *wing* as a meronym? With hyponymy, we were able to make a case for the relationship being linguistic (although some scholars disagree). The case is much harder with meronymy. We will return to this question just below.

A second problem is determining what counts as a part. Does it have to be a necessary part? That is, if a wheel is part of a car, would something cease to be a *car* if had no wheels but was raised above the road by magnetism? Is *daughter* a meronym of *family*, even though there are perfectly good nuclear families which have no daughters? Does a flock of sheep have an individual sheep as a part or not? Does a forest have a tree as a part? It would be odd to say *That forest has a tree*, or *That tree is a part of Sherwood Forest*, and yet you cannot have a forest without trees. Similarly, are you a part of the population of the country you inhabit? Although you cannot have a population without people, it is not clear that 'has-a' or 'part-of' are the relevant relationships between the two notions. Is a daisy part of your lawn, or not, because if it was not there, the lawn would still exist (and perhaps be a better lawn)?

A third problem is the problem of transitivity of meronymy. If your body has an arm as one of its parts, and the arm has a hand as one of its parts, and the hand has a finger as one of its parts, and the finger has a nail as one of its parts, then it appears that it must be true that a nail is a part of your body. Yet *My body has a nail* would be a very odd utterance, and *This nail is part of my body* would not be much better. This is perhaps the strongest reason for supposing that meronymy is a linguistic relationship: logically the 'part-of' relationship has to be transitive, but linguistically it is often awkward to use phraseology which implies that.

4.4.5 Networks

What we see from all these various relationships between words is that the words of English (or of any other language) exist in a network, and that the definitions of the individual words are to some extent limited or circumscribed by the definitions of other words in the same network. In Saussurean terms, words gain a **value** from other words in the same network. Such networks are multifaceted and complex to describe, and are linked directly to culture in unpredictable ways. A couple of brief examples may help make the point,

One of Saussure's own examples is that *mouton* in French and *sheep* in English have different values, because *mouton* can refer to the living animal or its flesh used as food, whereas in English we have *sheep* for the living animal, but *mutton* for the flesh of the sheep as food. The meaning of *sheep* in English is different from the meaning of *mouton* in French because they have different values because of contrasting words which take up some of the semantic space that is available in another language. If we push this further, we find some surprising and some unsurprising things. Among the unsurprising things is that we have no word in English for the meat of a lion. We do not, as a cultural norm, eat lions, and so have no need for such a word. Perhaps more surprising is that we have no specific word for the meat of a chicken or a duck. We do eat those, but we are quite happy to use the name of the animal as the name for the meat. In fact, there is a very limited set of animals for which we do have a special meat-word, perhaps, in general usage, only *beef, pork, mutton* and *venison*. Even *lamb* is used both for the living animal and for its meat. We clearly need to ask what is special about those animals that they deserve meat-words. The answer is probably that they were the animals that provided most of our meat intake at the time the vocabulary was established. But if we take it that the relevant time was sometime shortly after the Norman Conquest, the hunting of deer was illegal, and venison should not have been providing much meat for most of the population. It would only have been providing meat for the upper classes, and they would have been the people who understood or spoke French (which is where the words *beef, pork, mutton* and *venison* come from). That is, there is probably an instance here of language reflecting culture, but it is the culture of a specific set of people at a specific time.

As a second example, consider the words for family relationships. We have the words *brother* and *sister*, but we do not have – as some other cultures do – specific words for 'older brother', 'younger brother', 'older sister' and 'younger sister'. We must conclude that, in our culture, birth order is less significant than it is in cultures which mark such differences in their vocabularies. We have the two words *aunt* and *uncle*. We do not have words which allow us to differentiate between an uncle who is a brother of our mother and an uncle who is the brother of our father. We do not have different words for an aunt who is a parent's sister and an aunt who has married a parent's brother (although in the works of Jane Austen you can see the two being addressed differently). In Danish, there is a difference between an *onkel* ('married-in uncle'), a *farbror* ('father's brother') and a *morbror* ('mother's brother'). Since many people in England spoke some Danish or had Danish family in the eleventh century, and since French operates just like English in having single terms to cover all of this, we must assume that English culture was happy to adopt a system where being a member of the family was more important than the particular line of descent.

The study of **semantic fields** like this provides an interesting way of considering the network of words that are linked, directly or indirectly, in our vocabularies, and the way that our language reflects our culture (or the culture we had when the network of words was established). When used comparatively, it can show how speakers of different languages perceive the world differently, in the sense that their language provides them with a certain categorisation, not that they cannot understand an alternative categorisation once it is made overt.

4.5 Semantic features

Consider the words in (8). The sets have been carefully chosen to make a point.

(8) bull   cow   calf
     man   woman   child
     ram   ewe   lamb
     stallion mare   foal

On the basis of this data, you might think that English has three sets of words for different kinds of animal: one for the adult male, one for the adult female, and one for the offspring (without reference to sex). Furthermore, it seems reasonable to suggest that *calf*, for instance, is defined by being bovine and non-adult. An easy way to show this is in terms of semantic **features** (sometimes called semantic components). If we set up the features [±bovine], [±human], [±ovine], [±equine], [±adult], [±male] and [±female], we can define each of the words presented in (8) in terms of these features, and show how the field of animal names in English is structured. (We might decide that it is redundant to have both [±male] and [±female], although it will become obvious later that there might be advantages to this.)

Of course, things are not that simple. Let us consider a set of circumstances which illustrate this point.

First of all, most of these sets have a word which indicates the whole set – that is, there is a word which is the superordinate term for the three words in each set given above. We have the words *person*, *sheep* and *horse*, for instance. In the bovine section, the superordinate term is probably *cow*. This is the only example in (8) where the superordinate term is the same word-form as one of its hyponyms, but it is not the only case, if we look further. If we add canines, then we find that *dog* is the name for the male (consider *dog fox*), as well as being the superordinate term. So sometimes the superordinate is also the term for the male, sometimes it is also the term for the female. There is no overall generalisation. In terms of our features, this means that *cow* fits both [+bovine, +adult, +female] and [+bovine] with no further specification of adulthood and sex. We might want to say that generic *cow* is [±male] or we might want to say that it is [0male]: either will create problems.

Now consider the word *colt*. It clearly belongs in the equine row, but a colt is older than a foal, and is specifically male; the female equivalent is *filly*. We might feel that we have to add two extra columns to the set in (8) at this point, and such a conclusion would be supported by the fact that we also find *heifer*, which is a young female cow. Dictionary definitions of *filly* and *heifer* do not always match in detail, but as far as we have defined them here, they would fit into the same slot, which we might loosely define as 'teenager'. We now have the situation in (8').

(8')	*animal type*	*generic*	*adult, male*	*adult, female*	*teenage, male*	*teenage, female*	*young*
	bovine	cow	bull	cow		heifer	calf
	canine	dog	dog	bitch			pup(py)
	equine	horse	stallion	mare	colt	filly	foal
	human	person	man	woman			child
	ovine	sheep	ram	ewe			lamb

One of the things that becomes clear from (8') is that there are some **lexical gaps** in the system: there are some slots in the matrix for which we do not have words. We might think that we could fill the teenage, male bovine slot with *bullock*, but a bullock has been castrated. There are other words for castrated animals, such as *wether*, and, in one use, *hog*, *ox*. We can also see that, although *child* is a superordinate term for both *girl* and *boy*, there are no corresponding hyponymic terms in the other four series. On the other hand, we do not necessarily differentiate between a male teenager and a female teenager for people, though we have the words to do so for horses. Perhaps *youth* would fill the male slot for humans. *Young man* and *young woman* seem to carry different kinds of connotations with them: perhaps they are most often heard in secondary schools, or perhaps they are mostly used in address by (disapproving) elders.

If we add further families to the set in (8') we can find more lexical gaps. We can also find synonyms. We would expect two words that fill the same slot to be synonyms. For example, *pig* and *hog* can both be generic terms for the porcine family. We also have words such as *steed* and *nag*, which might fit in the same slot as *horse*, but which have positive and negative connotations, respectively. *Shoat* and *weaner* are both used for newly weaned pigs. *Hogget* is used differently by people in different parts of the world: for some it is porcine, for some it is ovine. In either case it is older than the very young animal, and not specified for sex (rather like *teenager*).

If we add some animals that are not part of the British farmyard, things become complex in a different way. Bears have *boars* and *sows*, like pigs, but their babies are *cubs*, while pigs do not have cubs. Elephants, on the other hand, have *bulls*, *cows* and *calves*.

What does not become clear from all this is that the parts of the matrix for which we have terms are precisely those parts which are economically useful. We call all bovines *cows* because the cow is the more economically useful of the pair. When we don't care about an animal's sex, we tend to use the term for the male as the generic, as with dogs and lions. (8′) is further elaborated in (8″) to illustrate such factors.

(8″)

animal type	generic	adult, male	adult, female	castrated male	teenage	teenage, male	teenage, female	young
bovine	cow	bull	cow			(bullock, steer)	heifer	calf
canine	dog	dog	bitch					pup(py)
equine	horse	stallion	mare	gelding		colt	filly	foal
feline	cat	tom	quean					kitten
gallinaceous	hen	rooster, cock	hen			cockerel		chick
human	person	man	woman	eunuch, castrato	teenager			child; girl; boy
leonine	lion	lion	lioness					cub
ovine	sheep	ram	ewe	wether	hogget			lamb
porcine	pig, hog	boar	sow	hog				piglet, weaner, shoat
ursine	bear	boar	sow					cub

The great benefit of a featural analysis like the one illustrated here is that it allows us to capture a number of parallels and collocational facts that will be difficult to see if we do not use the features. For example, if we want to fill in the parallel that *stallion* is to *ram* as *mare* is to ~, the tables above allow us to fill in the word *ewe*. We can say *This mare is pregnant*, and also *This lioness is pregnant*, but not, under normal circumstances, *This tom is pregnant* or *This stallion is pregnant*. We do not say *This hen is pregnant*, but that is to do with the fact that gallinaceous animals are not subsets of placental mammals. Similarly, *purr* collocates with the words in the feline set, but not in the canine set or the porcine set, *is the sire of* collocates with male (and not castrated) set, but not with the young set, and so on. This also indicates that the sets of words could be extended. We could add a column for the typical noise made by the animal in question, another for the place where it lives, another for the name for a collection of the animals, in some instances a collection of new-borns (for example, *farrow* for pigs).

But there are also disadvantages of such a system. The most obvious one is the status of the 'animal type' feature. In most cases, a positive value for any of these features implies a negative value for all the others – they are incompatible terms. That is, at least, not very economical.

But even if this can be reformulated in some way to avoid the problem, a feature like 'bovine' carries most of the meaning of the words in that set, and masks the fact that we do not necessarily know just what it is that makes a creature bovine.

Furthermore, not all areas of vocabulary can necessarily be set up in a table like that in (8″). Consider the set of citrus fruit. We know some of these very well: *orange, lemon, lime, grapefruit*. But it is not necessarily clear what features of components should be seen as distinguishing these words. And once we start adding *tangerine, ugli fruit, tangelo, mandarin(e), satsuma* most of us would be at a loss, even if we recognise the fruit or at least know how to use them. And very few of us would know just what it is that distinguishes a *kumquat* from any of these.

In any case, it is not clear what information in a table like (8″) is of most use to us in interpreting these words. Perhaps the features that we really pay attention to are the softness of cats, the tongues of dogs, the snouts of pigs, the fact that we can ride on horses. Yet these features, however important they are, can be ignored by speakers on occasions. The typical reaction of a pre-school child in Western Europe (where men do not traditionally wear skirts) if they see a man in a kilt is to say 'Look, Mummy, a man in a skirt', rather than, for instance, 'What does that lady have in her sock?' Wearing a skirt is, in that area, something that women do, but is obviously not necessarily criterial to the definition of *woman* for small children.

Perhaps most importantly, from a theoretical point of view, if not from a practical point of view, is that it is not clear how to interpret the feature system. It was suggested above that a noun like *person* might be [±adult, ±male]. That is, we assume that either value for these other features is possible. But what, then, of *hermaphrodite*? A hermaphrodite has features of both males and females, and if hermaphrodites are [±male, ±female] it is because they have features of both, rather than a free choice between them. We cannot compute a system where '±' sometimes means 'either-or' and sometimes means 'both-and'. There are surely ways round such problems, but it remains true that care must be taken within a feature system to know how many contrasting values there are for the various features, and precisely how these are to be interpreted.

4.6 Categorising words

Words whose meanings can be determined (to a greater or lesser extent) by a set of semantic features lead us to consider that words might have hard and fast meanings, meanings which can be expressed by providing the appropriate semantic elements. Such words often lend themselves to a definition *per genus et differentiam*, as the Romans expressed Aristotelian practice: they can be defined by providing a superordinate term and then the information that distinguishes this word from its co-hyponyms. Thus a colt may defined as being a young male horse (or, equivalently, a young stallion), where *horse* is the superordinate term, and *young* and *male* differentiate the colt from other types of horses.

But even words which can be defined in such ways are not necessarily categorised in such ways by speakers. Consider the word *bird*. We might try to define it as a feathered biped (although, give the current view of some dinosaurs, perhaps rather more information is required to make sure that just birds are covered by the definition), but it seems that most people work rather differently with the category of bird. For most Europeans, at least, birds are feathered creatures which fly, lay eggs, build nests and sing songs. They are also typically of a certain size, so that a sparrow is rather more bird-sized than a condor. In fact, people seem to have an ideal bird in mind when they think of a bird (this has become known as the **prototype**), with most birds failing to match the prototype in some way or another: an eagle is too large for the prototype and probably too dangerous, an ostrich doesn't fly, a penguin does fly, but under water, and so on. The prototypical bird for a North American is said to be the North American robin; for Europeans, it might be a blackbird. If you ask a group of people to write down as many bird names as they can in a short time, the more prototypical ones are likely to be the most frequent of the list; if you time speakers to find out how quickly they respond to a question like *Is the starling a bird?*, you find that more prototypical birds get faster positive responses than less prototypical birds. Round the edges of the category, there are words which belong only marginally to the category, or which belong more strongly to another category, but have things in common with birds. A plane can be called a *bird*, but we are aware that this is not literal; a bat is not a bird; a satellite can be called a *bird*, but is not very like a real bird, and so on. It is probably the case that an emu is a better bird for Australians than for Europeans.

4.7 Multiple meanings

4.7.1 Monosemy, polysemy and homonymy

A word like *chiropodist* has only a single meaning; it is **monosemous**. By contrast, a word like *see* has multiple meanings, some of which are illustrated in the sentences in (9); it is polysemous.

(9)   a. Can't you see that he's tricking you?
       b. I can see a mountain on the horizon.
       c. I have to see the dentist tomorrow.
       d. I see that Scottish independence is on the agenda again.
       e. I see your point.
       f. I'll raise you two and see you.
       g. I'll see if he's in.
       h. She's seeing a young man who works at the university.
       i. Will Lady Elizabeth see me?

It is no coincidence that *see*, a very common word, has more poly-semes (polysemous meanings) than *chiropodist*, a very rare word. Frequent usage leads to more different shades of meaning. But precisely how many polysemes any given word has is a matter of theoretical stance and analysis, not a matter that is given by the way the language is used. Some scholars take the view that as few distinct polysemes of any word should be recognised as is possible, others seem to seek as many as possible. We might argue that (9a) and (9e) both mean 'understand' and should be considered to be examples of a single polyseme, or we could argue that *see* in (9a) means 'realise' while *see* in (9e) means 'grasp, understand', and that two distinct polysemes are involved.

In either case, we probably want to distinguish between the mean-ings of *see* set out in (9), and the difference between *cricket* ('an insect') and *cricket* ('a sport'), between *duck* ('bird sp.') and *duck* ('lower the head suddenly'), *maroon* ('reddish brown') and *maroon* (on a desert island), *mast* (of a ship) and *mast* ('fruit of forest trees as food'), *shanty* ('a rough hut') and *shanty* ('a song'), *staple* ('fastener') and *staple* ('the main part of the diet'), and many other such pairs. The difference is that we treat *see* as a single lexeme with a lot of meanings, but we treat *cricket* as two distinct lexemes, each with its own meaning. We say then that the two lexemes are homonyms. Although the distinction might seem clear, it is far from clear in practice. One of the ways in which we might know that we have two distinct lexemes is that they have different sources, that is, different etymologies: *shanty* ('hut') is a version of an Irish Gaelic expression, while *shanty* ('song') is a corruption of a French word. The trouble with this criterion is that it suggests that we can know that two words are homonyms only if we know their history. Even in English that can be a problem, but it assumes that in many cases in a language like Basque where we do not have a lot of related languages to make comparisons with, we might never know whether words are homonyms or polysemous words. In such cases, we might feel that the large dif-ference of meaning between, for instance, the insect and the sport for *cricket*, is enough to tell us whether we have homonymy or polysemy. But now consider *board* ('plank') and *board* ('food', as in *bed and board* or *boarding house*). These two meanings seem a long way apart, but they are related. A plank with supports under it makes a table, and food is eaten off a table. Does knowing this change our notion of whether the words should be seen as homonyms or not?

In some cases, we have two different lexemes by virtue of the fact that they belong to different word-classes (as with *duck* and *maroon*). It might seem that this would guarantee homonymy. But *standard* (as in *standard language* on the one hand and *standard-bearer* on the other) come from a common source, despite the different word-classes, and are often treated under the same headword in dictionaries (perhaps only as a space-saving measure).

As a different kind of example, consider *bird* in *to do bird* ('to be in prison') and *bird* ('feathered biped'). Again the meaning is very different, but *to do bird* is rhyming slang, and the full version is *to do bird lime*, which rhymes with *time*, and it means 'to do time', which is another expression meaning 'to be in prison'. In *bird lime*, *bird* means 'feathered biped', but by the time it has passed through the mechanism of rhyming slang its meaning has become unrecognisable. Is this polysemy or homonymy?

In any case, we need to be a bit careful with homonymy. Some authorities distinguish between homographs and homophones. *Lead* ('a metal') and *lead* ('go before') are **homographs** – they are written the same way – without being **homophones**, that is, without being pronounced the same way. *Pair* and *pear* are homophones – they share the same phonemic structure – without being homographs. In the examples used above, all the words have been both homophones and homographs, but given the vicissitudes of English spelling, it is wise to be able to distinguish.

It might, in principle, be possible to look at this the other way round, and ask whether there are limited strategies which give rise to polysemy. To some extent, the answer is 'yes', but not entirely.

The obvious cases of polysemy are those where the new meaning arises through a figurative extension of the meaning. The major relevant figures of speech are metaphor and metonymy (with synecdoche as a type of metonymy).

4.7.2 Metaphor

In a metaphor (/ˈmetəfɔː/), something is said or assumed to be something else, which is incorrect on a literal level, but draws attention to some similarities between the two things. A brief example will make things simpler. If you say *My brother is a pig!* you do not mean that he has trotters, likes rolling in mud and is likely to be slaughtered for bacon. Unless you yourself are a pig, *My brother is a pig* is literally false. However, by stating the equivalence between your brother and the pig, you draw attention to certain similarities between the behaviour or appearance of your brother and the culturally normalised expectations of the behaviour or appearance of a pig. You might wish to draw attention to your brother having a dirty face, living in insalubrious surroundings, not having good table manners, being greedy and so on.

There is, as you might expect, a terminology associated with this. The word *pig* is the **linguistic vehicle** of the metaphor, the meaning 'pig' is the **source**, and 'my brother' is the **target**, the thing you aim to associate with the source. Note the implication here that metaphors exist in meanings, not in words. The fact that pigs are dirty, greedy and rude is something we conventionally associate with pigs, but it is (if we still believe in the distinction – see Section 4.3) encyclopedic information, not part of the definition of *pig*. Furthermore, it is selective encyclopedic information, in that we would not call someone a pig because they were unexpectedly intelligent or were good at finding truffles, even if this is encyclopedic information we might have about pigs.

We might not always understand the implicit comparison in a metaphor, even when we assume that some metaphor exists. We may not know why we would call the lead performer in a line-up the *top banana* (are they yellow, easily peeled, green when unripe, easily digested?) or why we would say *It is raining cats and dogs*, but we might suspect a hidden metaphor. If we cannot interpret the metaphor, then we might prefer to call these expressions idioms (see Section 1.3).

Metaphors are ubiquitous in everyday language. Some have become so much a part of our language that we fail to notice them at all. For example, there is a general metaphor in English that *up* is the same as *good*, and we get expressions such as those in (10).

(10) He's a high-flyer.
       He's moved one more step up the ladder.
       Her obvious good intentions raised my spirits.
       She's on the up and up.
       Smith's is a high-class butcher's.
       They're having a high old time.
       United are 2–1 up at the moment.

We also have metaphors such as life is a journey (*He came from a poor family*, *She has come a long way*, *He is heading for disaster*, *From the beginning to the end of her life* and so on), or affection is heat (*Our love has grown cold*, *The warmth or our affection*, *Our relationship heated up* and so on).

4.7.3 Synecdoche

Synecdoche (/sɪˈnekdəki/) is also known by the Latin name *pars pro toto* (that is, the part for the whole). When the captain of a ship shouts for *All hands on deck!* it is not just the hands that are wanted, it is the people who have the useful hands. The real hand (with fingers) is just one part of what is meant by *hand* in context, and *hand* is a case of synecdoche. The exocentric compounds illustrated in (3c) in Chapter 2, sometimes called by the Sanskrit name of bahuvrihi compounds, all work by synecdoche. If we say *Wiser heads than yours have struggled with this question*, we do not just mean that the heads were involved, but that wise people have considered the question, and the head is a part of the person.

4.7.4 Metonymy

Synecdoche is sometimes classified as one type of metonymy. In metonymy (/meˈtɒnəmi/), one thing is compared with another that is cognitively adjacent or contiguous to it. This adjacency is hard to define precisely, but we can illustrate it. If we say *I like Mozart*, we probably do not mean that we like the person, but that we like the music written by Mozart. The linguistic vehicle *Mozart* denotes the person (the source), but is used to denote the music (the target). If I say *I am parked next to the bank*, it is not the speaker, denoted by *I*, who is parked, but the car driven by the speaker. If we say *Westminster has passed a new law*, it is not the city that has passed a law, but the people associated with the city, namely the politicians, who have passed the new law. The adjacency is different in all these cases: in one case it is a cognitive closeness caused by the source having produced the music, in another it is the source having been the driver of the car that has parked, in a third it is adjacency in space, politicians in Britain being associated with Westminster, where Parliament sits. These types of adjacency by no means exhaust the possibilities, but merely illustrate that there are many possibilities, including, if we think synecdoche is a type of metonymy, being a part of something. There is even an argument that all words are metonymical, because words are cognitively close to the things they denote by virtue of that denotation. This means that metonymy is just as pervasive as metaphor, possibly more so.

It may, nevertheless, be difficult to distinguish metaphor from metonymy. If we talk about the *head of a table*, we are presumably using a metaphor, because we are implicitly comparing (or overtly stating an equivalence between) the importance of the head to the body, and the importance of the position at the table to the rest of the table. If we speak of the *head* on a glass of beer, we are again using a metaphor, because we compare the position of the head at the top of the body to the position of the froth on the beer. But what if we speak about *the head of a bed*? Do we mean that (perhaps because of the pillow) it resembles the head of a person (metaphor), or do we mean that it is the position where the head is placed in a bed (metonymy)? The distinction may not be clear. Both are figurative, that is, they are not literal interpretations of the linguistic vehicle, but at times distinguishing between them can be awkward.

4.7.5 *Figurative usage and polysemy*

One of the major sources of polysemy is figurative extension of the use of a word. Because figurative uses are everywhere, we often do not notice them. Consider, for example, the case of *house*. How would you define *house*? You might say that a house is a building in which people live. In that case, a *hen-house* must be a figurative usage (metaphor). If we think a house is a building in which something lives, then *hen-house* is no longer a figurative usage, it is literal, but *coffee-house* is a figurative usage, as is *House of Commons*. If you define *house* as any building, though, all of these may be literal though *house* in *house wine* is still metonymy. What is a figurative meaning depends crucially on what you think the literal meaning of a word is – and that may not be easy to decide.

Polysemes may arise from things other than figurative usage. *Loaf* in *Use your loaf* may be a polyseme of *loaf* in *A crusty loaf*, but it does not arise through figurative usage, but through rhyming slang (*loaf of bread* rhymes with *head*). *Dog* as in *dog fox* and *dog* as in *Have you put the dog out?* (where the *dog* in question might be a bitch) may not arise through figurative usage.

One point which should be considered seriously before we leave this topic is whether polysemy and homonymy are at all relevant for the discussion of meaning. For an item to be polysemous, or for two items to homonyms, we assume that there is something like the lexeme. In polysemy we attribute multiple meanings to the same lexeme, in homonymy we attribute different meanings attached to indistinguishable forms as arising because there are two (or more) lexemes involved. In a description based on lexemes, this is not problematic, and the description in this book has been based on lexemes. But what if we want to say that lexemes are irrelevant to semantics, and that the various distinguishable meanings are the fundamental units of semantics? Then *dog* ('male canine') and *dog* ('canine') are fundamental units, and we do not have to decide how many lexemes are involved (and we do not have to distinguish between polysemy and homonymy). How this would then interface with a morphology that distinguishes centrally between lexemes and word-forms would have to be worked out, and consideration of this would go far beyond what is possible in a book of this nature. The question remains a serious one, however.

4.7.6 Coercion

There is another way in which lexemes can gain multiple meanings, which is usually kept separate from polysemy because the meanings are grammatical rather than lexical. This is called **coercion** because a word which is assumed inherently to have a certain set of grammatical features changes those features when forced to by the context. The question of coercion will be dealt with again later (see Section 6.5.11), so only some brief examples will be given here.

Verbs are usually assumed to be inherently transitive or intransitive: *fall* is intransitive, *persuade* is transitive. In many languages of the world (for example, Hungarian, West Greenlandic) verbs are overtly marked with inflectional morphology to show whether they are transitive or intransitive or to change their transitivity; this is not the case in English. In a few cases in English, transitivity is marked derivationally or lexically: *fall* is intransitive, *fell* ('to cause to fall') is transitive; in standard English *lie* is intransitive, *lay* is transitive (*The baby lies in its cot*, *The mother lays the baby in its cot*). More usually, however, transitivity is not marked, and the only way we have of telling whether a verb is transitive or intransitive is to see whether or not it has a direct object. *Run* is intransitive in *He runs every morning* and transitive in *He runs 5 miles every morning*; *grow* is intransitive in *Babies just grow* and transitive in *Last year we grew tomatoes*; *smell* is intransitive in *The rubbish smells* and transitive in *She smelt a rat*. If we assume that one of these usages is intrinsic, the other reading arises through coercion.

Similarly, adjectives are either gradable or ungradable. One thing can be bigger than another (*big* is gradable), but secrets cannot be more atomic than other secrets (*atomic* is ungradable). However, even though *French* is usually ungradable (things are either French or they are not), we can say *She is more French than the French* (meaning that, even though she is not French, she behaves in a way which fits with our notion of how the French should behave to a greater extent than many French people: perhaps she dresses chicly, embraces acquaintances she meets in the street, uses a lot of gestures when she speaks, supports the French rugby team). This gradable reading is gained through coercion.

4.8 The meanings of word-elements

However words mean what they mean, or however we wish to represent the meanings of words, the meanings of word-elements such as prefixes and suffixes work in different ways. Partly this is a result of their different nature: because they have to apply to large number of bases they have relatively general meanings, often relatively grammatical meanings (especially with inflectional morphology). We still have to deal with questions of **monosemy** and polysemy, though, and also with homonymy and with figurative extensions.

The simplest affixes to deal with are monosemous. Consider, as an example, the suffix *-ess*, which always means 'female', although the connotations of *-ess* in *authoress* and *Princess Charlotte* may be different. Equally, the prefix *mini-* (as opposed to the noun *mini*), always means 'smaller than some norm'. The meanings of such affixes can be combined with the meanings of their bases in relatively straightforward ways, so that *authoress* means 'female author' (leaving connotations out of the picture) and *mini-skirt* means 'a skirt which is smaller than might – by the usual norms of the society – be expected for a skirt'. The process for merging the meaning of the base and meaning of the affix is similar to the process for merging the meaning of an adjective with the meaning of a noun to work out what *female author* or *small skirt* might mean. What is more, the meanings of these affixes, as it happens, are rather like the meanings that can be attributed to entire words, so they are relatively lexical.

In contrast, consider the suffix *-ed*, as it arises in *imagined*. The meaning here is much more grammatical: in the sentence *You imagined it!* the meaning is 'past tense' (or, more likely, some internal formulation which involves things like 'completed action', 'no longer current' and the like, which can be conveniently glossed as 'past tense'). But now we meet a problem. Because in the sentence *You must have imagined it!* the suffix no longer means 'past tense' but 'past participle'. One of the questions that we might need to address is whether *-ed* is polysemous or whether we have two homonymous *-ed* affixes. The argument for two suffixes would be their different meanings and different functions in the paradigms; the argument for a single suffix would rely on their matching forms (at least in regular verbs), and the idea that that the meaning 'past participle' can – in most cases – be deduced from the presence of the verb HAVE immediately before it. We might also want to say that there is some shared meaning (perhaps 'completed action'). To make matters even more complex, now consider *He was furious because of some imagined insult.* Here we might want to say that *imagined* is an adjective. It is not clear whether this is the same *imagined* that we find in *The insult had been imagined*, where some authorities see a passive participle, distinct from the past participle. Again we need to know about polysemy versus homonymy, but here we have the extra problem that some see *imagined*, the adjective, as distinct from *imagined* in any of its verbal forms, because they consider the *-ed* in this case to be derivational rather than inflectional. If it is derivational (and the verbal one is indeed inflectional), we still have to decide whether the *-ed* in, say, *blue-eyed boy*, where the *-ed* is added to a noun phrase rather than to a verb form, is the same *-ed* as creates the de-verbal adjective or not. I do not provide a solution here, because I am not convinced that there is a single solution that everyone can agree about. What I want to draw attention to is the fact that questions of polysemy and homonymy are as important in dealing with the semantics of affixes as they are in dealing with the semantics of words, and just as difficult to resolve.

Finally, consider the suffix *-age*, as in *marriage* (where the base is a verb; no position is taken here on *-age* added to nouns as in *parsonage*, *patronage*, *voltage*). This, too, has a number of meanings, though there is probably agreement here that the various meanings (or readings) are matters of polysemy. There is a certain amount of agreement within Cognitive Linguistics that the different readings of an affix like this one are related to each other by metonymy, although that position remains controversial. For examples of the various readings, see those given in (11).

(11)	Her carriage was pulled by two black horses.	'vehicle which carries'
	She has an excellent carriage.	'way of carrying herself'
	The law is very precise about the carriage of goods.	'the act of carrying'
	The postage was exorbitant.	'amount paid for posting'
	The stoppage was removed surgically.	'something which stops something'
	Their marriage was a harmonious one.	'period or state of being married'
	Their marriage was yesterday.	'event during which they were married'
	We have to account for breakages.	'things broken'

The thing to note about these various readings is that they denote things which necessarily arise in relation to performing the action of the verb. If something is carried not simply by a human, then the thing which does the actual carrying is part of the act of carrying; you can post letters and parcels, but you have to pay for that, and the payment is part of the scenario of posting mail; if a flow is stopped, then something must have stopped it; marriage might be basically an act of getting married, but in our society that usually involves a ceremony, and the result of the action of getting married is a state of being married; if something is broken, then the thing that is broken is important; and so on. There are two possible claims here, both of which have been made within Cognitive Linguistics: the first is that for any given affix which has a number of polysemes, the polysemes are in a metonymical relationship with each other; the second is that the readings of affixes are always metonymically related to the denotation of the base. It might be safer to say 'figurative' rather than 'metonymical', because sometimes the polysemes of affixes appear to be metaphorical: *Mondayitis* compares the feeling that Mondays impart to many people in our society to a disease, for instance.

All of this has implications for the way in which we deal with the linguistics of affixational meaning. If we assume that figurative interpretations are built into human cognition, and can be found in places that are not linguistic (for example, in paintings), then we can assume that it is not the job of linguistics specifically to account for figurative interpretations – it is a wider cognitive problem. If that is the case, any meaning that arises due to a figurative extension is not part of the linguistic structure of the linguistic item concerned, but is due to the way human cognition functions. The fact that a *carriage* is (or can be) a vehicle is something about the world that human beings can deduce, but not a part of the linguistic meaning of *carriage*, which is simply 'act of carrying', or, more abstractly, 'nominalisation of *carry*'. Clearly, the matter is more complex than this simple statement makes it sound. There are many affixes that can be glossed as 'nominalisation of a verb', and they do not all have the same range of meanings (most of them do not mean 'amount paid for the carrying out of the action of the verb', for example). The attested readings are driven by some mechanism which is probably based on parallels with other familiar examples. Nonetheless, if we want to distinguish between a linguistic meaning and an encyclopedic meaning, in some more sophisticated view of what these might imply, the figurative uses can be seen as part of what we know (the encyclopedia) rather than things which the grammar and the lexicon need in order to function (the linguistic or lexical meaning).

4.9 Summary

This chapter has been about the network of meaning relationships that connect words to each other. Sometimes the various relations seem to overlap, sometimes they pull in very different directions, but in either case our impression of the word as a whole is informed by the various links that are available. One of the things you absorb gradually, either when learning your first language or when learning a second or foreign language, is something of the range of associations that different words bring with them, whether they are syntagmatic or paradigmatic, whether they are of denotation or connotation, whether they are literal or figurative. Because dictionaries and thesauruses cannot provide a full set of such links, you have to be very careful in interpreting such reference works if you want to use a word that is otherwise unfamiliar to you. Because there are so many semantic links between words, it is sometimes argued that no true synonyms can ever be found. Depending on your definition, that may be true.

Exercises

1. Consider each of the following forms (or find your own), all of which have more than one meaning. Are we dealing with polysemous lexemes, or pairs (perhaps triplets) of homonymous lexemes? How do you decide?

   boa, earth, patent, proof, reproduction, watch

2. Can you draw up a table for family relationships like that in (8)? If not, what is the problem? If you can, what kinds of meanings do you have, and do those correspond to your intuitions about the relevant words?
3. Find five pairs of homographs that are not homophones, and five pairs of homophones that are not homographs.
4. What counts as a *berry* in English is an interesting question. Check dictionaries and recipe books to see whether the same items are included in the two places. Alternatively, try the same procedure with *fruit* and *vegetable*.
5. Is meronomy a type of metonymy? Why (not)?
6. Make a case that the English word *chair* is either monosemous or polysemous. Try to answer points which might disagree with your position.
7. Find a short passage of English prose, and find all the figurative uses or expressions within the passage. Can you classify them?

8. Consider each of the following sentences. They may or may not be acceptable. Explain why they might be thought odd, using the terminology introduced in this chapter.
   (a) That isn't a Dachshund, it's a dog.
   (b) My sausage dog is a Dachshund.
   (c) Kentledge is a type of ballast, not a hop-growing area.
   (d) She may not be married, but she certainly isn't single.
   (e) He's the most married bachelor I know.
   (f) The sea isn't blue today, it's green.
   (g) He lives in a real pigsty.

Recommendations for reading

There are many textbooks on semantics which cover the area of lexical semantics, which is the topic of this chapter. Among the most approachable are Cruse (1986) and Murphy (2010). A classic in the field is Lyons (1977), though it provides a denser explication than the others mentioned. The example of the kakapo in Section 4.3 is taken from Bauer (2005), which also considers some other examples. Two works on different aspects of figurative speech that are worth reading are Lakoff and Johnson (2003) and Littlemore (2015). For a summary of work on the figurative readings of word-elements, see Bauer (2017b). On readings of nominalisations, see Bauer et al. (2013). On prototypes, see Taylor (2003), which also deals with some of the other topics covered in this chapter. On the sheepdog with a vocabulary of 200 words discussed in Section 4.4.1, see Kaminsky et al. (2004). Clark (1995: 95–100) gives evidence of similar behaviour in children.

5 Orthographic and phonological structure

5.1 Introduction

English spelling has a very bad reputation. George Bernard Shaw once suggested that the word *fish* could be spelt <ghoti> in English (<gh> as in *enough*, <o> as in *women*, <ti> as in *nation*). He was wrong, but the example has stuck. And examples with various pronunciations of <ough>, as in *Although the ploughboy coughed and hiccoughed his rough way to Scarborough*, are adduced as evidence of the stupidity of the English orthographic system. Yet, however accurate these observations may be, they affect only a small part of the spelling system, and some of it – most of it – is a lot more sensible.

In order to discuss spelling and sound, we need a link to a specific model of English pronunciation. Since the pronunciation of English is very different in Sydney, Washington DC, Edinburgh and Cape Town, it cannot simply be assumed that what is true of one variety of English is true of all. The pronunciation model used here is a rather conservative southern English model, based on the dialect known to linguists as Standard Southern British English. The pronunciation is sometimes called 'Oxford English', 'BBC English' or 'RP' (which stands for 'Received Pronunciation'). None of the labels is satisfactory, but 'RP' will be preferred here. It is the pronunciation illustrated in the major English pronunciation dictionaries and other reference works. Although there is some variation within RP, it is very minor in comparison with the variation found across the British Isles or across the English-speaking world. Occasional reference will be made to other pronunciations. If you do not speak RP (and the chances are that you do not), you may need to make some adjustments to fit your own pronunciation.

5.2 Spelling and vowel length

The first point to consider is **vowel length**. To understand this, we have to understand that RP (like older varieties of English) has two sets of vowels, which we can call short and long (although equivalent labels such as **lax** and **tense, checked** and **unchecked** are sometimes used). The short vowels are the vowels in the lexical sets KIT, DRESS, TRAP, STRUT, LOT and FOOT (**lexical sets** – see Wells 1982 – are sets of words which share a common vowel sound, illustrated in the keyword used to name the set). They are, as the label suggests, relatively short, and when stressed they must be followed by a consonant in an English word: we can have *dress* and *trap*, but no words like */dre/ or */træ/. The long vowels come in two sets, the monophthongs, which occur in words like FLEECE, START, THOUGHT, GOOSE, NURSE, and the diphthongs, which occur in words like FACE, PRICE, CHOICE, GOAT, MOUTH, NEAR, SQUARE, CURE. In the **monophthongs**, the tongue and lips remain in a relatively constant position throughout the articulation of the vowel, whereas in the **diphthongs** the tongue and/or the lips must move during the articulation of the vowel. The long vowels, when stressed, can occur in word-final position, as in /fliː/, /kæŋgəˈruː/, /traɪ/ and so on. Some varieties of English, such as Scottish English, no longer retain this vowel length distinction, but many still do.

One of the oddities that English inherited from Latin (which is where our alphabet originated) is that we use the same vowel letters for short vowels and for long vowels. The <a> represents a short vowel in *cat*, but a long vowel in *spa* and in *cape* (not the same long vowel sound, but both are long). If our spelling system has to indicate which is which, it needs some way of doing this.

One possibility, though rarely used, is simply to put the vowel last in a word. Since a short vowel must be followed by a consonant sound, any final stressed vowel must be long. Thus the vowel sounds represented by the final vowel letters in *do, flu, go, he, she, ski, spa* are all long.

The second way to show vowel length is to use a representation involving two vowel letters for a long vowel. Examples of words which use this technique are *aunt, brooch, faith, faun, hearth, Keith, meet, point, road, root, seat, shriek, sue, toe, youth*. There are some exceptions, often due to historical changes. They include things like *build, cough, friend, good, head, heifer, leopard, plait, said, sieve*, all of which contain short stressed vowel sounds in RP.

Long vowels can also be written with a vowel letter plus a <w> or a <y>. Examples of this usage are *boy, buy, fawn, grew, now, say, throw*. Exceptions include *knowledge*.

In RP, long vowels can be written with a vowel letter plus <r>. In many other varieties of English, this combination represents a short vowel and /r/, but the /r/ was lost in pronunciation from about the seventeenth century in London and eastern England. In the case of <er>, <ir>, <ur>, these have merged in RP as /ɜː/ in words like *fern, fir, fur*. In standard American English, the vowel is the same in all of these, but there is still an /r/ pronounced. In Scottish English, <er> is pronounced differently from the other two (in some varieties, all three are distinct), so that *fern* and *burn* do not rhyme. The spellings <ar> and <or> now represent /ɑː/ and /ɔː/ respectively in RP. Some other cases are in the list of examples below. Where these originate as short vowel + /r/, the spelling is often that which indicates a short vowel – this will be explained further below. Examples are *corn, cur, fair, farm, firm, hear, heard, scar, tier.*

We can see another technique used in English spelling to distinguish long vowel sounds from short vowels sounds, if we look at the examples in (1).

(1) *Short vowel*   *Long vowel*
    matting   mating
    letter   meter
    bitter   biter
    hopping   hoping
    cutter   cuter

Here we see that if we want to keep a short value for a stressed vowel written with a single vowel letter, we can double the consonant letter immediately following it. Where there is only one consonant letter following the vowel letter, the vowel letter is read as long. Conversely, to keep a stressed vowel long, there must be at most one consonant letter following it. If there is otherwise no vowel letter following the relevant consonant letter, we add <e>. In children's spelling lessons, this is sometimes referred to as 'magic e' which 'makes the vowel say its name'; it is also referred to as 'silent <e>'. We can see the effect of magic <e> in (2).

(2) *Short vowel*   *Long vowel*
    cap   cape
    met   mete
    sit   site
    hop   hope
    cut   cute

Consonant doubling requires some explanation. Some letters cannot double: <ng>, <sh>, <th>, <v> and <w> (double <v> would simply turn into <w>) and <x> (*Exxon* is an invented trade name). *Never* has a short stressed vowel, *fever* has a long one, and *lever* has a short vowel in American English but a long one in British English. Long vowels before <sh> (and there are very few) need some other way to show their length, as in *leash*; alternatively, they maintain a French spelling, as in *douche*. The letter <j> rarely doubles, but consider *raj* and *hajj* (with alternative spellings), which work much as expected. *Creche* is pronounced either with a long or with a short vowel.

Some letters have unexpected double forms: <k> is doubled as <ck>, <ch> is doubled as <tch>, so we can contrast *bicker* (short vowel) with *biker* (long vowel), and *latch* (short vowel) with *ache* (long vowel). *Rich*, without a doubled consonant at the end, is just like *bet*, which also has a short vowel and no doubled consonant at the end. Doubled /ʤ/ is usually spelt <dge>, which assumes a normal spelling of <ge> for this sound, as in *cadge* versus *cage*.

The trouble with consonant doubling is that it really works only with Germanic words. With words of other origins, it may work – if the word has been sufficiently built into the English system – or it may not. *Pedal* is usually pronounced /pedəl/, but *bipedal*, in RP, seems to prefer /baɪˈpiːdəl/ (though American English seems to be different); *pedal* is a Latin word. The prefix *meta-*, a Greek prefix, as in *metaphor*, is pronounced with a short vowel. But the name of the Greek letter *theta* is pronounced with a long vowel. This means that the pronunciation of VCV cannot be guaranteed without at least some knowledge of the origin of the word.

More generally, a sequence of two consonant letters tends to indicate that the stressed vowel preceding them is short: *asphalt, camber, candour, capture, conker, elven, finger, lumber, mantra*, and so on. Note that many of these are not Germanic. We can explain this as follows. Any single intervocalic consonant belongs to the following syllable, so that the stressed syllable is left **open** (with no final consonant – no **coda**). Short vowels in stressed monosyllables cannot occur in this context, and we assume that this is generalised to multisyllabic words. However, if there are two (or more) consonants, the first can close the first syllable, and the second forms the onset to the second syllable. A closed syllable can contain a short vowel, and so the stressed vowel is read as short. Consonant doubling is a way of making it look as though there is a coda consonant in the first syllable (even though it is not pronounced), and so acts as a visual clue to the short vowel.

This does not explain all consonant doubling in English (in particular, it does not deal with cases like British <traveller> but American <traveler> where the relevant vowel is not stressed or cases like British

<instil>, American <instill>). Nevertheless, consonant doubling will often show spellings to be more regular than they might otherwise appear.

5.3 Some potentially confusing spellings

Some of the unexpected spellings of English can be explained by the way English has developed historically. For example, the spelling <kn> at the beginnings of words like *knight* and *know* exists because these words were once, hundreds of years ago, pronounced with a /k/. The word corresponding to *knight* in German (albeit with a different meaning) is *Knecht* ('labourer, jack (in cards)') and in Danish it is *knægt* ('lad, rascal, jack (in cards)'), and in both cases the [k] is pronounced. The same is true of the silent <w> at the beginning or *wring, write, writhe* and so on. The modern Danish word corresponding to *writhe* is *vride* ('wring, wrench, writhe'), and the <v> is pronounced.

Other cases are much more complicated. The letters <oo> once represented a long vowel, and that is why the vowel letter is doubled. In some words, <oo> still represents a long vowel, now pronounced /uː/, as in *food, loom, coop, soothe*. In many other instances, though, the vowel corresponding to the <oo> spelling became short. When that happened, two things could happen. Either it stayed as a back vowel, as in words like *book, good, took*, or, along with many other words that had a short [u] pronunciation at the time, it became a central vowel, in Modern English usually transcribed as /ʌ/. Examples are *blood, flood*. In a few words, such as *roof, room*, either /uː/ or /ʊ/ can be heard from different speakers in modern English.

In monosyllabic words, not many letters are doubled at the end of the word to keep the vowel short. We find, for example, *log, nib, pin, set, bid* with short vowels but only a single consonant at the end. A few letters can be doubled, particularly when this is needed to ensure that there are three letters in the word: *add, ass, ebb, egg, inn, butt, snuff, tell*. The general rule here, as elsewhere, is that a double letter indicates a short vowel preceding, but there are some cases where this does not happen. The first is <a> before <ll> as in *all, tall, small* and so on. In most cases, we get the long vowel /ɔː/. We can postulate an intermediate stage in the seventeenth century where we found [aʊl], which merged with what was written <awl> so that *tall* and *crawl* came to rhyme. The change is not absolute: *shall* is still pronounced with /æl/, and *Pall Mall* (once pronounced /pelmel/) usually has /æ/, although shopping *mall* has /ɔː/. This change in pronunciation also applies where there is only a single written <l> if there is a following consonant letter, as in *alter, baldric, salt, talk, walk.* There are places, especially with more recent words, where the spelling is followed and we get /æ/ in *alkali, contralto, gallery, medallion, Pallas, shallow, Trafalgar* – none of these at the end of a word.

The second set of exceptions concerns words with final <ss>, such as *class, pass,* and final <ff> as in *staff.* This is part of a wider change, again in the seventeenth century, whereby the stressed <a> vowel lengthened before /f/, /θ/ and /s/. Not only do we get /glaːs/, /staːf/, we also get /aːftə/, /laːf/, /paːθ/, /paːst/ and so on. Some speakers have /plaːstɪk/ instead of the more usual /plæstɪk/. But this rule was never completed, and there are some words where it never applied, and also some words which became part of English after the relevant period, where the rule could not apply. In the case of *ass*, the problem that /aːs/ sounds like *arse* may have discouraged this pronunciation (and led to *ass* being largely replaced by *donkey* – literally, 'little Duncan'; for the pronunciation of the vowel, compare *monkey*). *Mass* still has the possibility of /maːs/ for the church service, though it is always /mæs/ in *mass media. Asterisk, bastille, chastise, lass* (originally a northern word), *mastiff, masturbate, Pasteur* (but not *pasteurise*), for example, retain /æ/. *Drastic* and *lath* still vary. You will note that this is not only a relatively late change (which is why it did not reach the USA), but a southern change, so that northern accents of English, including Scottish English, retain /æ/ in these places.

5.4 The Great Vowel Shift

Between the time when Chaucer was writing and up until about the time when Shakespeare was writing, English long monophthongs underwent a huge change in pronunciation. Before this time, the correspondence between the long vowels and their spelling was more or less as it was in Latin (and to a large extent still is in most European languages, as well as other languages that use the Roman alphabet). In Italian, the vowel letters are called, approximately, [a], [ɛ], [i], [ɔ], [u], which contrasts with the English /eɪ/, /iː/, /aɪ/, /əʊ/, /juː/. The vowel shift (generally called the **Great Vowel Shift** – GVS) can be represented as a very systematic change to the pronunciation of the vowels, although it must be remembered that the entire process took about 200 years. The process is illustrated in Figure 5.1 (in a simplified form), with solid lines showing the vowel changes that were part of the GVS, and dotted lines showing subsequent developments. This change has had a number of effects on the way in which English is written as well as pronounced. Some of these effects are discussed below.

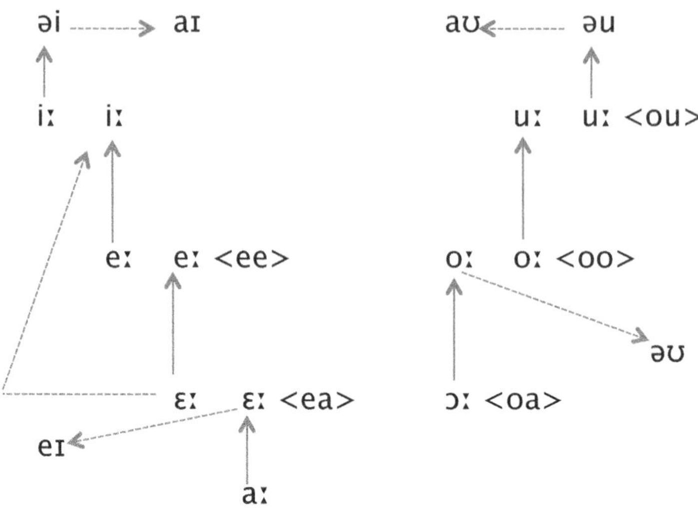

Figure 5.1 The Great Vowel Shift

In Middle English (that is, before the GVS), some word-pairs were related in that one had a long vowel where its partner had the corresponding short vowel. In modern English, that spelling relationship is often still there, with the short vowel pronunciation often still similar to the pre-GVS pronunciation, but the long vowel sounds are now different even if the letters are not. Examples are given in (3).

(3) *Short vowel*   *Long vowel*
     bitten   bite
     divination   divine
     explanatory   explain
     jocular   joke
     obscenity   obscene
     profundity   profound
     pronunciation   pronounce
     tonic   tone
     typical   type
     diagnostic   diagnose

For many centuries before and after the Great Vowel Shift, Latin was the language of the church and the law. The pronunciation of Latin that was in use in the church and the law changed in line with the changes of the GVS. In later periods, it was observed that ecclesiastical and legal Latin had deviated from what was known of the pronunciation of

Classical Latin, and a new reformed Latin pronunciation was imposed. The result is that there are often two pronunciations of Latin words in English, the traditional (the GVS changes apply) and the reformed (attempting to copy original Latin). This is seen most often with the letters <i> and <a> (the others are rarer or do not change). Some examples are provided in (4).

(4)

Letter	Example	Traditional	Reformed
<i>	alumni	əlʌmnaɪ	əlʌmni:
	fiat	faɪæt	fi:ət
	regina	rɪdʒaɪnə	rɪdʒi:nə (regi:nə)
	via	vaɪə	viə
<e>	deus (ex machina)	di:ʌs	deɪʌs
<a>	apparatus	æpəreɪtʌs	æpəra:təs
	data	deɪtə	da:tə
	imperator	ɪmpəreɪtə	ɪmpəra:tə
	(alma) mater	meɪtə	ma:tə

In some words, often borrowed words, there has been uncertainty as to whether there should be a long vowel or a short one. This is typically true where the spelling is ambiguous. The result is sometimes that both are found in English, but with the long vowel showing the value that has been affected by the GVS. Some examples are shown in (5), but you can probably think of plenty of others.

(5)

Word	Short vowel	Long vowel
Megan	megən	mi:gən
nematode	nemətəʊd	ni:mətəʊd
patent	pætənt	peɪtənt
penalise	penəlaɪz	pi:nəlaɪz
scenic	senɪk	si:nɪk

As a special case of this type of distinction, we find cases where different dialects of English use vowels of different lengths. In particular, American English seems to prefer a long vowel when borrowing from a foreign language, while British English prefers a short vowel. Often, but not always, the resulting variants resemble long–short brought about by the GVS. Some examples of this are given in (6).

(6)

Word	British	American
adios	ædiɒs	ædiəʊs
baroque	bərɒk	bərəʊk
Ludwig	lʌdvɪg	lu:dvɪg
pasta	pæstə	pa:stə
yoghurt	jɒgət	jəʊgət

Note, though, that where British English has the possibility of the spellings <ae> or <oe> and American English just uses <e>, American English sometimes prefers the short pronunciation, as in (*o*)*estrus*, *anap(a)est*.

One of the curious effects of the Great Vowel Shift is that words borrowed (especially from French) after the shift have a different spelling–pronunciation link than those borrowed before. Words borrowed before the vowel shift, went through the vowel shift, and the values for the long vowels were changed in the expected ways. Words borrowed after the vowels shift, however, were borrowed with a French spelling and kept the modern pronunciation. The result is that there are sets like those in (7) where the same spelling in a French loan word is pronounced in two ways in English.

(7)   *Old borrowing*   *New borrowing*
      beauty   beau
      employee   fiancée
      oblige   prestige
      prise   cerise
      sage   camouflage
      suit   suite
      Valentine   quarantine
      voucher   boutique

5.5 Consonants

5.5.1 Some spelling conventions

The spelling of the consonantal parts of English words largely follows the phonology closely, but there are a few places where the spelling is worthy of particular comment, and those will be dealt with first.

The use of <ck> for double <k>, <tch> for double <ch>, <dge> for double <ge> was commented on in Section 5.2. The use of double consonant letters to mark preceding short vowels was discussed at the same point. Nothing further needs to be said about those here.

The sounds /θ/ and /ð/ are not consistently distinguished in English spelling. In Old English, there was only one phoneme, which was voiced intervocalically. That is why *breathe* (and similar words) now has /ð/, even though the sound represented by the final <e> is now lost. But even in the verb to *mouth*, there is a final /ð/, despite the fact that there is no <e> to mark it. Initially, /ð/ appears only in grammatical words, as in (8).

(8)   the
       this, that, these, those
       thou, thee, thy, thine, thyself
       they, them, their, theirs, themselves
       there (and compounds, like *therefore, thereafter*)
       thus, though, then, than, that (conjunction), thence (and com-
       pounds, like *thenceforth*)
       Note that *through* begins with /θ/ although it is a preposition, and
       though (and *although*) is pronounced with /θ/ in some places.

Lexical words beginning with <th> always have /θ/, which is why
thy and *thigh, though* and *thought, then* and *thing, them* and *theme, these* and
thesis begin with different consonant sounds. Since *thy* is so rarely used
these days, there are few minimal pairs between /θ/ and /ð/, but those
speakers who pronounce *either* with /iː/ will have a minimal pair with
ether, and *wreath, wreathe* provide a minimal pair for all speakers. Where
<th> appears in the middle of words, it tends to be /θ/ in Greek words
(such as *author* and *method*) but /ð/ in Germanic words (such as *heathen*
and *mother*). There is sometimes variation between /θ/ and /ð/ in the
pronunciation of <th>: *oaths, earthen* and *with* are among the words
which might have either pronunciation, although the variation in *with*
tends to be regional rather than individual. In a few words, <th> represents /t/, as, for instance, in *Thames, thyme*. In *Anthony*, some people use
/t/, and some use /θ/ under the influence of the spelling.

The phoneme /ʒ/ arises late in English, originating in French words,
and has a limited distribution and inconsistent spelling. Its spellings are
set out in (9), and it should be noted that these nearly all come from
French or Latin.

(9)   <g>, before <e>in French words like *beige, bourgeois, prestige*. In
       final position, /ʤ/ can replace /ʒ/.
       <g>, before <i> in the French word *regime*.
       <ge>. In the French suffix *-age*, in modern loans, as in *barrage,
       collage, camouflage*. Where the suffix is English (as in *anchorage*), the
       pronunciation is /ɪʤ/. The word *garage* is sometimes pronounced
       /gəˈrɑːʒ/, sometimes /ˈgærɑːʒ/ and sometimes /ˈgærɪʤ/, with
       the first the most French pronunciation, the last the most assimi-
       lated pronunciation.
       <j>, initially in French words which are modern loans: *jabot,
       jardinière*.
       <s>, before <i> or <u> as in *invasion, measure, treasury, usual*.
       <t>, before <i> in the word *equation*, which is irregular, and is
       pronounced with /ʃ/ to match the spelling in some varieties.

<z>, before <u> in a very few words, including *azure* and *seizure*. <zh> in loans from other languages, like *Zhivago, zho*.

The letter <c> can be pronounced /s/ or /k/. It is pronounced /s/ when it comes before <e> or <i> in words from Latin or French (*centre, conceive*), and /k/ when it comes before <a>, <o> or <u>, before another consonant, or at the end of a word (*capture, convict, accuse, tragic*). The combination <sc> is pronounced /s/ or /sk/ in a parallel way: *sceptre, science,* but when not in a Latin or French word, or when not before <e> or <i>, it is /sk/: *Oscar, scabies, scar* and so on. It occurs rarely the end of a word, as in *disc*, which is increasingly spelt <disk>. The occasional pronunciation as /ʃ/ (as in *conscience*) is irregular. The sequence <sch> is regularly /sk/ in Greek words (*scheme, school*), but /ʃ/ in words borrowed from German or Yiddish (*Porsche, schnapps, schnozzle, Schubert*) and irregularly in the traditional British pronunciation of *schedule*.

Conversely, /k/ may be written <c> before <a>, <o> and <u> in Latin or French words, finally in words originally derived from Greek, and in the combinations <sc> and <sch> as above, or <k>, <ck> and irregularly <kk> (as in *brekky* 'breakfast'). The sequence <sk> usually indicates a Scandinavian word in initial position, as in *sky, skin* (but not in *skeleton*). The cluster /kw/ is nearly always written <qu>, but <que> can be /k/ in French loans, like *masque*.

As is the case with <c>, <g> has one pronunciation before <e> and <i> in French and Latin words, and another before other vowels. This is made more complex by the pronunciation of <g> as /ʒ/ illustrated in (9), and the fact that in Germanic words the same rules may not apply, so that <gill> spells /gɪl/ (of a fish – a Scandinavian word) and /dʒɪl/ ('fluid measure' – a French word). Germanic words in which <g> is /g/ before an <e> or an <i> include *gear, get, giddy, girl, give*. The word *yogi* illustrates an exotic loan word in which the <g> is still /g/.

5.5.2 *Initial consonant clusters*

At the beginnings of words, where there are clusters of consonants, these fit fairly strict rules. Some foreign words break these rules, others are manipulated to comply with them.

If a word begins with a voiceless plosive (/p/, /t/, or /k/) then there are four potential following consonants in the cluster, as illustrated in (10). The parenthesised item in (10) is borrowed from Spanish, but fits the pattern.

(10)   l   r   j   w
    p   please   pray   pewter   (pueblo)
    t   –   tray   tune   twinkle
    k   clean   crime   cute   quick

Note that the /j/ in such clusters does not have its own representation: it is most often part of the <u> /juː/. Note the variable spellings of /k/.

There are no instances of a plosive being followed by a fricative. Where <ts> is borrowed in a loan word, the pronunciation /ts/ has been avoided, at least until recently. *Tsetse fly* is traditionally pronounced /tetsi/, *tsar* is pronounced /zɑː/ and *tsunami* is pronounced /suːnɑːmi/. Recent pronunciations are more likely to follow the spelling.

Corresponding to (10), we find similar patterns with voiced plosives, as in (11).

(11)   l   r   j   w
    b   blow   bray   beauty   (bwana)
    d   –   dray   dune   dwindle
    g   glean   grey   (gules)   (Gwendolen)

Where we have fricatives in first position, the options are more limited, as shown in (12).

(12)   l   r   j   w
    f   flea   free   few   (Fuego)
    θ   –   three   thew   thwack
    s   slay   –   suit   switch
    ʃ   –   shrimp   –   (Schweizer)
    h   –   –   huge   when (for some speakers)

The distribution /s/ is exceptional, and more will be said about that below. The fact that /s/ occurs before /l/ and /ʃ/ before /r/ has some effect on loan words. The country formerly known as *Ceylon* is often called /ʃriː læŋkə/, despite the spelling (although the pronunciation following the spelling, which breaks the normal patterns of English, is now frequently heard in news broadcasts). The fricative /ʃ/ is found before /l/ only in Yiddish loan words like *schlep*, *schlock* and German loan words such as *Schleswig*.

The fricative /s/ can also occur followed by another fricative, but only in the cluster /sf/ (which, because it occurs in Greek words, is spelt <sph> as in *sphere*) and the single loan word *sthenic*. Note that some people pronounce loan words such as *svelte* and *Svengali* with /sf/ (to make them agree with the general rule), but some speakers pronounce the /sv/ suggested by the spelling, despite the wider pattern.

The same fricative can also be followed by nasals, as in *smug* and *snug*.

The biggest oddity of /s/, though, is that it can so frequently be added in front of a voiceless plosive to make a two-consonant cluster, as shown in (13), and in front of a two-consonant cluster to make a three-consonant cluster, as shown in (14).

(13) spill
     still
     skill

(14)   l   r   j   w
     sp   splay   spray   spew   –
     st   –   stray   stew   –
     sk   (sclerosis)   scream   skew   squid

Some people feel that /sp/, /st/, /sk/ should be considered to be single consonants (like /tʃ/ and /dʒ/) to help explain the oddity of this pattern. Clusters of /sb/, /sd/, /sg/ do not occur, because the elements in the cluster have to have the same value for voicing, and since /s/ is voiceless, the others also have to be voiceless (see also the discussion of /sv/ just above). There are extremely rare cases of /s/ + nasal + /j/: a *smew* /smjuː/ is a kind of merganser, and *snew* /snjuː/ is a dialect form for the past tense (sometimes for the present tense) of the verb 'to snow'. *Sleuth* has an old, but possible, pronunciation /sljuːθ/. Initial clusters with any non-plosive consonant and /j/ are becoming rarer. Not only *suit* (now most often /suːt/), but *Susan*, the prefix *super-*, and, in the middle of words, *assume* used to have /sj/, and *lewd*, *lucid*, *lute* and *illuminate* used to have /lj/. Longer ago, *rule* had /rj/, but this is now heard only in regional dialectal forms. *Zurich* used to be pronounced with a /j/. In standard American English, /j/ is lost following /t/, /d/, /n/ so that *tune*, *dune*, *news* are pronounced with no /j/. Such usage is spreading elsewhere.

Spellings which seem to imply clusters which are not part of the English system are usually misleading as to the pronunciation. For example, the initial <p> in *pneumonia, psychology, pterosaur* is not pronounced in English (though it was in Greek), and neither is the initial <b> in *bdellium*. *Mnemonic* has no initial /m/ in English. The name *Dvorak* is pronounced with a /d/, but is usually pronounced with a vowel between the /d/ and the /v/. *Vladivostok* is pronounced with the foreign /vl/. Because /rh/ is not a possible onset cluster, <rhododendron> cannot be pronounced with /rh/. Although we have <wr> and

<kn> in *wraith* and *knowledge*, these cannot be direct representations of phonological clusters and the first letter of each is silent. There is an increasing tendency to pronounce things as they are spelt, but the English system still creates an extremely strong pressure.

Note that, occasionally, we are misled by the spelling rather than because a cluster is impossible. An initial /hj/ is possible in *huge*, but it is not written <hy>. Initial <hy> is pronounced /haɪ/, as in *hyena*. So the car brand *Hyundai* is usually pronounced with initial /haɪ/, even though the <hy> represents a Korean /hj/.

5.5.3 Final consonant clusters

Final consonant clusters are much more complex, and will be dealt with far more programmatically. There can be final clusters of up to five consonants, as illustrated in (15). These are in monosyllabic words, and so the clusters follow a stressed vowel; there are fewer possible clusters following an unstressed vowel.

(15) 2   apse, best, felt, hold, paths, tells
      3   asks, belts, elves, lapsed, mulct
      4   prompts, sculpts, texts
      5   lengths (/leŋktθs/), sixths (/sɪkstθs/), twelfths (/twelftθs/)

All five-consonant clusters have alternatives with just four consonants (or fewer), and are heard with five only when the speaker is trying to be particularly clear in pronunciation. All four- and five-consonant clusters have an inflectional affix on the end, and the system in morphologically simple words is much less complex. Some scholars feel that these suffixes need to be treated differently in the system of consonant clusters from those phonemically identical sequences which arise in monomorphemic words. Such scholars treat *apse* differently from *caps*, and *mulct* differently from *milked*. It is notable that under this system, the most complex clusters tend to be in learned words.

Note that older speakers distinguish *tense* (/tens/) from *tents* (/tents/), *prince* (/prɪns/) from *prints* (/prɪnts/), while younger speakers tend to have these words as homophones with three consonant clusters.

Four basic rules of consonant clusters can be considered.

1. It is not possible to have two of the same consonant together in a cluster. Gemination sometimes appears over syllable – and morpheme – boundaries (in words like *busstop, meanness, openness, strifeful, wholly*) but not within a syllable.
2. If a nasal consonant occurs immediately before a plosive in the same

cluster (in the same syllable), it must have the same place of articulation: *lump*, *hound* and *think* (/θɪŋk/) have normal clusters, but we cannot have */ŋp/, for instance, and a cluster like that in *harmed* /hɑːmd/ can only occur when the plosive is a separate affix.

3. If a cluster contains two or more adjacent plosives or fricatives, they must agree in voicing. A final /st/ is allowed (in *best*), but not a final */sd/. There are a handful of exceptions, and they all have variants which fit the rule. *Breadth*, *width*, *hundredth* and *thousandth* may end in /dθ/ or /tθ/ (and occasionally /dð/, though that is rare). Stops or fricatives can disagree in voicing in adjacent syllables (for example, *adhere*, *disdain*), but even then agreement is sometimes possible, so that *absurd* can be /əbsɜːd/, /əpsɜːd/ or /əbzɜːd/.

4. Consonants in clusters following a vowel come in a relatively fixed order, which we can write as VLNO. The V stands for the vowel, the L for /l/, the N for a nasal consonant, and the O for any **obstruent** (where obstruent means any plosive or fricative or affricate). Varieties of English that have /r/ after the vowel (North American standard varieties, Scottish and Irish English, Devon English and so on) can rewrite the formula as VRLNO. There can only be one consonant in each of the RLN slots, but there can be several in the O slot, and not every slot is necessarily filled. This formula is an overall pattern, and there are, of course, restrictions within this, so that final /tʃt/ is allowed (*pitched*) but /tʃs/ is not.

Although these clusters usually reflect the spelling and are heard when clear single-word pronunciations are provided, in connected speech (even precise connected speech, but more frequently in fast speech) consonants may be elided or assimilated to surrounding consonants. The compound *hand-gun*, for instance, is likely to be pronounced /hæŋgʌn/, with loss of the final /d/ of *hand* and assimilation of the /n/ to /ŋ/ before /g/. Such processes are so normal that we rarely notice them. Such processes can also create new clusters (even new consonant types). *Because*, for example, may be pronounced [pxəz], even though English does not 'have' the sound [x], and so cannot 'have' a [px] cluster.

5.6 Unstressed vowels

The vowel sounds dealt with above have nearly all been stressed. In this section, unstressed vowels are the focus of attention. It is a matter of some controversy how many levels of stress we need to distinguish in English, but here three will suffice. The first is the stressed vowels dealt with earlier; the second is the vowels which have the quality of one of those stressed vowels, but have less prominence, which we can call secondary stressed; and the third, the ones to be dealt with here, have reduced vowels that cannot be stressed. The case of syllables with no vowel sounds at all will also be briefly considered here. Some people talk about a fourth level of stress where stress and intonation intersect, and there is intonational pitch movement on a stressed syllable, but we need not worry about such instances here, except to say that when a word is said in isolation, the pitch movement associated with intonation magnifies the effect of the stressed syllable, and makes it clearer which syllable is involved. A word like the noun *counterclaim* has a sequence of stressed–unstressed–secondary stressed in the same word, and we can transcribe that as /ˈkaʊntəkleɪm/, with the full vowel in the final syllable not marked as stressed.

It should be said at this point that not all varieties of English function in precisely the same way with regard to stress. Some varieties, such as Singapore English, have no really unstressed vowels; some north of England varieties have rather more secondary stressed vowels, replacing some of the unstressed vowels of RP with secondary stress. The name *Charlotte* is /ˈʃɑːlət/ in RP, but may be /ˈʃɑːlɒt/ in such varieties.

We begin with the comma vowel, transcribed /ə/. This sound can be written with any of the vowel letters (sometimes with a sequence of more than one, sometimes with an <r> included), so that it is not possible to judge the spelling from the pronunciation, or the pronunciation from the written vowel letter. We find the same sound written with different letters in the words in (16).

(16) *Words pronounced with /ə/*

<i>	terrible (also pronounced with /ɪ/)
<e>	bigger, mitre
<a>	about, capitulate
<o>	to (in, for example, *ten to three*), second
<u>	suffice, jodhpurs
<ou>	colour
<io>	nation
<eu>	grandeur
<ai>	villain
<oi>	porpoise, tortoise (this is now sometimes pronounced with /ɔɪ/)
<oa>	cupboard
<y>	analysis, pyjamas (/ɪ/ is also possible in these words)

Another way to see the multiple spellings of the same sound is shown in (17), where the words rhyme with each other (or in some instances are homophones) despite the different spellings.

(17) adviser   advisor
      altar   alter
      barter   martyr
      beggar   mega
      bigger   figure
      data   dater
      elephant   element
      higher   Messiah
      liar   lyre
      mailer   tailor
      postman   postmen
      sailor   sailer
      Sarah   fairer

Homophonous sequences at the beginnings of words are given in in (18).

(18) aboard   obnoxious
      accord   occur
      affect   effect (these are now sometimes deliberately distin-
                 guished, but still give rise to spelling mistakes)
      allay   obey (sometimes with /əʊ/)
      corrupt   curtail
      pacific   perform
      project   subject (both verbs; these can be kept distinct by full
                 vowels)

This vowel can also be found in complex words where the stress is moved by the processes of derivation. Some examples are given in (19), where the relevant vowel letter, the one pronounced with /ə/, is underlined.

(19) c<u>o</u>nfer   conf<u>e</u>rence
      c<u>o</u>nfirm   conf<u>i</u>rmation
      explain   expl<u>a</u>nation
      mel<u>o</u>dy   m<u>e</u>lodious
      subst<u>a</u>nce s<u>u</u>bstantial

Word-final /ə/, and especially phrase-final /ə/, has a more open pronunciation than the vowel in the middle of a word, and in some varieties,
notably in some varieties of Australian English, may be taken to belong
to the STRUT vowel or even the START vowel (so that the final two vowels
in *koala* may be felt to belong to the same phoneme). Where the commA
vowel is lengthened but not made more open, it may be perceived as

being the NURSE vowel, so that a word like *villager* may be taken to end in /ɜː/. There are two possibilities here: either this is a misperception due to assuming vowels from different subsystems can replace each other, or the vowel has moved to a different subsystem, and is no longer an unstressed vowel. The latter possibility may hold even where there is variation between an unstressed vowel and one with full vowel quality.

The happY vowel is found spelt <y>, <ey>, <i>, <ie> or <e> at the ends of words, such as *happy, chutney, doggie, epitome, Iraqi*. The quality of this vowel is variable. For some old-fashioned speakers of RP it may be the same as the pronunciation of the KIT vowel. For some speakers from the north of England, it may be pronounced like the KIT vowel, or even like the DRESS vowel. For most speakers from the south of England, and also for speakers from Australia and New Zealand, it sounds in quality like the FLEECE vowel. In this book it is transcribed with the quantity (length) of the KIT vowel, but the quality of the FLEECE vowel, as /i/, but this has the disadvantage of suggesting a clearly distinguishable pronunciation. Whatever its actual quality, it belongs in the system of unstressed vowels. For most speakers, there is a distinction between the FLEECE vowel in final position and the happY vowel in final position, as shown in (20) – although not all speakers maintain the difference in all of these pairs.

(20) *Final* FLEECE   *Final happY*
    cooee   hooey
    internee   attorney
    sari   sorry
    trochee   trophy

As well as occurring word-finally (sometimes followed by inflectional affixes), the happY vowel also occurs word-medially, before another vowel, as in *glorious, harmonious, react* and so on.

Although it does not occur in the rather conservative RP being described here, many speakers of English, especially from the English south-east and from Australasia, have an unstressed vowel which arises historically from (and is reflected orthographically in) the vocalisation of /l/ (that is, what was once /l/ becomes a vowel sound). For such speakers, the word *smile* is pronounced something like /smaɪo/ and *bottle* something like /bɒto/. What is here transcribed as /o/ is a vowel of variable pronunciation, but back, relatively close and often rounded, which may overlap with the FOOT vowel, but is more usually auditorily distinct from that vowel. Speakers who vocalise /l/ in such ways may also have a number of new diphthongs in words like *help, twelve, hold, cull* and so on.

The KIT vowel and the FOOT vowel may also occur in unstressed syllables, though in slightly different ways. RP speakers may maintain a difference between *villagers* and *villages*, where the former has commA and the latter KIT before the final /z/. However, an increasing number of speakers do not distinguish these (or if they do, they change the value of the last vowel in *villagers* to /ɜ:/). In the same way as we talk about the KIT vowel, we can talk about the horsES vowel in this situation, and say that the horsES vowel may overlap phonemically with the KIT vowel, but need not.

The KIT vowel often occurs as the reduction of the PRICE and DRESS vowels, when stress is moved off those vowels by derivational processes. Examples are given in (21).

(21) *Full vowel*   *Reduced KIT*
     mime   mimetic
     recognise   recognition
     resign   resignation
     definition   define
     telegraphy   telegraph
     prophetic   prophet

The FOOT vowel may be replaced by a vowel which is variable between the quality of FOOT and the quality of GOOSE, but with the length of FOOT. This is sometimes transcribed /u/ (and so compares directly with the happY vowel). This vowel arises before another vowel sound, in words like *annual, fluidity, situation, superfluous*. It occasionally is also found before a consonant, as in *Lucille, Lucretius, Rumania* (when this is spelt, as it now usually is, with an <o>, the pronunciation may change). It is now also replacing /ʊ/ in words like *erudite* and possibly also *adjutant*, while /ə/ is more common in words like *century*, which are rather more frequent. Something which is clearly the FOOT vowel in fully unstressed syllables is thus getting rarer. Nonetheless, /ʊ/ is still found in words like *hopeful, stressful*, with the suffix *-ful*.

There are also syllables where any vowel is optional. The clearest examples of such times are provided by words like *bottle* and *button*, where there may or may not be a (short, unstressed) vowel after the /t/. It has already been said above that the /l/ in such positions may, for some speakers, become a vowel (which we transcribed /o/). An /n/, however, is retained, and if there is no vowel before it, fills a syllable by itself. Consonants which do this are termed **syllabic consonants**. Varieties of English vary in the extent to which they allow syllabic consonants, and there may be variation linked with speech style even with a variety. Some speakers distinguish *lightning* (that occurs with thunder) from *lightening* ('getting lighter') by a syllabic consonant in the latter. Some speakers have a syllabic consonant in *bottom* and *spasm*, while others have a vowel before the /m/). Some American speakers interpret the sound at the end of words like *butter, cover* as a syllabic /r/, and even non-rhotic speakers may feel they have a syllabic /r/ in *for instance* or *vigorous*. A common expression like *of course* is often heard without an initial vowel, but a syllabic fricative (either /v/ or /f/). The deletion of the first vowel in *suppose* and *support* may leave behind a syllabic /s/, although the /s/ in such instances can also be non-syllabic. Finally, it is also possible to have a totally silent syllable (though whether it can then be called a syllable becomes dubious), as in *thank you*, reduced to /kju/, where the beat for the *thank* may still be perceptible.

5.7 Summary

In this section, the orthographic structure and the phonological structure of words have been briefly considered, with a focus on the way in which orthography and phonology interact, and thus how the writing system represents phonemes. In all of this, the history of the language is of vital importance, since the relationship between orthography and phonology varies depending on the etymological source of the words concerned. Nevertheless, an understanding of the ways in which the orthography works can help with an understanding of how to write English or how to pronounce the written word. Since many of us meet words in writing that we do not normally meet in speech, the writing provides our only clue to the pronunciation, but has to be interpreted with care.

Exercises

1. Why was Shaw wrong about *ghoti* being a viable spelling of *fish*?
2. The presence or absence of /j/ before /uː/ distinguishes British and US standard forms of English, and also varieties within North America and within Britain. The rules are rather different in stressed and unstressed positions. Either by listening to speakers from different regions, or by consulting pronunciation dictionaries of British and North American varieties of English, see if you can discover when the /j/ is and is not pronounced. Consider the following words. Do the rules from these words generalise to other similar words?

   > abuse, chute, cute, dune, enthuse, gules, jute, lewd, music, new, nude, puke, rude, sue, tune, Zurich

3. Consult a pronunciation dictionary of English, and find two-syllable words, stressed on the first syllable and with an unstressed second syllable. What final consonant clusters do you find in unstressed syllables? (You should find a way to take a sample from the dictionary you consult, rather than trying to read the whole work. You might want to restrict yourself to clusters after /ə/.)

4. Why are some items parenthesised in (11) and (12)? Are they all parenthesised for the same reason? Are you familiar with the parenthesised words? Does this affect your evaluation of the examples?

5. If /sp/, /st/ and /sk/ are single consonants rather than consonant clusters in English, what are the benefits for the analysis of English, and what are the drawbacks?

6. If you are teaching a five-year-old (or an adult foreign learner) to read and write English, how should you deal with /ə/? What problems are you likely to face?

7. Look at the way <g> is pronounced before <i> and <e>. Has this been simplified in the text? If so, how? How would you advise a foreign learner of English to pronounce <g> in such contexts?

8. The letter <s> is sometimes pronounced as /s/ between vowels (for example, in *desiccate, beside*) and sometimes as /z/ (for example, in *design, resist*). Are there rules on how to pronounce it?

9. Find ten examples of a short, stressed vowel followed by a single consonant letter in English. Can you make any generalisations about why the vowel is not long in such cases?

10. Take a sentence of English and consider where the spelling is regular and where it is irregular.

Recommendations for reading

On lexical sets, see Wells (1982). On the pronunciation of English, in particular the pronunciation of RP, see Gimson (2001). For a detailed presentation of English spelling, see Carney (1994). For the pronunciation of individual words of English, see any of a number of pronunciation dictionaries, including Jones et al. (2002), Upton et al. (2001) and Wells (2008). For American English, Kenyon and Knott (1953) is still useful, though out of date, and it is particularly useful for variation within the US. The British pronunciation dictionaries often give information on American pronunciations, too. Ordinary dictionaries also provide information on pronunciation, but many of them do not provide the same amount of detail, or use idiosyncratic transcription systems.

6 Some puzzles in English words

6.1 Introduction

In this final chapter, several topics that have already been broached are revisited, with the aim of showing that there are aspects of English words about which we are still ignorant, despite many years of study. The choice of topics is determined largely by the author's personal interests and expertise; there are many other puzzles out there. In many cases, though, it is only when you consider the problems in some detail that the puzzles become apparent. The aim in this chapter is not to solve the puzzles, but to show why particular areas do not give rise to single, easily confirmable solutions. Solving any of these puzzles, assuming it can be done in ways that do not depend entirely on controversial theoretical assumptions, might have implications for other puzzles as well as providing better descriptions of small areas of English grammar. This chapter is, then, to phrase it differently, a call for further research into problems concerned with English words, which may have implications for studies of similar phenomena in other languages.

6.2 N+N where the first N is plural

The general rule for sticking two nouns together in English, whether they are written as one word or as two, is that the first, the modifying noun, occurs in the base form. Thus we have *book-shelf* (and not **books-shelf*), we have *mountain time* (and not **mountains time*), we have *toothbrush* (and not **teethbrush*).

So what are we to make of the fact that a *timetable* is not the same as a *times table*, that the alveolum is regularly called the *teeth-ridge*, and that people who sell weapons are called *arms dealers*? If these are nouns, and are plural, why are they plural, when are they made plural, and what is the difference between a singular and a plural noun in such constructions?

Let us begin with the question as to whether we are dealing with nouns. In most cases, there is no evidence to suggest otherwise, but in a few instances we can challenge this notion. Consider *times table*. The *times* in *times table* comes from *six times four is twenty-four* and other equivalent formulae. Although this is originally a plural noun (if you write four six times and add them all together, you will get twenty-four), it has arguably become a separate item. The *OED* calls *plus* and *minus* in mathematical formulae 'prepositions', and the same analysis might be applied to *times*. The final -*s* is part of this – it is *one times five*, not **one time five* – and there is a verb *to times*, which derives from the usage – *Now times that number by seven* – which implies that the final -*s* is not inflectional. In the light of this, we can argue that *times* in *times table* is not (or is no longer) a plural noun. This example is isolated, and there are few similar cases, but consider *downstairs toilet, indoors pool* (although *indoor pool* seems to be preferred, even though the final <s> is not a plural marker).

When we ask whether we are dealing with plurals, we have rather more obvious cases to deal with. First, we have a whole series of words which are marked as having a possessive in the modifier rather than a plural. This may sound just like a plural, but the orthography suggests otherwise. Some examples are given in (1).

(1)   bull's-eye
       cat's-eye
       dog's breakfast
       frog's-mouth
       hare's tail
       wolf's bane

If the forms in (1) illustrate the fact that we can find possessives in this position, the forms in (2) are less clear.

(2)   beeswax
       coltsfoot
       hogshead
       lambswool
       sportswear

These are written as though they are plural, but they seem to make better sense if they are possessive. *Menswear* must be genitive, even though it is not written with an apostrophe. Given how variably the apostrophe is used in the public domain, it would be dangerous to assume that any of these is a plural, although such an analysis cannot be conclusively ruled out. An interesting case is provided by *girl's school, girls school, girls' school* where the varying spellings (and we might add *girl school* to the list) illustrate writers' insecurity with the construction. Another class of exceptions is provided by expressions such as those in (3).

(3)   linguistics book
       mathematics tutorial
       phonetics laboratory
       physics lecturer
       radiophonics workshop

Although the modifiers here look like plural nouns, they are not plural. We cannot count *one mathematic, two mathematics*, we say *Phonetics is the study of speech sounds* and not **Phonetics are the study of speech sounds.* The final *-s* in these words has the function of making the base adjectives into nouns, not a function of pluralising nouns. The modifiers are nouns, but not plural ones. Note that even where there is an *-ic* noun which can be pluralised, as with *statistic*, there is rarely any doubt as to whether the noun with an *-s* is singular or plural.

These counter-examples still leave us with a host of cases which are clearly nouns and clearly plural. One comment that is often made about such instances is that it is easier for irregular plural forms to appear in such constructions than for regular plural forms. So, the claim goes, we can have *mice droppings*, but not **rats droppings.* While it is hard to show that *rats droppings* really is impossible (as opposed to extremely rare), it is certainly true that we can find *mice droppings*, and we can accept this statement as far as it goes. However, the purpose of this statement is to support a theoretical point about morphological theory, and it deserves some close scrutiny.

First, then, while we can find *mice* and *teeth* in modifying elements, it is a lot harder to find *feet* and *geese*: we have *footwear, foot warmers* and *footprints*, even where multiple feet are involved; a *goosegirl* used to look after lots of geese. While *men* and *women* can be used in the first elements of compounds, it is always when the compound is coordinative, and is plural: *one gentleman farmer, two gentlemen farmers, one woman doctor, two women doctors.* But it is still *two lady doctors*, and things like *boy geniuses* do not have plural first elements. When it comes to forms which are irregular but do not involve umlaut, the plural does not seem to be common at all: a *wolfhound* was bred to hunt *wolves*, a *thief-catcher* may catch many *thieves, leafmould* comes from the decay of multiple *leaves* and so on. In fact, even with *mice, mouse droppings* is a more usual expression than *mice droppings*, and *louse-infested* is more usual than *lice-infested* (this example has an adjectival head, but is the most obvious example of the use of *lice* as a modifier).

Even nouns which are inherently plural differ as to whether they keep their plural marking in modifying position. We find *gallows humour, innings defeat, mains water, measles epidemic, mews flat, people-mover* with apparently plural-marked modifiers, but *oat-meal, scissor-cut, staircase, troop-carrier, trouser-press, wage-earner* where the plural marker is apparently avoided. While it is true that it is in principle possible to distinguish *arms control* (involving weapons) from *arm control* (involving a limb) or *brains trust* (involving people) from *brain trust* (involving the organ) or *club house* (involving people in a club) from *clubs house* (involving playing cards), in practice most such cases sound forced and are unlikely to cause real misunderstanding.

Nevertheless, it does seem that some uses of final *-s* in modifiers have the function of specifying the lexeme involved. A *newspaper* would have to involve *news*, while a putative *newpaper* would not; a *savings account* unambiguously has a noun in the first element, not an adjective (although the pattern is not generalised); a *glasses case* is usefully different from a *glass case*, a *clothes basket* would not usually be a *cloth basket*, a *Commons debate* is not a *common debate*. Although it seems that such examples would provide a solid motivation for a construction with a plural modifier, they are not particularly frequent, and the unmarked modifier is found in apparently parallel instances such as *gut reaction, spirit level, stocking trade*.

In past generations, linguists had to rely upon their intuitions about the relative frequencies of constructions like these. Today we have access to large public corpora – computer-searchable bodies of text which allow an accurate picture of the way in which such modifiers are used. Accordingly, you are now in a position to check similar constructions for yourself.

It is often said that the *-s* in such cases is a genuine plural, and is used to show the multiple entities involved. Superficially, this is nonsense, in that there are any number of cases where a modifier with no plural marking refers to multiple entities. Consider, for example, *book-shelf* (holds many books), *car park* (does not park just one car), *flower garden* (contains lots of flowers), *microwave oven* (has more than one wave), *photograph album* (holds many photographs), and so on. In a few cases, we might even argue that there is an *-s* with no plural meaning: does a *sportsman* necessarily play more than one sport, or a *craftsman* master more than one craft? However, if we look at genuine examples of usage, we begin to notice some correlation. The examples in (4) all come from the British National Corpus (BNC – Davies 2004).

(4) burns unit
     careers office
     claims court
     contents page
     drugs problem
     loans fund
     records management
     resources development
     roads programme
     schools council
     trades unions

It is noticeable that in all of these examples there is a case to be made that the plural meaning in the first element is intended. If we contrast this with the same words without plural marking, we get the examples in (5), again from the BNC.

(5) burn marks
     career development
     claim form
     content word
     drug trafficking
     loan agreement
     record company
     resource management
     road accident
     school meals
     trade union

Trades union and *trade union* appear to be synonymous. Although *drugs* often means 'illegal drugs' while *drug* often means 'legal drug', that is not the case here, where illegal drugs are involved in both examples. There is a semantic difference between *record* and *records*, and between *content* and *contents*. In the other cases, either it is not clear from the isolated example whether a single entity is involved or whether there are multiple entities, or it is clear that a single entity is involved (a *loan agreement* probably involves a single loan, for example). So while a non-plural form in the first element does not necessarily imply that only one entity is involved, a plural first element does seem to imply that more than one entity is involved.

While it may make sense to have a construction which confirms the importance of plurality in the first element, it is less obvious why we would need this when the older construction allows for precisely that interpretation. Moreover, most of the scholars who have considered this construction are of the view that it has been increasing during the last century or so. While it is not unusual to see a common construction becoming rarer, the increase in a rare construction seems to require some justification. Of course, it happens, or we could never gain new constructions. The question is what it brings to English speakers that makes it increasingly used. This is particularly important since the unmarked first element remains more common, and since we occasionally find (as with *trade(s) union* above) apparently synonymous pairs with or without a plural-marked modifier.

We have no real answer to such questions. We can speculate that the few well-established examples that appeared to have a plural *-s* in the first element allowed for the structure, and the structure was then used precisely when the plurality of the first noun was unchallenged. We can suggest that the confusion between plural and possessive marking made the apparently plural first element a larger set than it might otherwise have been. But overall, this construction remains something of a puzzle because it is so unpredictable.

6.3 Comparatives and superlatives

6.3.1 Two puzzles

In (6) there is a sentence with a gap for an adjective to be inserted.

(6)   Buildings like this are _____ than you might think.

If the adjective is *big*, you will probably insert *bigger*; if the adjective is *important*, you will probably insert *more important*; if the adjective is *common*, you may be in doubt as to whether to insert *commoner* or *more common*. So straightaway there are two puzzles here. The first is that something that appears to be morphological in some circumstances appears to be syntactic in others; that is, comparison can be marked within the word (in which case we talk about synthetic or morphological marking) or in a separate word (in which case we talk about analytic or periphrastic or syntactic marking). The second puzzle is how we know when to use morphological marking and when to use syntactic marking.

The answer to the second puzzle is that we don't know, but it raises all kinds of questions for the way in which we use language.

The first puzzle is a puzzle for how we organise grammars. There seems to be a general assumption in linguistics that there is a firm boundary between morphology and syntax, and there is a well-established theoretical position, called **lexicalism**, that rules in the syntax cannot affect things in the morphology or use morphological information to inform the way the syntax works. For example, no syntactic rule can be of the form 'if the noun is a derivative, do X, but if it is morphologically simple, do Y'. Comparative marking challenges this position, because it seems to imply a rule that says 'if *common* is not already marked for comparative in the morphology, then add *more*'. Comparatives are not the only challenge to lexicalism (or to variants of lexicalism), but they exemplify the situation nicely.

Having categories which are sometimes marked morphologically and sometimes marked syntactically is not particularly rare. In French (and several other Indo-European languages) tense/aspect is sometimes marked within the word (synthetically) and sometimes by using a sequence of words (analytically). For example, the difference between French *chantait* ('he/she/it was singing') and *a chanté* ('he/she/it sang') illustrates this, and, incidentally, reflects a similar situation in English. We must, then, accept a situation where a similar or the same category is marked analytically and periphrastically in the same language; the puzzle is how to deal with this within a linguistic theory. That question goes well beyond the remit of this book.

The puzzle of how we know whether to express the comparative analytically or periphrastically, on the other hand, is one that looks as though it belongs in this book. It turns out to be extremely complex.

6.3.2 *Factors influencing morphological and syntactic use*

If you look up the answer in a basic grammar of English for foreigners, you will probably find a generalisation to the effect that three-syllable adjectives or longer ones take *more* (*most* in the superlative), that monosyllabic adjectives take *-er* (*-est* in the superlative) and that there is variation among disyllabic adjectives. As a very rough guide to help with production, this is a good start. As a description of how speakers actually use these, it is clearly inaccurate. It does suggest that an important factor in deciding which method to use to mark the comparative is the phonological length of the adjective (whether of the base adjective or of the suffixed adjective is less clear). We will see that there are other factors which play a role.

To illustrate the inaccuracy of this overall statement, consider the examples in (7), all of which come from the BNC.

(7) I am the unhappiest creature in the world
'Curiouser and curiouser,' she said. 'What strange goings-on.[']

> I'm the most beautifulest girl in the world!
> More bright in zeal than the devotion
> She says it is more bad to be frightened than to die.
> the closer he came the more sure she was that this was her husband

But even if the syllable-based generalisation were correct, it leaves wide open the question of what influences the variation in disyllabic adjectives. Here there are a number of factors, and the discussion below will only scrape the surface of the possible factors. Rather than aim for exhaustiveness, the description here will try to show just how different the factors involved can be.

Some of the factors are phonological. Consider the question of where the stress falls in the disyllabic adjective. It can fall either on the first or on the last syllable, and where it falls seems to make a difference. To illustrate this, the frequencies in the BNC for the comparative and superlative forms of ten adjectives of each type are given in (8) and (9).

(8)   *BNC frequencies for comparison marking on end-stressed adjectives*

Adjective	-er	-est	more	most
benign	0	0	21	5
concise	0	0	17	1
correct	0	0	30	8
hirsute	0	0	0	0
humane	0	0	48	4
intense	3	2	164	74
polite	5	13	23	9
profound	11	15	107	42
remote	78	71	174	40
sincere	1	11	11	12
	98	112	595	195

With final-stressed adjectives, 79 per cent of the comparative or superlative forms are periphrastic.

(9)   *BNC frequencies for comparison marking on initially stressed adjectives*

Adjective	-er	-est	more	most
busy	96	222	8	3
clever	74	48	20	1
friendly	50	30	68	10
narrow	415	76	13	2
porous	0	0	6	0
savage	0	0	10	27
secret	0	0	12	29
simple	944	969	60	27

stupid	7	16	17	13
stylish	0	0	13	15
	1,586	1,361	227	127

With the adjectives that have initial-syllable stress, 10.7 per cent of the comparative and superlative forms use the periphrastic form. These numbers are suspect: they are based on only ten examples of each type, and there is huge variation between the individual types (the number of synthetic examples for *simple* alone might throw out the numbers); and, indeed, some other surveys have reached the contrary result. Nevertheless, this is sufficient to suggest that stress placement in the adjective may be one relevant factor.

Final consonants may also have an effect. Although the BNC has multiple examples of *more modest* and *most modest*, it has no examples of *modestest*. This might look like a case of haplology, where *estest* is disallowed because of the repetition of consonants, but two things suggest that it is not. The first is that the BNC has two examples of *honestest* (admittedly, a small number, but enough to suggest that it is not impossible) and the second is that the BNC has no hits for *modester* (nor for *honester* or *unjuster*), where haplology cannot be the answer. Since no affix is involved here, whatever is limiting the use of -*er* and -*est* here seems to be phonological (although there are so few disyllabic, gradable adjectives ending in -*st* that it is hard to be sure).

Certainly, the suffix in disyllabic adjectives (where there are suffixes) can be influential. Consider disyllabics ending in -*y*. We can distinguish at least three different types: those where -*y* is part of the base, and not an affix, those where -*y* is itself an affix, and those where the -*y* is part of an -*ly* affix. If, again, we try to look at the numbers for small data-sets from the BNC, we find the answers in (10)–(12).

(10) *Comparison markers for adjectives where -y is not part of a suffix*

Adjective	-er	-est	more	most
busy	96	222	8	3
empty	11	6	3	1
happy	872	290	14	27
heavy	789	246	5	1
holy	13	24	4	11
pretty	85	101	4	0
ready	24	6	54	1
silly	15	24	1	0
sorry	17	3	13	2
ugly	29	42	3	5
	1,951	964	109	51

(11) *Comparison markers for adjectives where -y is a suffix*

Adjective	-er	-est	more	most
bloody	7	37	2	1
crazy	18	19	2	0
dirty	43	44	0	0
funny	54	117	6	0
handy	13	0	1	1
healthy	379	42	26	8
lazy	9	11	1	1
noisy	26	21	6	2
sticky	6	9	5	0
sunny	20	17	1	0
	575	317	50	13

(12) Comparison markers for adjectives where -y is part of the suffix -ly

Adjective	-er	-est	more	most
costly	14	27	87	17
cowardly	0	0	1	1
friendly	50	30	68	10
heavenly	0	0	0	2
likely	16	41	3,688	1,383
lively	59	42	46	13
lonely	0	0	7	4
lovely	32	89	7	20
orderly	0	0	20	1
prickly	1	0	0	1
	172	229	3,924	1,452

Again, variability between individual adjectives is the major finding (and again, this means that a sample of ten adjectives is probably too few to be anything more than suggestive), but it seems that *-ly* adjectives are more likely (!) to take periphrastic comparison than the other two types, and that synthetic comparison is more likely where *-y* is not a suffix than where it is. Suffixation matters.

As another piece of evidence that some of the restrictions are morphological, consider the comparative of adjectives in *-ous*. The only adjective found in the BNC that forms its comparative in this way is *curious*, and that is a literary joke from Lewis Carroll. Examples like the ones in (13) are thus particularly noteworthy.

(13) You're already rich and famous, [...] and you're going to be richer and famouser. (Lawrence Block (2003), *Small Town*, London: Orion, p. 335)

"I've been up for three hours, nervouser than a nun at a penguin shoot," she said. (John Sandford (2007), *Golden Prey*, New York: Putnam, p. 19)

Such examples show that you cannot expect to find total predictability in the use of periphrastic or synthetic comparatives, but also make the point that in this particular instance, the use of the synthetic comparative is extremely unusual, and when it arises indicates some non-serious goal on the part of the user.

Sometimes the restrictions may be syntactic, though this is harder to show with just a few examples. It seems that adjectives submodified by, for example, *apparently, even, rather, supposedly* and so on are more likely to take comparison with *more* than they would be in other constructions. Of course, the other types of restriction still hold sway, so that *rather more likely* is probably preferred to *rather likelier* just because *more likely* is preferred to *likelier* (although both can be found in either construction). That is why broad conclusions cannot be drawn on the basis of small amounts of data.

On top of all this, there are probably dialectal differences and personal differences. There are certainly differences determined by what is in the preceding context. If you have just heard a lot of *more* forms, you are more likely to use a *more* form (assuming it to be possible) than if you have just heard a lot of *-er* forms.

This indicates just how complex the whole area is, and why simple rules for the use of the two types of form cannot be given. Perhaps more surprising, it seems to be assumed in most (though not all) of the research

- that superlatives work just like comparatives
- that different speakers use the same factors to determine the form of comparative or superlative marking
- that the same rules apply to the same adjective in all its meanings (that is, the rules apply to, say, *remote*, independent of whether it occurs in *remote areas* or *remote cousin* or *remote behaviour*).

Because superlatives overall tend to be rarer than comparatives, and because *most A* can have so many different meanings (compare *the most remote island I have ever visited, that is a most remote possibility, most remote islands are quite small* where an *-est* form is possible in only the first of the three constructions), studies of superlatives tend to be relatively little undertaken and less reliable.

The implications of all this are enormous. If all these factors (and, indeed, others not mentioned here) can influence the choice of comparative or superlative marker, how do speakers learn which to use when? We can probably provide a mathematical model of the interplay of the factors, but does that mean that speakers (however numerate or innumerate they may feel themselves to be) are closet statisticians in their language use, keeping track of these various factors and calculating the form to use on any given occasion? Alternatively, might it be the case that speakers do not know about all these factors, and actually react to a much smaller set? It could certainly be the case that speakers produce output which appears to show the influence of all these factors even though they themselves are actually using some different method for determining which form to use, a method which we perhaps are as yet unaware of. The major puzzle here is a psycholinguistic one – how do speakers cope with such complex variation?

6.4 Coordinative compounds

There are multiple types of coordinative compounds in English, and yet some of those that are most common elsewhere in the world are almost entirely missing. They give rise to three major questions: what types can we distinguish (and is distinguishing them helpful)? Are they compounds? How are they different from those blends which also have coordinative semantics? We will consider these in order.

6.4.1 What types can we distinguish?

What unites coordinative compounds is that the two (sometimes more) elements are equivalent. We shall see that even this is difficult to be sure about sometimes. We can find coordinative compounds which are nouns, verbs or adjectives. Some of these may be considered to belong to the same types, some types are restricted to a given word-class. Most coordinative compounds in English are nouns, and we will start with those. One of the most important types of coordinative compound in other languages (usually called by the Sanskrit name dvandva) is the type where words denoting two distinct entities are coordinated to denote the sum of the two. Thus, in languages which have this type, we typically find words like *sheep-goats* (meaning 'sheep and goats') or *father-son* (meaning 'father and son' as a social unit). English has such types mainly with proper names, as in (14), although *murder-suicide* seems to fit the category.

(14) a. HarperCollins,   Mercedes-Benz,   Mouton   de   Gruyter,
      Times-Warner

    b. Alsace-Lorraine, Budapest, Minneapolis-Saint Paul, Nelson-Marlborough, Schleswig-Holstein

In the set in (14a) we find names which belong to firms which have merged with each other. In the set in (14b) we find place-names. Many of these are loans in English, but in New Zealand English there are several examples, including *Otago-Southland*, and *Napier-Hastings*. It is not clear why this pattern should be more prominent in New Zealand than elsewhere. We might also consider 'double-barrelled' surnames such as *Fotherington-Smythe* to belong to this category.

Much more common in English are coordinatives where the two elements name different aspects of the same entity. Some examples are in (15).

(15) a. boy genius, gentleman farmer, manservant, servant girl, woman doctor
      b. bull elephant, dog fox, hen pheasant, tom cat
      c. dinner-dance, fighter-bomber, fridge-freezer, houseboat, penny-farthing, sofa-bed, tractor-trailer, washer-drier
      d. director-producer, hunter-gatherer, lawyer-accountant, owner-occupier, painter-poet, singer-songwriter
      e. cod fish, collie dog, elm tree, widow woman
      f. bull-mastiff, collie-shepherd, south-west

In (15a) we have a number of examples where the main function of one of the nouns seems to be to mark gender. *Servant girl* is extraordinary in this set, because we might expect *girl servant* (compare *maidservant*).

In (15b) we have equivalent terms for non-humans. Many scholars see these as a separate type, similar to adjective + noun compounds rather than to noun + noun compounds – a view which goes back to the Sanskrit grammarians. The only difficulty with this view is in determining the borders of the category. For example, it may not be clear whether the words in (15e) should also be seen as part of this set.

In (15c) we have single entities that are named by two of their parts or functions. A *fridge-freezer* has two separate parts, a fridge part and a freezer part, and the whole is named by these two major constituents; a *washer-drier* has two functions, which may be carried out in the same (part of the) machine. *Fighter-bomber* and *houseboat* are less clear members of the set. *House* and *boat* can be seen as the two functions of a *houseboat*, or it could be seen as a boat which is distinguished by resembling – or possibly having some of the functions of – a house (in which case it is not coordinative). These two classifications may be found in the literature. A *fighter-bomber* might be seen as a plane which fulfils the two functions named, or it could be seen, like *bull-mastiff* in (15f), as a hybrid between the two types.

The examples in (15d) are all labels for people, and all name two different functions that these people carry out – those functions are, typically, jobs, but a form like *mother-innkeeper* where *mother* is not a job in the same sense, would also be possible, or *chess player-philatelist* where the functions are (probably) hobbies. Compounds of this type are often called **appositional compounds**, though it is not clear that apposition is involved.

The examples in (15e) are often called **tautological compounds**, because every cod is a fish, so that once we have called it a *cod*, the word *fish* is tautological. While *widows* were not always female by definition, today they are, so that *widow woman* seems to fit into the set.

The last set in (15f) are hybrids, and denote something that is neither of the creatures named, but a cross between them. It is an oddity of English that we seem to prefer blends for such cases, so that *labradoodle* is more typical name for a cross-breed than *collie-(German) shepherd*. We call a cross between a zebra and a horse a *zorse*, and usually use *zebra-horse* in a phrase such as *zebra-horse hybrid*, where it functions as an attributive.

In some of these cases, subdivisions of the sets have been proposed, but we do not really need a finer division than that presented in (14) and (15) to illustrate something of the complexity associated with coordinative compounds. To these we can add the types in (16) where, although two nouns are coordinated, the compounds appear to be used exclusively in attributive position (and are thus sometimes considered to be adjectives).

(16)   a.   Arab-Israeli conflict, father-daughter dance (esp. US English), love-hate relationship, patient-doctor interaction

      b.   Dutch-English dictionary, London-Paris flight, subject-verb agreement

Examples like those in (16a) are sometimes called **co-participant compounds**, and those in (16b) are called **translative compounds**.

Some of these types can also be found among adjectives and verbs, too, though it is often controversial whether these examples are really coordinative. Adjectives are illustrated in (17), verbs in (18).

(17)   a.   philosophical-historical, red-hot, shabby-genteel

      b.   blue-green, medium-rare

      c.   manic-depressive, passive-aggressive

(18) a. blow-dry, drop-kick, fly-drive, freeze-dry, shrink-wrap, sleep-walk, strip-search, stir-fry

    b. go-go, pass-fail, stop-go, stop-start, win-win

Note that *shabby-genteel* seems to mean 'genteel though shabby', *manic-depressive* seems to show alternating states (rather than the presence of both simultaneously), and that the examples in (18b) are used attributively. The examples in (18a) are not all the same, but we can argue as to whether *freeze-dry* means 'to freeze and dry' or 'to dry by freezing' (similarly *blow-dry* and *stir-fry*). *Drop-kick* and *fly-drive* both seem to mean two distinct actions, adjacent in time, which together make up a new one, whereas *sleep-walk* has the two actions occurring simultaneously.

6.4.2 Are they compounds?

Although the relevant items have been termed 'compounds' here, and that is the most usual analysis, there is a minority point of view according to which these are simply coordinated elements, and that coordination is always syntactic. So just as we can coordinate without an overt coordinator elsewhere in syntax (this is called **asyndetic coordination**), as in *She wore a warm red coat, They are pigs, swine,* comparable to *She wore a warm and red coat, They are pigs or swine,* so we can have *We bought a new fridge-freezer* or *We bought a new fridge and freezer.*

There are at least two pieces of evidence that they might be compounds. The first is that many of them are item-familiar fixed expressions, which we do not expect ordinary coordinated items to be. *You are a coward and a blackguard* sounds like two different accusations; *you are a coward-blackguard* sounds odd, because we do not recognise it as a fixed expression, perhaps because we do not recognise it as a category of people. The counter-evidence to this suggestion is that at least the category in (15d) does seem to be rather freely extendable: *scholar-athlete, nerd-genius, painter-writer-musician, doctor-screenwriter* are attested examples; if double-barrelled surnames belong in this category, then they are freely available; and adjectives like those in (17a) can easily be multiplied, as when Polonius lists various types of play including those in (19).

(19) pastoral-comical, historical-pastoral, tragical-historical, tragical-comical-historical-pastoral (William Shakespeare, *Hamlet,* II.ii)

The second piece of evidence concerns the order of the elements. In syntax, *A man and a dog walked down the lane* is equivalent to *A dog and a man walked down the lane:* the order is not significant. That being the case, if these forms are syntactic, we might expect to find *songwriter-singer* as easily as *singer-songwriter*. While this is true in some instances (*philosophical-historical* is probably equivalent to *historical-philosophical*, and *boy-toy* and *toy-boy* are both found with the same meaning), most of the examples have a fixed order. This may be related to the notion of head. Syntactic coordination is usually assumed not to be headed: neither *red* nor *warm* is the head of the adjective phrase in *warm red coat*. But at least some of the types presented here behave as though they may be headed, and the fixed order is one of the things that shows this. On the other hand, it is not necessarily clear what the head will be. If these are compounds and behave like other compounds (indeed, like most word-formation in English), we would expect the head to be the rightmost element. But is a *lawyer-accountant* basically a lawyer, basically an accountant, or really someone who balances both professions equally? Would an *accountant-lawyer* be different? If one of your lecturers augments their salary by singing in a pub, are they a *lecturer-singer* or a *singer-lecturer* or either? Speakers may have clear intuitions on such matters (which may or may not agree with what linguists expect).

6.4.3 *How do they differ from coordinative blends?*

We have already seen that speakers seem to prefer blends to coordinative compounds for the names of hybrids, at least of animals. This seems to be a relatively recent trend. We have words like *mule* and *hinny* for hybrids which are traditionally important, and *cockerpoo* (which is a clipping compound, not a blend) is an example of a more recent one. Nevertheless, the blend seems to dominate these days. However, another novel trend is for the elements in such blends not to be randomly ordered. The difference between a *tigon* and a *liger* is which is the sire and which is the dam (sire first, dam second), a *cama* is a hybrid between a male camel and a female llama, a *leopon* is a hybrid between a male leopard and a lioness. This seems to be imposing headedness on a pattern which was once considered non-headed (so a *beefalo* is not necessarily from a male domestic bull and a female buffalo). That does not mean that it is easy to know which element is the head. And blends are found even where male and female are not relevant, and where headedness cannot be determined by the same rule, as with *citrange, peacherine, plumcot, tangelo*. Again, note that older words like *ugli fruit* ('hybrid of grapefruit and tangerine'), *loganberry* ('hybrid of raspberry and American dewberry') do not use blends.

This might suggest that coordinative compounds and coordinative blends divide up the territory between them, each having its own domain. And it seems that a *singer-songwriter* cannot be a **singwriter*. But we do have the term *foolosopher*. The question is, is that a coordination of *fool* and *philosopher* like *painter-poet*, or is it a hybrid between *fool* and *philosopher* like *peacherine*? And, crucially, can we tell the difference between these two analyses non-circularly?

To complicate matters further, note that there are two further constructions which have similar semantics. The first is illustrated by *kitchen-cum-dining room*. There is no apparent reason why this could not be a coordinative compound, but the element *cum* (a preposition borrowed from Latin, where it means 'with') seems to be just as natural. While the spelling seems to suggest that *kitchen-cum-dining room* is a lexical item (or a morphologically constructed word), it might also be considered as a piece of syntax, although *cum* does not seem to be used to coordinate complete phrases like *the best man, really rather stupid* or *kill a mockingbird*: that is, we do not seem to find **the best man cum the brother of the bride* (although we could replace *cum* in this with *and*, or it would be fine if we omitted the second *the*).

The second of these extra constructions is overt conjunction. Consider the example in (20), where *cum* does not seem possible, but a coordinative compound might be.

(20) a utilitarian concrete-and-glass building (Matthew Palmer (2015), *Secrets of State*, New York: Putnam, p. 40)

It seems unlikely that each of these constructions applies to unique non-overlapping domains. At the moment, though, we do not know what the preferred domains for each of these constructions is, where they can overlap and where they do not. This is the same problem that arises in several places: when do we use a compound, when do we use an adjective + noun construction; when do we use a blend, when do we use a compound; when do we use fore-stress on an adjective + noun construction and when do we use end-stress? Such questions provide a research programme for some time to come.

6.5 Changes without changes of form

If we look across languages, it is the normal pattern for major changes in bases to be signalled by affixes. Consider changes to word-class, for instance. In English there are many affixes (especially suffixes) whose major job seems to be to indicate what word-class a particular word is to be interpreted as having. If we start with the noun *form*, we can make it an adjective by adding *-al*, then make that adjective a verb by adding *-ise*, and then make that verb a noun by adding *-ation* or make the adjective *formal* a noun by adding *-ity*. What is more, although some suffixes carry their own clear meaning, the major function of an affix like *-al* seems to be to indicate the word-class rather than to add to the meaning. Deviations from this pattern are not unknown, but are relatively rare. For instance, in many Polynesian languages it seems misleading to say that any word belongs to a particular word-class; rather, the word-class is determined by the syntactic pattern in which the word arises. If it is in subject position, it is a noun; if it modifies a subject, it is an adjective; if it is marked for tense/aspect, it is a verb. English is rather different (although perhaps less so than some other languages). The word *parental* is an adjective, the word *personalise* is a verb, and often the same can be said of words that have no affix determining word-class. For example, *big* is an adjective, *come* is a verb and *woman* is a noun.

In such a situation, it is surprising to find that there are many processes which seem to link words of identical form but belonging to different word-classes or with clearly distinguishable meaning or functions. Yet English has several such instances. They are often given different names, partly depending on whether they are viewed as syntactic or morphological processes, partly depending on the theoretical perspective that is taken to them. They share a semantic or functional purpose and the lack of affixation.

We will first look at the various instances, and then ask how they differ from each other. Part of the puzzle here is that they should exist at all – why not use affixes? Part of the puzzle is why there should be so many similar processes, linking homophonous forms.

6.5.1 Nouns and verbs

To distinguish homonymous nouns and verbs, either the noun will be preceded by the indefinite article and the verb by *to* or, equivalently, the words will be marked by a closing bracket and a word-class tag, thus: *mark*]ᵥ.

Some examples of corresponding homonymous nouns and verbs are given in (21), where the examples are of different types.

(21) a collapse   to collapse
      a go   to go
      an impact   to impact
      a love   to love

The example of *love* in (21) arises in a different way from the other examples, in that it comes about because of the loss of inflections in Old English, which led to the noun and the verb forms being homophonous.

Some authorities like to keep this type distinct from the other types, on the basis of the historical difference, but the distinction is invisible in modern English, and examples like *love* will be treated on a par with examples like *collapse* here. The difference between *go* and *impact* is that speakers probably have a feeling that *a go* (as in *have a go*) is derived from the verb, while the verb *to impact* is felt by many to be derived from the noun. With *collapse*, it may not be clear which comes first. It is not entirely clear to what extent the difference matters, nor to what extent we can be sure whether the historical process is from noun to verb or from verb to noun. The use of an original noun as a verb often gives rise to prescriptive opprobrium (as with the case of *to impact*). As Bill Watterson's Calvin says to Hobbes, 'verbing weirds language'. The use of an original verb as a noun seems to raise fewer hackles, although it is not very long since talk of *a long commute* was considered odd.

To the extent that the direction of change can be deduced, it is usually taken that the definition of the derived form assumes the base form, so that $panic]_V$ can be usefully glossed as 'to show panic', but $panic]_N$ would not usually be glossed as 'the result of panicking'. It is also generally assumed that the base form is the more frequent. Where etymological information is available, the date of first attestation of each use of the form may also provide relevant information, although the information is subject to the vicissitudes of collecting appropriate forms throughout the history of English. Where these factors agree, directionality can be assumed; it is often the case that they do not.

6.5.2 Nouns and adjectives

There are various types of overlap between nouns and adjectives, of which three main ones will be given here.

The first of these is the use of an adjective with a definite article, as in *the good, the bad and the ugly, the rich and famous, the poor are an embarrassment to the state*. This construction is not possible with the indefinite article (**a good, a bad and an ugly*), nor can it take a plural marker. Where such adjectives take plural agreement, people are denoted: *The good are undervalued.* Where singular agreement is found, a quality and not a person is denoted: *The good is oft interred with their bones.* Although this type of construction is widely available, and is reflected by comparable constructions in many Indo-European languages, it is not universally acceptable. For the French poet, *L'important c'est la rose* ('the important is the rose'), but in English we would have to say *The important thing is the rose.*

The second construction is shown by adjectives such as *daily, digestive, intellectual.* These adjectives can occur in any noun phrase, with pre- or post-modification, and with any determiner, and the forms can have a plural form, as in (22).

(22) The dailies were delivered to the door.
      This sweet digestive sat on her plate.
      A famous intellectual of international standing addressed the meeting.

The third type is rather more controversial. Here the basic form looks like a noun, but it is used attributively to modify another noun and may sometimes be used predicatively as well. Consider the word *steel*. Although this is basically a noun, it can occur in expressions like those in (23).

(23) a steel trap
      The door is steel.

The difficulty with such examples is that N+N constructions have previously been called compounds (see Section 2.3) and we do not want to have two descriptions for the same expression. The borderlines are hard to draw, if a distinction is to be made. *Crocodile tears* is probably a compound, but in *a crocodile handbag, crocodile* may be an adjective and some dictionaries describe the modifiers in *alligator clip* and *crocodile clip* (which mean the same thing) differently.

In any case, it is not clear that anything that is used attributively is, by that very fact, an adjective. Consider the examples in (24); it is not clear that we need to analyse the modifiers in these examples as adjectives rather than as adverbs, prepositions and phrases. They certainly do not behave like stereotypical adjectives: they are not gradable, they cannot be compared, they do not have predicative usage.

(24) a don't-look-at-me-in-that-tone-of-voice glare
      an off moment
      our before-tax profit
      the down train
      the downstairs bathroom
      the then king

With constructions like *a hard-won victory* it is not clear whether we should treat *hard-won* as a syntactic construction or whether we should treat *hard-won* as an adjective, presumably created by a process of word-formation. All this says that, although we may be sure that we have a class of adjectives in English, the borders of the class are extremely fuzzy, and correspondingly, it is hard to say whether things which have some but not all of the features of adjectives should be classed as adjectives or not.

6.5.3 Adjectives and verbs

There are several ways of making causative verbs from adjectives in English, including those illustrated in *broaden, domesticate, enliven, enrich, falsify, realise*. But the causative verb corresponding to the adjective *empty* is *to empty*. The same is true with *calm, dirty, smooth, soundproof, waterproof*. Intransitive verbs can also be homophonous with an adjective, as with *dry, narrow, yellow*. *To dry* and *to empty* can be intransitive or transitive.

6.5.4 Adjectives and adverbs

Although there are many adverbs which are basic words with that function (words like *here, not, now, then, there*), the general rule in English is that adverbs of manner are derived from adjectives by the use of the *-ly* suffix. It is virtually automatic that an adjective has a corresponding *-ly* adverb; there are thousands of them. Accordingly, it is more interesting when this system breaks down. For example, though *hardly, lately, really, roughly, scarcely* seem to be adverbs formed from adjectives, the meaning is not appropriate (or at least, is not appropriate in their most usual readings).

One of the problems for the analyst is that we have, in English, a number of forms which, even if the meanings do not always agree, can function as adjectives and adverbs. These include the examples in (25).

(25) *Adjective*   *Adverb*
    a hard floor   It hit him hard.
    a just decision   She just showed up one morning.
    as pretty as a picture   That was pretty stupid.
    his late wife   He arrived late.
    She drives a fast car.   She drives fast.
    the jolly sailor   He looked jolly stupid.
    an upstairs room   They went upstairs. (Compare (24) above)
    the wrong idea   She did it wrong.

Not all speakers have the same set of words that can be either adverbs or adjectives. Some that vary are illustrated in (26).

(26) *Adjective*   *Adverb*
    a daily limit of two   We see these things daily.
    tablets
    a friendly hug   She hugged me friendly.
    a leisurely stroll   They strolled leisurely along the promenade.
    a quick trip   Kiss me quick!

6.5.5 Nouns, verbs and adjectives

One particularly problematic set of data relates to forms in *-ing*. In sentences like *I am driving to Edinburgh*, the *-ing* form is usually treated as a verb. In sentences like *My driving has improved since I took the lessons*, *driving* is seen as a noun. In sentences like *The driving rain soon soaked through my clothes*, *driving* is often seen as an adjective. In the grammar of Classical Greece and Rome, these forms were seen as participles, and of a different word-class from either noun or verb (Greek and Roman grammar did not recognise a category of adjective). Where, as is usual today, participles are seen as forms of verbs, there is, at least, a problem of description. What is clear, though, is that *driving* in *driving lesson* and *driving* in *driving rain* belong to different word-classes (and that difference is reflected in the difference in stress in the two expressions: stress on *driving* in *driving lesson*, stress on *rain* in *driving rain*), and that each is related somehow to a form of a verb.

Similarly, but in not such a complicated fashion, the form *shared* in *They shared their meal with us* and *shared* in *We enjoyed a shared meal* are distinguished as verb and adjective. Again, the same form appears to belong to separate word-classes.

6.5.6 Nouns and more nouns

Any proper name can be used as a common noun, though in English these are still written with an initial capital letter, which makes them look like names. Some examples are given in (27). (See also the examples in Section 1.2.)

(27)   I don't know any Benedicts.
        That wasn't the Elizabeth I meant.
        There's a Paris in France and another in Texas.
        We need another Churchill.
        All the Smiths have those startling green eyes.

Although it is traditional in English dictionaries for foreign learners to divide nouns into countable and uncountable, there are very few nouns which can be used as one but not as the other. The difference between the two types is set out in (28) using *cat* as a countable noun and *knowledge* as an uncountable noun.

(28)   *cat   knowledge
        two cats   *two knowledges
        many cats, *much cat   much knowledge, *many knowledges
        *some (/səm/) cat   some (/səm/) knowledge

Until relatively recently, we could have added *a number of cats, an amount of knowledge*, but these days people often use *amount of* with countables.

However, there are many words which are standardly used both ways, so that *cake, two cakes, many cakes, much cake, some cake* are all perfectly normal (and the same would be true with *beer, cheese, potato, wine* and a host of other words). But most nouns that are uncountable can be made countable if they are used to mean 'types of ~', For example, *bread* is often said to be uncountable, and *loaf* countable, but *In the supermarket they had dozens of breads* with *bread* used countably is perfectly normal. Equally, if you can imagine anything being used as food, it is possible to use it uncountably: in a child's story about termites, it would be normal to have one termite asking another if they would like some chair, or how much chair they would like for dinner. So just about any countable noun can be used uncountably and vice versa. If they cannot (and *knowledge* is an example of word which it is hard to use countably), it is because of the semantic peculiarity of the notion, rather than because it is bad grammar.

6.5.7 *Verbs and more verbs*

Only a few verbs are overtly marked for the difference between transitive and intransitive: *lie* and *lay, rise* and *raise* are corresponding intransitive and transitive pairs (see Section 2.5.1). Occasionally, distinct verbs are used for the intransitive and transitive, as in *The crops died, They killed the crops.* Most verbs are not marked for transitivity (sometimes called 'causativity'), as is illustrated in (29).

(29) *Intransitive*   *Transitive*
      We can walk to the park.   We can walk the dog in the park.
      I can't see.   I can't see the mountains.
      Children just grow.   We grow our own tomatoes.
      The building collapsed.   They collapsed the tent.
      The fire is smoking.   We will smoke the herrings.
      The balloon burst.   She burst the balloon.

Not all verbs can be intransitive or transitive (*arrive* is not standardly used as a transitive verb, *consume* is not standardly used as an intransitive). But where both uses are found, it is typically the case that the verb keeps the same form. Similarly, ditransitive verbs are not specifically marked, as shown in (30).

(30) *Transitive*   *Ditransitive*
      He got his Master's from Bristol.   He got me the information I'd
                                            asked for.

      She found some mushrooms.   She found me some clothes.
      They gave a great performance.   They gave him a round of
                                            applause.
      The job offers prospects.   They offered her a scholarship.

Ditransitive usage is much rarer than transitive usage, and is not
always predictable, but it is not specifically marked, so that intransitive,
transitive and ditransitive verbs can be homophonous, and do not differ
in their inflections.

6.5.8 Adjectives and more adjectives

While typical adjectives are gradable (so that we can not only have
big, but *bigger, very big* and so on), others are not, so that **dentaller, *more
dental, *very dental* are, if not totally impossible, very unlikely. However,
adjectives which we would normally consider non-gradable are sometimes used in constructions which indicate gradability. Some examples
are given in (31).

(31) She's more French than the French.
      He was more dead than alive.
      I've never met a more married man.
      They moved with utterly feline grace.

6.5.9 Prepositions and other things

Occasionally we find prepositions (possibly adverbs) with the same form
as words which may be of different word-classes. Examples are in (32).

(32) *Preposition*   *Other word-classes*
      She walked down the slope.   He downed a beer.
                                            a down payment (compare (24)
                                            above)
                                            They've got a down on me.
                                            Put it down!
      She walked round the table.   They rounded the corner.
                                            theatre in the round
                                            knights of the round table
                                            They glanced round.

Not all prepositions show the same range of uses, not even basic prepositions, and there are many gaps, but the patterns are possible.

6.5.10 Use and mention

The words *if* and *but* are conjunctions of different types, and when used in sentences they occur in that function, as in *If you call, he'll come, but he won't come willingly*. However, in sentences like *I want no ifs or buts*, or *But me no buts*, *if* and *but* are cited or mentioned rather than used. Linguists would usually put such items in italics, to indicate this status (see Section 1.1). Mentioned items usually function as nouns, but occasionally can function as verbs (as in the initial word in *But me no buts*) or adjectives (with the provisos in Section 6.5.2).

6.5.11 Putting this in a theoretical framework

Linguists usually distinguish between two separate types of construction here, one classed as conversion (or some other term which has theoretical implications) and one called coercion. Conversion is usually considered to be a type of word-formation, whereas coercion is usually considered to be a syntactic phenomenon. The distinction is easily motivated, but it is not entirely clear to what extent the distinction is justified or to what extent it hides similarities of behaviour.

If conversion is seen as a type of word-formation, it is because it has two features that are typical of derivation: it causes changes in word-class, and it is sporadic (the process does not apply blindly to all bases). Just because we can have *a love* and *to love*, it does not follow that we can have *a prove* and *to prove* or *a trove* and *to trove*. If coercion is viewed as a syntactic process, it is because it does not involve any morphological modification (the forms are the same) and because, in most cases, it appears to be absolutely automatic. If we can have *We must look after the poor*, we can substitute any adjective for *poor* (as long as it can apply to humans): *manipulative, misunderstood, obese, scary, tall*.

Conversion is sometimes called **zero-derivation**. Those who use this label view it as a process of derivation, but with an affix that has no form. To parallel *black* + *en*, *domestic* + *ate*, *false* + *ify*, we have *smooth* + Ø or *empty* + Ø. The Ø (zero) is a suffix with no form. Zero is just another affix, like all the others that share the burden of making causative verbs from adjectives. If that is the case, then we might analyse *French* in *more French* as *French* + Ø. We might then assume that the process was either inflectional or derivational, depending on the characteristics we see as important. However, in this case, there are no parallel overt affixes to support the analysis. We are breaking the rule that we cannot have an affix whose only form is zero (sometimes called the **overt analogue criterion**).

Another view of conversion is that it is not a derivational process, but an inflectional one, that we have *love* with nominal inflections or *love* with verbal inflections, and it is the inflections (even if they are not overt) which make the difference. Again, a parallel analysis of coercion might be made, but this time there is no change of word-class with different inflectional paradigms to justify the analysis.

A third analysis of conversion is that it is **functional shift**, that is, a form is given another function; again, this could be applied to coercion. An intransitive verb is shifted to function as a transitive one, just as an adjective is shifted to function as a noun. An alternative terminology is that conversion is **relisting**, that is, what was an adjective is also listed as a noun. That analysis, too, might apply to coercion.

A final possibility, gaining in popularity, is that conversion is a matter of gaining a figurative reading, typically so that the derived form in conversion is related by metonymy to the base form. Again, the same analysis might be applied to instances of coercion.

This makes it seem as though the only difference between conversion and coercion is whether there is a shift in word-class or not. Where there is, we have conversion, where there is not, we have coercion. For the most part this is true, and if it is true, we might argue that the difference in label merely reflects this difference, and we could just as well talk about conversion across word-classes and conversion within word-class. The crucial type here is the example of *the poor* versus *the intellectual*. As was shown above, *the poor* is very restricted in the pattern of noun phrase it can occur in, while *the intellectual* is much freer. But that may not be crucial; rather, the important factor is the relative ease of forming the *poor* type, as opposed to the unpredictability of the *intellectual* type. The first is usually taken as coercion and the latter as conversion. But again, the arguments do not seem to be convincing in saying that conversion and coercion are different constructions rather than the same type applied with different degrees of predictability.

This does not solve the question of the participles. If we assume that a participle is an inflected form of a verb, then these constructions do not take a lexeme and turn it into another lexeme (or another use of the same lexeme), they take an inflected form and turn it into a different lexeme. An alternative solution might be to see these things as principally adjectives, and say that BE + adjective_in_ing is a construction which creates a continuous form, and that HAVE + adjective_in_ed is a construction which creates a perfect. The noun *coming* would equally have to come from the adjective *coming*. Such an analysis, while possible, seems weak, since forms in -*ing*, for example, sometimes are used as nouns with little sign of them being adjectives and vice versa. *Interesting* is usually an adjective rather than a noun; *meeting* is usually a noun rather than an adjective. Other things being equal, an analysis that moves items from the most complete set of forms to the less used forms (in this case from verb to noun and from verb to adjective) would be more convincing. If it were not that the verbal -*ing* carries what is usually thought of as an inflectional marker, this would be the obvious analysis.

The puzzle here is not so much a matter of description – we could describe the facts in numerous different ways, and various analyses can be found in the literature. The puzzle is in recognising a single construction type as opposed to two contrasting construction types (possibly more). The arguments for that are far less clear-cut. Hand in hand with this puzzle, and strongly related to it, is the puzzle of dealing with the facts in a theoretical framework. Can we determine which theoretical framework provides the best description (if that is a meaningful question), and what would lead to a better theoretical explanation?

6.6 Summary

In this chapter, four particular puzzles dealing with English words have been considered. The puzzles range from determining what the actual facts we are trying to describe and explain are (for example, when is a plural used in the first element of a N+N structure and what is its implication) to how we can theorise the facts that we are faced with (as with conversion). Although four particular aspects of English words have been chosen to illustrate these points, it has been something of a theme of the book that there are multiple ways of viewing much of what is going on, and that the reasons behind the facts that we can observe (to the extent that we can even be sure of what we are observing – as we saw with comparative marking) are often obscure. This might seem like a very confusing, possible disheartening, situation to be in. But it also means that there are opportunities to find better ways of making observations, better ways of thinking about the way in which descriptions and explanations are couched, better ways of viewing how the brain copes with the very complex area of the way in which words function in our language.

In the last few decades, linguists have viewed the brain, or that part of it that deals with language, in two distinct ways. One is that the brain attempts to minimise the amount of memorisation required and maximise the amount of computation of forms, the other is that the brain readily allows for large amounts of memorisation. Extreme positions might make for eye-catching theories, but they seldom reflect reality. The truth is more likely to be somewhere in between. But how the workload is distributed, and how we might determine how the workload is distributed, are open questions. An alternative view is that we should not consider the way in which the human brain actually deals with such material, but simply look for a way to describe, as economically and as simply as possible, the outputs that speakers produce (and that listeners understand).

Whichever approach we might wish to take, and whatever developments in this area of study will arise over the next half-century or so, it seems inevitable that the controversies and the alternative views will continue, and that the need for people with an overview of opinions and a commitment to developing our understanding of the area will continue to be felt.

Exercises

1. At the end of Section 6.4.2 there are a series of questions about coordinative compounds. Either attempt to answer these as a class, or try to elicit opinions from your peers who are not members of this class – flatmates, co-workers, members of your sports team and so on. Think about how you will try to elicit the answers without priming the interviewees. Note that those without access to native-speaking informants will not be able to answer this question.

2. *Drugs*, *jobs* and *schools* seem to occur relatively easily as first elements in N+N sequences. How many examples can you find? Contrast these with examples of the same words with no final -*s*. Do they occur in the same positions or not? Is there a potential reason for any differences you find? You may want to look at some corpus to gather data for this question.

3. Find any disyllabic adjective which, in your judgement, can take either -*er* or *more*-marking for the comparative, and which has at least two obviously different meanings – perhaps literal and figurative. Either look for examples in some large corpus or try to elicit judgements from friends and acquaintances as to whether the -*er* or the *more*-form is more natural. Does the meaning make any difference?

4. How would you decide whether *steel* in *steel cutlery* is an adjective or a noun?

5. Can you think of any arguments for or against the position that *parental* is just an adjectival form of the lexeme PARENT, and that *a parent, to parent* and *parental* are inflectionally distinct forms of a single lexeme?

6. Find five examples of noun–verb conversion and see if you can determine whether the verb is converted from the noun or the noun from the verb.

7. In the examples in (32), what are the other word-classes that share forms with the preposition? Have any been omitted?

8. Choose five *-ing* forms or regular *-ed* forms, and check their use in a corpus to see how they are most used – as verbs, adjectives or nouns. Is the answer the same for all five? Does the answer depend upon what kind of verb is used (for example, transitive or intransitive, denoting an action or a state)? Does the answer depend on the individual verb chosen?

Recommendations for reading

Most of the material discussed here is canvassed and summarised in Bauer et al. (2013). On plural forms in N+N structures, see Bauer (2017a) and, for a contrasting analysis, Pinker (1999). Most of the literature on this topic is now rather out-dated. It seems that plural modifiers were seen as rather more exceptional before about 1970, which suggests that there is recent change in English in this area. On comparatives, Mondorf (2009) is recommended, but there is a large literature on the subject. On coordinative compounds, see Wälchli (2005), Bauer (2008), Renner (2008) and Bauer (2017a). On conversion see Bauer and Valera (2005) and Bauer (2018). *L'important c'est la rose* is a song written by Louis Amade and Gilbert Bécaud, first recorded in 1969.

Glossary

ablaut (see also **umlaut, vowel mutation**)
– a type of vowel mutation which is motivated by the morphology and not by the phonology (contrast **umlaut**). The difference between *sing* and *sang* is an example of ablaut.

acronym (contrast **initialism**)
– an **alphabetism** that is pronounced as a word in its own right. *Laser*, which comes from *Light Amplification by Stimulated Emission of Radiation*, is an acronym.

action nominalisation
– *nominalisation* refers to the creation of nouns from words of other **word-classes**, or the nouns produced in this way. An action nominalisation is a nominalisation derived from a verb which can be used to refer to the action of that verb. *Reformation* is an action nominalisation that can refer to the action of reforming.

affix
– a cover term for both **prefixes** and **suffixes**.

allomorphy
– when a **morpheme** has two or more distinct **forms** which arise in different environments, we talk of allomorphs of the morpheme, and allomorphy is the phenomenon of having allomorphs. The forms *em-* and *en-* are allomorphs of the same morpheme occurring in, for example, *emplane* and *entrain*.

alphabetism
– a word derived from the letters (usually initial letters) of a longer phrase. **Acronyms** and **initialisms** are types of alphabetism.

ambiclipping (contrast **back-clipping, foreclipping**)
– a **clipping** which has lost material from both ends of the original word. *Flu* from *influenza* is an ambiclipping.

antonymy
– a meaning relationship based on oppositeness of meaning. Some scholars use the term antonymy only where gradable antonymy is involved, others use it for all kinds of oppositeness. The words that are opposites are called 'antonyms'. **Gradable antonyms** are words which provide a scale of oppositeness, such that there are intermediate points on the scale. *Happy* and *sad*, *shallow* and *deep*, *short* and *tall* are pairs of gradable antonyms.

apophony – see **vowel mutation**

appositional (**compound**) – see **compound, appositional**

arbitrary (contrast **motivated**)
– a **form** is arbitrary to the extent that it is not **motivated**. A word like *pig* is arbitrary in its form in that there is nothing in the sounds or letters of the word *pig* to indicate that it has anything to do with porcine animals.

asyndetic coordination
– asyndetic (/æsɪnˈdetɪk/) coordination is coordination without any overt coordinator (such as *and, or*). *Friends, Romans, countrymen lend me your ears!* has three plural nouns in asyndetic coordination.

attributive (contrast **predicative**)
– used before a noun to modify it. *Red* is attributive in *my red shoes*.

back-clipping (contrast **ambiclipping, foreclipping**)
– a **clipping** that has lost material from the end of the original word. *Jumbo*, derived from *jumbo jet*, is a back-clipping.

back-formation
– the formation of a new word by the deletion of material from an original word. The material deleted is usually an **affix**, or is considered to be an affix. The verb to *baby-sit*, derived from *baby-sitter*, is a case of back-formation.

backronym
– derived jokingly from *back* and *acronym*: a word which purports to be an **acronym**, but where the coiner found a suitable final form and then provided the phrase to fit. The *USA PATRIOT Act* (apparently supposed to correspond to *Uniting and Strengthening America by Providing Appropriate Tools Required to Intercept and Obstruct Terrorism*) is reported to be a backronym.

base
– the **form** to which a morphological process applies. Typically, it is the word to which an **affix** is added. The base in *friendly* is *friend*; the base in *friendliness* is *friendly*.

blend
– a word coined by merging two other words so that the beginning of the first word and the end of the second word remain in the blend. The word *tigon* is a blend of *tiger* and *lion*, and denotes a hybrid between the two big cats.

borrowing
– a word is borrowed from another language when it is adopted into the borrowing language, not necessarily with precisely the same meaning as it has in the original language.

canonical
– a particular usage is canonical if it fits with all the criteria expected of the pattern in which the particular usage occurs. This implies that there are members of a class which do not meet all the criteria for membership of the class, but some sub-set of those criteria.

checked versus **unchecked** – see **vowel length**

clipping (see also **ambiclipping, back-clipping, foreclipping**)
– a word that is shortened, but retains its initial meaning. *Phone* from *telephone* is a clipping. An **embellished** clipping is word which is first shortened, and then lengthened, typically, but not exclusively, with a *-y* (*-ie*) or an *-o*, as in *muso* < *musician* + *o* or *Aussie* < *Australian* + *ie*.

clitic
– an element which has some **features** of a word and some of an **affix**. Like an affix, a clitic cannot stand alone; like a word, it often has a syntactic function. The *'m* in *I'm* and the *'s* in *John's* are examples of clitics in English.

coda
– in a syllable, the coda is the material that follows the nucleus (which is usually the vowel). In *grand*, the coda is /nd/.

coercion
– when the meaning of a word is extended to take in some grammatically distinct but semantically related sense, we talk of coercion. Examples include changes in countability (*several butters, much elk*) or transitivity (*walk the dog, have you paid?*).

collocation
– a habitual co-occurrence of words, such as *happy* with *birthday*.

combining form
– (a) an element of a neo-classical compound such as *psych-* and *-ology* in *psychology*; (b) see **splinter**.

comparative
– **form** of an adjective that allows the speaker to compare two entities along some scale. *Bigger* in *This house is bigger than yours* is a comparative form. **Double comparison** is the use of both *more* and *-er* to mark a comparative adjective: *He is more stupider than I thought.*

complementary terms
– opposites that cannot be true of the same entity at the same time, and which divide the universe of relevant entities into exhaustive classes. *Dead* and *alive*, *married* and *single*, *boar* and *sow* are examples of complementary pairs.

compound
– a **lexeme** made up of two or more elements each of which can be used as a lexeme in its own right. *Windmill* is a compound made up of the elements *wind* and *mill*.

> **appositional**
> – one that names an entity by naming two (or more) facets of that entity. A *singer-songwriter* is simultaneously a singer and a songwriter, and the two facets of their behaviour are used to name them.
> **coordinate** – see **coordinative**
> **co-participant**
> – one which names the people of items which jointly take part, as in *Arabi–Israeli talks* where Arabs and Israelis take part.
> **copulative** – see **coordinative**
> **elative**
> – one where the left-hand element expresses a high degree or large amount of the right-hand element in a picturesque way. *Stone-cold* is an elative compound.
> **endocentric** (contrast **compound, exocentric**)
> – one which is a **hyponym** of one of its elements: a windmill is a kind of mill, so *windmill* is a endocentric compound.
> **exocentric** (contrast **compound, endocentric**)
> – one which is not a **hyponym** of any of its elements: a hatchback is neither a kind of hatch nor a kind of back, so *hatchback* is an exocentric compound.
> **primary** (contrast **compound, synthetic**)

– one which does not have a head element derived from a verb. Examples include *windmill* and *blackbird*.

root – see **compound, primary**

secondary – see **compound, synthetic**

subordinative (contrast **coordinative**)
– one in which one of the elements (the left-hand one in English) modifies the head element (the right-hand element). *Windmill* and *blackbird* are subordinative compounds.

synthetic (contrast **compound, primary**)
– one in which, in English, the right-hand element is derived from a verb, and the interpretation of that compound is determined by the verb and the arguments it takes. *Bus-driver* is a synthetic compound, because *driver* is derived from the verb *to drive*, and the interpretation of the compound necessarily refers to the subject (*-er*) and the object (*bus*) of the verb *drive*.

tautological
– one which is made up of a **hyponym** and its **superordinate** term, such as *elm tree*, where *elm* is a hyponym and *tree* is its superordinate.

translative
– those like *English–French (dictionary)* or *Paris–Rome (flight)* which show literal or metaphorical movement from one place to another.

verb-centred – see **compound, synthetic**

verbal-nexus – see **compound, synthetic**

connotation
– the emotional force which accompanies a word, for the individual or for the community.

consonant mutation
– the change of the nature of a consonant as part of a process of word-formation. The difference between *wolf* and *wolves* involves consonant mutation.

construction
– a fixed pattern of linguistic elements that is associated with a fixed meaning. Constructions may be very general or very specific. There is a construction of the **form** NP V-*ed* possessive *way* PP (e.g. *She hummed her way down the hall, My father splashed his way across the carpark*) which carries a meaning of movement, even though the verb is not a verb of movement.

converse terms
– denote the same event but view that event from different perspectives. *Buy* and *sell* are converse terms.

conversion
– a change of **word-class** of a **form** without any concomitant change of form. *Love* can be a noun or a verb, and the change from one to another is attributed to conversion.

coordinate (compound) – see **coordinative**

coordinative
– a process or word-formation is coordinative when its elements are of equivalent status and neither modifies the other. Typically, this means that the elements can be understood as being linked by *and*. *Minneapolis– St Paul* is a compound whose meaning can be glossed as 'Minneapolis and St Paul', and is a coordinative **compound**.

co-participant (compound) – see **compound, co-participant**

copulative (compound) – see **coordinative**

denotation
– a relationship between a **lexeme** and the world, such that the denoting lexeme draws attention to some facet of the world and names it.

derivational morphology (contrast **inflection** *or* **inflectional morphology**)
– the creation of new **lexemes** from smaller meaningful elements; the elements that allow this. The creation of the lexeme WHITEHALLESE from an existing name and the **suffix** *-ese* is a case of derivational morphology, and *-ese* itself is a piece of derivational morphology.

derivational paradigm
– a recurrent **paradigm** of words which contrast in the **derivational morphology** added to the **base**.

derivative
– a word created by a process of **derivational morphology**.

descriptive (contrast **prescriptive**)
– a statement about language is descriptive if it merely makes an observation about the way the language is used.

dictionary (contrast **lexicon**)
– 'dictionary' is used in this book to refer to dictionaries that appear in print or online and are human compilations of linguistic knowledge.

diphthong
– a vowel sound during the course of which the tongue and/or the lips move. The vowel sounds in *go, buy* and *say* are diphthongs in RP.

distal (contrast **proximal**)
– a word has distal reference if it points to something away from the speaker and near to the listener or to a third person. *That* is a distal demonstrative.

double comparison – see **comparative**

dual-route model
– any model of the way in which humans produce and understand words which assumes that people may either look up complex words as units or work out what complex words must mean on the basis of their internal elements.

dvandva
– a dvandva (compound) is a **coordinative compound** which refers to two distinct entities which unite in a new entity. Dvandvas are rare in English, but *Minneapolis-St Paul* is a dvandva.

elative (compound) – see **compound, elative**

embellished (clipping) – see **clipping**

endocentric (compound) – see **compound, endocentric**

etymology
– etymological study traces the history of words: their origins, and the ways in which they have changed their **form** or meaning.

exocentric (compound) – see **compound, exocentric**

exotic word
– a term used for a word **borrowed** from a language which is not a usual source of **loan words**.

extender
– a meaningless element added between a **base** and an **affix**. The <l> in *Congolese* is an extender.

feature
– a construct of the analyst to indicate properties belonging to the units being analysed. A semantic feature is used to show properties of words (e.g. [+male] might be a feature of the word *man*), and phonological features are used to show properties of sounds (e.g. [-voice] might be a feature of the sound [t]).

figurative
– in a figurative use of language some expression does not denote what it appears to denote but instead denotes something that is in

some way related, and where the relationship can be calculated by the speaker or listener on the basis of general principles of cognition. **Metaphor** and **metonymy** are two of the major figurative uses of language.

foreclipping (contrast **ambiclipping, back-clipping**)
– a **clipping** that has lost material from the start of the original word. *Phone* from *telephone*, is a foreclipping.

form
– physical shape: here, of linguistic elements, either phonological (a spoken form) or orthographic (a written form).

formula
– a fixed way of expressing a particular idea. Greetings and farewells are often formulaic, as are things like *I'm sorry for your loss.*

functional shift – see **conversion**

genitive
– the name of a case which marks possession. The **Saxon genitive** is the genitive marked with an <s>, as in *the cat's* rather than with *of,* as in *of the cat.*

gradable (**antonyms**) – see **antonymy**

grammatical word
– a word which performs a grammatical function, that is, words like articles (*the, a*), prepositions (*to, in*), auxiliary verbs (*does* in *Does she like it?*) and so on.

Great Vowel Shift (GVS)
– a major change to the pronunciation of long vowels in English over a period of over 200 years.

headed
– a **construction** is headed if it is subordinative and not **coordinative**.

headword
– the word in a **dictionary** which begins an entry. *To put up* may be listed under the headword *put.*

holonym (see also **meronymy**)
– denotes the whole of which a **meronym** denotes a part. *Bird* might be a holonym for *wing.*

homographs
– distinct words which are written the same way whether or not they

are pronounced the same way. *Cricket* ('sport' or 'insect') and *lead* ('base metal' or 'show the way') are homographs.

homonyms
– sets of words with the same **form** but different meaning. It is sometimes useful to distinguish between **homographs** and **homophones**.

homophones
– distinct words which sound the same, whether or not they are written the same way. *Right* and *write*, and *cricket* ('sport' or 'insect') are homophones.

hyper(o)nym – see **superordinate**

hypocoristic
– a **form** that is used as pet name. *Billy* is a hypocoristic related to *William*.

hyponymy
– a semantic relationship based on subclassification. A cat is a kind of animal, so *cat* is a hyponym of *animal*.

idiom
– a **construction** whose meaning can only be understood globally, and not in terms of the elements which make it up. *To shoot the breeze* has to be interpreted as a whole ('to chat') and cannot be understood in terms of the meanings of *shoot* and *breeze*, and is an idiom.

incompatibility
– two words have incompatible meanings if they cannot both apply simultaneously to the same entity. *Red* and *black* are incompatible because if you say *My car is red* that excludes the possibility that *My car is black*.

inflection *or* **inflectional morphology** (contrast **derivational morphology**)
– the creation of new **word-forms** from smaller meaningful elements; the elements that allow this. The creation of the word-form *collapsed* from an existing verb and the **suffix** *-ed* is a case of inflectional morphology, and *-ed* itself is an inflection or a piece of inflectional morphology.

initialism (contrast **acronym**)
– an **alphabetism** whose **form** is pronounced as the names for a series of letters. *KGB* is pronounced /keɪ dʒiː biː/ and is an initialism.

internal modification
– any process of creating new words that involves changing parts of the

phonological structure of the **base**. This includes **consonant mutation** and vowel mutation, or change in **stress**.

lax – see **vowel length**

lexeme (contrast **word-form**)
– a word in the sense that *collapse, collapses, collapsed* and *collapsing* are all the same word. We can write the lexeme as COLLAPSE.

lexical gap
– a slot in the network of **lexemes** which we might expect to be filled, but where we find no filler for the gap. For instance, although we have words like *chair* and *bed* which might appear to be **hyponyms** of the same word, there is no word to fill the slot for the **superordinate** term. Although we have words to distinguish male and female siblings, we have no words to distinguish male and female cousins.

lexical set
– a set of words which share a phonological **feature** such as containing the same stressed vowel. The original idea comes from Wells, though extra sets have been added by various scholars.

lexicalism
– the theoretical position that the internal structure of words cannot influence the syntax and that the syntax cannot influence the internal structure of words.

lexicon (contrast **dictionary**)
– in this book, the mental **dictionary**, or what corresponds to a dictionary, but is a mental construct in speakers and listeners.

loan word
– a word which has been **borrowed** from another language.

main (**stress**) – see **stress, main**

mention (contrast **use**)
– a linguistic item is mentioned when it is talked about in a text. In the entry for **meronymy**, the words *wing* and *bird* are mentioned.

meronymy (see also **holonym**)
– a semantic relationship of part to whole. *Wing* is a meronym of *bird*, because a wing is a part of a bird.

metaphor
– a figure of speech in which one thing is stated to be another, which it is thought to resemble. Calling a child a *little monkey* is a metaphor.

metonymy
– a figure of speech in which one thing is called by the name of something closely related to it. Saying that someone has *taken to the bottle* shows metonymy of the bottle for the strong liquor in the bottle.

modal verb
– one of a set of verbs which has no third-person *-s* **form**, no *-ing* form, and which acts as an auxiliary verb showing obligation, possibility and necessity. Verbs like *can* and *must* are modal verbs in English.

monomorphemic
– containing only one **morpheme** or meaningful element. *Cat, if* and *elephant* are monomorphemic words of English.

monophthong
– a vowel sound during whose articulation the tongue and the lips remain in a fixed position. The vowels sounds in *pit, hot* and *cut* are monophthongs for most speakers.

monosemy
– the principle that any word has only a single meaning.

morpheme
– the smallest recurrent, meaningful element in the make-up of a word. In the word *cats*, there are two morphemes, corresponding to the written elements *cat* and *s*.

motivated (contrast **arbitrary**)
– the **form** of a word is motivated if there is a reason why some or all of it has the particular shape it has. The motivation may come from the sound (as in *cuckoo*) or from the elements within the word (as in *stupidness*, where the *-ness* regularly marks words as being nouns with a particular meaning).

multi-word expression (MWE)
– an expression made up of at least two distinct words that is in some way idiosyncratic (and so word-like): it may have unpredictable meaning, it may have unusual syntax, it may provide an unexpected collocation and so on. Examples include *by and large, in an interesting condition* 'pregnant', *down at heel* 'shabby and poor'.

normative – see **prescriptive**

oblique
– the name of a case **form** in a system where accusative and dative are

not distinguished. Oblique contrasts with nominative, and possibly with **genitive**.

obstruent
– the set of plosives and the set of fricatives and the set of affricates together make up the set of obstruents.

open
– a syllable is said to be open if it ends with a vowel sound.

overt analogue criterion
– the overt analogue criterion says that you cannot have a **morpheme** whose only realisation is zero: every morpheme must have at least one overt **allomorph**.

paradigm (contrast **syntagm**)
– a paradigm (/ˈpærədaɪm/) is a set of expressions which contains contrasting items in one position. The set of **word-forms** *distribute, distributes, distributed, distributing* forms an **inflectional** paradigm in English, with the endings contrasting on a **base** form.

paradigmatic (contrast **syntagmatic**)
– items which contrast in a **paradigm** are said to be in a paradigmatic (/pærədɪgˈmætik/) relationship to each other.

part of speech – see **word-class**

phonotactics
– the study of the way in which sound units can be strung together in larger units. The phonotactics of a language is the way in which sound units can be strung together in that language. For example, English allows word-initial /sl/ and /ʃr/ but not initial /ʃl/ and /sr/ (which occur only in **loan words**).

phrasal verb
– a term used more or less specifically to refer to a **construction** made up of a verb plus a preposition/adverb/particle such as *look up* (an answer), *put down* (a sick animal), *put up* (a guest), *put up with* (hardship). Various subtypes are recognised by some authors.

polyseme
– each of the distinct meanings attached to a given **lexeme** is a polyseme of that lexeme.

portmanteau word – see **blend**

predicative (contrast **attributive**)
– a predicative adjective is one that is used in the predicate, e.g. *red* in *My new shoes are red.*

prefix (contrast **suffix**)
– an element that cannot stand alone as a word that is added before a **base**. In *prejudge* the prefix is *pre-*.

prescriptive (contrast **descriptive**)
– a statement about language is prescriptive or normative to the extent that it provides information on the way in which its author believes that the language ought to be used.

primary (compound) – see **compound, primary**

productivity
– productivity is concerned with the extent to which a given **morpheme** or other way of creating new words can be used or is used in the creation of new words. The **suffix** *-ness* is very productive in English, whereas the suffix *-th* (on *warmth*) is probably not at all productive (you cannot invent, for instance, *highth* or *bluth*).

prototype
– a prototype of a category is the most typical or central example of that category. A chair might be the prototypical piece of furniture, for instance.

proximal (contrast **distal**)
– a word has proximal reference if it points to something close to the speaker. *This* is a proximal demonstrative.

reading
– a word-formation process is said to have a number of readings when its meaning is determined by pragmatic features of the context rather than by semantic effects tied to the **base** and the process itself. The **suffix** *-er* in English can have a locative reading in *diner* ('a place to eat') and an agentive reader in *killer* ('a person who kills').

recognition point
– the point in a word at which, on hearing the word spoken, the listener can determine accurately what the word must be.

relisting – see **conversion**

reversative
– a word which denotes the undoing of an action, or the element in the word which provides this meaning. To *untie* is a reversative from *tie*, and

un- is the reversative **prefix** in *untie.*

root (**compound**) – see **compound, primary**

Saxon (**genitive**) – see **genitive**

secondary (**compound**) – see **compound, synthetic**

secondary (**stress**) – see **stress, secondary**

semantic field
– a set of interrelated words where the meanings of each of the words is constrained by the meanings of the surrounding words in the field.

source (contrast **target, vehicle, linguistic**)
– in studies of **figurative** language, the source is the meaning of the word which is used in place of the literal expression. If you call a friend a clown, 'clown' is the source.

splinter
– a part of a word used as an element in a **blend**. In *spork* the splinters are *sp* (from *spoon*) and *ork* (from *fork*).

spurious word
– a word which is found listed in **dictionaries**, but which may never have been used.

stress
– prominence given to a particular syllable in a word by virtue of greater loudness or length, or by pitch – either pitch movement or relative pitch which stands out from the pitch of surrounding syllables.

>**main**
>– the main stress, or the primary stress, in a word falls on the syllable in the word that is uttered with greatest degree of force, pitch movement, or length, that sets it apart from other syllables in the word. It is sometimes called lexical stress or word stress. In *premium* the main stress is on the first syllable, in *collapse* on the last.
>**secondary**
>– a lesser degree of stress, in this book associated with full vowel quality. A syllable which shows secondary stress carries some degree of stress, but not as much as the syllable that carries primary stress. In *consolidation*, the primary stress falls on /deɪʃ/ and the secondary stress on /sɒl/.

subjunctive
– an **inflectional** category marked on verbs, whose use in English is much reduced from the use in related languages. It is still used in

English in wishes (*God save the Queen!*) and in counterfactuals (*If I were you . . .*) and in a limited number of other uses.

subordinative (compound) – see **compound, subordinative**

substitution class
– a **paradigm**, but the term is usually used in syntax. For example, in *The victim drowned in a puddle of* — the gap can be filled with *water* or any other liquid, so that *beer, milk, petrol, water* and so on form a substitution class in this sentence.

suffix (contrast **prefix**)
– an element that cannot stand alone as a word that is added after a **base**. In *kingdoms* the suffixes are *-dom* and *-s*.

superlative
– a superlative **form** of an adjective allows the speaker to compare three or more entities along some scale. *Biggest* in *This is the biggest house I've ever seen* is a superlative form.

superordinate
– in **hyponymy** the superordinate term is the one that is subclassified by the hyponyms. *Animal* is a superordinate term for *dog, frog* and *giraffe*.

syllabic consonant
– one which fills a whole syllable without any vowel to support it. Some speakers have syllabic final consonants in *button, bottle* or *prism*.

synecdoche
– synecdoche (/sɪˈnekdəki/) is a figure of speech in which the whole of something is referred to be naming just a part of it. In *fifty head of cattle*, we name the head, but actually refer to the entire beast.

synonymy
– two words are synonyms if, in some context, they both mean exactly the same thing.

syntagm (contrast **paradigm**)
– a syntagm (/sɪntæm/) is a set of adjacent linguistic elements.

syntagmatic (contrast **paradigmatic**)
– adjacent elements in a linguistic structure enter into a syntagmatic (/sɪntæɡˈmætɪk/) relationship.

synthetic (compound) – see **compound, synthetic**

target (contrast **source, vehicle, linguistic**)
– in studies of **figurative** language, the target is the literal expression

which is replaced. If you call a politician a clown, *the politician* is the target.

tautological (compound) – see **compound, tautological**

telescope word – see **blend**

tense – see **vowel length**

translative (compound) – see **compound, translative**

transposition (see also **conversion**)
– the use of a word as belonging to a different **word-class** from that to which it usually belongs, with minimal change to the semantics. The label transposition is sometimes used when the change of word-class is signalled by affixation, and sometimes used when there is no morphological signal of the change of word-class.

umlaut (see also **ablaut, vowel mutation**)
– a type of vowel mutation originally caused by assimilation to a vowel in a following syllable. The distinction between *mouse* and *mice* is an instance of umlaut in English.

unchecked versus **checked** – see **vowel length**

unique morph
– an element which occurs in only one place in the language. The **suffix** *-red* in *hatred* and the word *kith* in *kith and kin* are examples of unique morphs.

unmarked
– has a host of related meanings, starting with the idea that the unmarked member of a pair has no piece of **form** showing its status, while the marked member does have some form showing its status. This tends to correlate strongly with the unmarked member of a pair having the wider distribution and being more common. *Happy* is unmarked in relation to *unhappy*, and is likely to be more common and occur in more different **construction** types.

use (contrast **mention**)
– a linguistic element which is a natural part of some structure is used. *Which* is an instance of language use in the last sentence, but an instance of **mention** in this sentence.

value
– the value of a **lexeme** is its function as constrained by the surrounding lexemes in a semantic field.

vehicle, linguistic (contrast **source, target**)
– the actual **form** which carries the meaning of the **source** to the **target** in studies of **figurative** language.

verbal-nexus (**compound**) – see **compound, synthetic**

verb-centred (**compound**) – see **compound, synthetic**

vowel length
– long and short vowels behave differently in English phonology. For example, stressed short vowels must be followed by a consonant in the same syllable. Long vowels are sometimes called free vowels, tense vowels or unchecked vowels, while short vowels are sometimes called checked vowels or lax vowels.

vowel mutation (see also **ablaut, umlaut**)
– alternation between vowel sounds associated with some morphological effect.

word family
– a set of words which share a common **base**. The words *book, books, booked, booking, bookish, booklet, book club, bookmark, bookshelf* and so on form a word family based on the item *book*.

word-class
– a word-class or part of speech is a set of linguistic items which form a **substitution class** at a very general level. Word-classes included nouns, verbs, adjectives, adverbs and so on.

word-form (contrast **lexeme**)
– a word in the sense that *collapse, collapses, collapsed* and *collapsing* are all different words. Word-forms are representations of **lexemes**.

zero-derivation – see **conversion**

References

Adams, Valerie (1973), *An Introduction to Modern English Word-Formation*, London: Longman.

Adams, Valerie (2001), *Complex Words in English*, Harlow: Longman.

Aitchison, Jean (2003; 3rd edn), *Words in the Mind*, Malden, MA: Blackwell.

Allport, D. A., and Elaine Funnell (1981), 'Components of the mental lexicon', *Philosophical Transactions of the Royal Society of London. Series B, Biological Sciences* 295: 397–410.

Bauer, Laurie (1983), *English Word-Formation*, Cambridge: Cambridge University Press.

Bauer, Laurie (2000), 'Word', in Geert Booij, Christian Lehmann and Joachim Mugdan (eds), *Morphology: An international handbook of inflection and word-formation*, Berlin and New York: de Gruyter, pp. 247–57.

Bauer, Laurie (2005), 'The illusory distinction between lexical and encyclopedia information', in Henrik Gottlieb, Jens Erik Mogensen and Arne Zettersten (eds), *Symposium of Lexicography XI*, Tübingen: Niemeyer, pp. 111–15.

Bauer, Laurie (2008), 'Dvandva', *Word Structure* 1: 1–20.

Bauer, Laurie (2017a), *Compounds and Compounding*, Cambridge: Cambridge University Press.

Bauer, Laurie (2017b), 'Metonymy and the semantics of word-formation', in Nikos Koutsoukos, Jenny Audring and Francesca Masini (eds), *Morphological Variation: Synchrony and diachrony*, Proceedings of the Mediterranean Morphology Meetings, vol. 11, pp. 1–13, <http://mmm.lis.upatras.gr/index.php/mmm/issue/view/352> (last accessed 1 April 2021).

Bauer, Laurie (2018), 'Conversion as metonymy', *Word Structure* 11/2: 175–84.

Bauer, Laurie, and Rodney Huddleston (2002), 'Lexical word-formation', in Rodney Huddleston and Geoffrey K. Pullum (eds), *The Cambridge Grammar of the English Language*, Cambridge: Cambridge University Press, pp. 1621–721.

Bauer, Laurie, Rochelle Lieber and Ingo Plag (2013), *The Oxford Reference Guide to English Morphology*, Oxford: Oxford University Press.

Bauer, Laurie, and Salvador Valera (eds) (2005), *Approaches to Conversion/Zero-Derivation*, Münster: Waxmann.

Baugh, Albert C. (1959; 2nd edn), *A History of the English Language*, London: Routledge & Kegan Paul.

Carney, Edward (1994), *A Survey of English Spelling*, London and New York: Routledge.

Carroll, Lewis (1872), *Through the Looking-Glass, and What Alice Found There*, London.

Clark, Eve V. (1995), *The Lexicon in Acquisition*, Cambridge: Cambridge University Press.

Cruse, D. A. (1986), *Lexical Semantics*, Cambridge: Cambridge University Press.

Crystal, David (1984), *Who Cares about English Usage?*, Harmondsworth: Penguin.

Davies, Mark (2004–), *British National Corpus* (from Oxford University Press), <https://www.english-corpora.org/bnc/> (last accessed 9 April 2021).

Denning, Keith, and William R. Leben (1995), *English Vocabulary Elements*, Oxford: Oxford University Press.

Derwing, Bruce (1973), *Transformational Grammar as a Theory of Language Acquisition*, Cambridge: Cambridge University Press.

Di Sciullo, Annamaria, and Edwin Williams (1987) *On the Definition of Word*, Cambridge, MA: MIT Press.

Dixon, R. M. W., and Alexandra Y. Aikhenvald (2002), 'Word: A typological framework', in R. M. W. Dixon and Alexandra Y. Aikhenvald (eds), *Word: A cross-linguistic typology*, Cambridge: Cambridge University Press, pp. 1–41.

Giegerich, Heinz J. (2012), 'The morphology of *-ly* and the categorial status of "adverbs" in English', *English Language and Linguistics* 16: 341–59.

Gimson, A. C. (2001; 6th edn), *Gimson's Pronunciation of English*, revised by Alan Cruttenden, London: Arnold. [Or any other edition after the first.]

Hay, Jennifer (2003), *Causes and Consequences of Word Structure*, London: Routledge.

Hippisley, Andrew (2015), 'The word as a universal category', in John R. Taylor (ed.), *The Oxford Handbook of the Word*, Oxford: Oxford University Press, pp. 246–69.

Hogg, Richard, and David Denison (eds) (2006), *A History of the English Language*, Cambridge: Cambridge University Press.

Huddleston, Rodney, and Geoffrey K. Pullum (eds) (2002), *The Cambridge Grammar of the English Language*, Cambridge: Cambridge University Press.

Jones, Daniel, James Hartman and Peter Roach (2002; 16th edn), *Cambridge English Pronouncing Dictionary*, Cambridge: Cambridge University Press.

Kaminsky, Juliane, Josep Call and Julia Fischer (2004), 'Word-learning in a domestic dog: Evidence for "fast mapping"', *Science* 302: 1682–3.

Kenyon, John S., and Thomas A. Knott (1953), *A Pronouncing Dictionary of American English*, Springfield, MA: Merriam.

Lakoff, George, and Mark Johnson (2003; revised edn), *Metaphors We Live By*, Chicago: University of Chicago Press.

Lass, Roger (1987), *The Shape of English*, London and Melbourne: Dent.

Lehnert, Martin (1971), *Reverse Dictionary of Present-Day English*, Leipzig: VEB.

Littlemore, Jeannette (2015), *Metonymy*, Cambridge: Cambridge University Press.

Longman Dictionary of Contemporary English (2009; 5th edn), Harlow: Pearson Education.

Lyons, John (1977), *Semantics* (2 vols), Cambridge: Cambridge University Press.

Marslen-Wilson, William D., and Pienie Zwitserlood (1989), 'Accessing spoken words: The importance of word onsets', *Journal of Experimental Psychology: Human Perception and Performance* 15: 576–85.

Mondorf, Britta (2009), *More Support for More-Support: The role of processing constraints on the choice between synthetic and analytic comparative forms*, Amsterdam and Philadelphia: Benjamins.

Moon, Rosamund (2015), 'Multi-word items', in John R. Taylor (ed.), *The Oxford Handbook of the Word*, Oxford: Oxford University Press, pp. 120–40.

Mugglestone, Lynda (2011), *Dictionaries: A very short introduction*, Oxford: Oxford University Press.

Murphy, M. Lynne (2010), *Lexical Semantics*, Cambridge: Cambridge University Press.

Payne, John, Rodney Huddleston and Geoffrey K. Pullum (2010), 'The distribution and category status of adjectives and adverbs', *Word Structure* 3: 31–81.

Pei, Mario (1967), *The Story of the English Language*, London: Allen & Unwin.

Pinker, Steven (1999), *Words and Rules*, London: Weidenfeld & Nicolson.

Plag, Ingo (1999), *Morphological Productivity*, Berlin and New York: Mouton de Gruyter.

Plag, Ingo (2003), *Word-Formation in English*, Cambridge: Cambridge University Press.

Poplack, Shana (2018), *Borrowing: Loanwords in the speech community and in the grammar*, Oxford: Oxford University Press.

Quirk, Randolph, Sidney Greenbaum, Geoffrey Leech and Jan Svartvik (1985), *A Comprehensive Grammar of the English Language*, Harlow: Longman.

Renner, Vincent (2008), 'On the semantics of English coordinate compounds', *English Studies* 89: 606–13.

Saussure, Ferdinand de [1916] (1969), *Cours de linguistique générale*, Paris: Payot. Also available in English as *Course in General Linguistics*, trans. Wade Baskin, London: Fontana, 1974.

Sledd, James, and Wilma R. Ebbitt (1962), *Dictionaries and That Dictionary*, Chicago: Scott, Foresman.

Stockwell, Robert, and Donka Minkova (2001), *English Words*, Cambridge: Cambridge University Press.

Strang, Barbara M. H. (1970), *A History of English*, London: Methuen.

Taylor, John (2003; 3rd edn), *Linguistic Categorization*, Oxford: Oxford University Press.

Upton, Clive, William A. Kretzschmar, Jr. and Rafal Konopka (2001), *The Oxford Dictionary of Pronunciation for Current English*, Oxford: Oxford University Press. See also the 2nd edn: Upton, Clive and William A. Kretzschmar, Jr. (2017), *The Routledge Dictionary of Pronunciation for Current English*, Abingdon: Routledge.

Wälchli, Bernhard (2005), *Co-compounds and Natural Coordination*, Oxford: Oxford University Press.

Wells, J. C. (1982), *Accents of English* (3 vols), Cambridge: Cambridge University Press.

Wells, J. C. (2008; 3rd edn), *Longman Pronunciation Dictionary*, Harlow: Pearson Education.

Wheeler, C. J., and D. A. Schumsky (1980), 'The morpheme boundaries of some English derivational suffixes', *Glossa* 14: 3–34.

Wray, Alison (2012), 'What do we (think we) know about formulaic language? An evaluation of the current state of play', *Annual Review of Applied Linguistics* 32/1: 231–54.

Index

References in *italics* are to places where terms are defined or explained.

EU Authorised Representative:

Easy Access System Europe Mustamäe tee 50, 10621 Tallinn, Estonia

gpsr.requests@easproject.com

Printed and bound by CPI Group (UK) Ltd, Croydon, CR0 4YY

19/04/2026

02092756-0001